# Storytelling and Conversation

Ceil Lucas, General Editor

**VOLUME 1**     *Sociolinguistics in Deaf Communities*
                 Ceil Lucas, Editor

**VOLUME 2**     *Multicultural Aspects of Sociolinguistics in*
                 *Deaf Communities*
                 Ceil Lucas, Editor

**VOLUME 3**     *Deaf Children in Public Schools*
                 Claire L. Ramsey

**VOLUME 4**     *Pinky Extension and Eye Gaze: Language Use in*
                 *Deaf Communities*
                 Ceil Lucas, Editor

**VOLUME 5**     *Storytelling and Conversation: Discourse in*
                 *Deaf Communities*
                 Elizabeth Winston, Editor

# Storytelling and Conversation

## Discourse in

## Deaf Communities

*Elizabeth Winston, Editor*

GALLAUDET UNIVERSITY PRESS

*Washington, D.C.*

**Sociolinguistics in Deaf Communities**

A Series Edited by Ceil Lucas

Gallaudet University Press

Washington, D.C. 20002

ISBN 1-56368-081-5

ISSN 1080-5494

Cover Design by Joseph Kolb

Interior Design by Richard Hendel

Composition by BookMasters, Inc.

Figures 2 and 3 on p. 43 are reprinted from *Frog, Where Are You?* by Mercer Mayer, published in 1969 by Dial Books for Young Readers, a division of Penguin Putnam USA. Reprinted by permission of the publisher.

# Contents

Editorial Advisory Board, vii
Contributors, viii
Editor's Introduction, ix

**PART ONE: INTERNAL CONTEXT**

Talking about Space with Space: Describing Environments
in ASL, 3
    *Karen Emmorey and Brenda Falgier*

Event Packaging in British Sign Language Discourse, 27
    *Gary Morgan*

Storytelling in the Visual Mode: A Comparison of
ASL and English, 59
    *Jennifer Rayman*

Affect, Emphasis, and Comment in Text Telephone
Conversations, 83
    *Meryl Glaser*

**PART TWO: EXTERNAL CONTEXT**

Sign Languages as a Natural Part of the Linguistic
Mosaic: The Impact of Deaf People on Discourse
Forms in North Bali, Indonesia, 109
    *Jan Branson, Don Miller, and I Gede Marsaja*

Italian Sign Language and Spoken Italian in Contact:
An Analysis of Interactions between Deaf Parents
and Hearing Children, 149
    *Sabina Fontana*

GET-TO-THE-POINT: Academic Bilingualism and Discourse
in American Sign Language and Written English, 162
    *Karen Christie, Dorothy M. Wilkins, Betsy Hicks
    McDonald, and Cindy Neuroth-Gimbrone*

Footing Shifts in an Interpreted Mock Interview, 190
    *Melanie Metzger*

Index, 219

# Editorial Advisory Board

# Contributors

Jan Branson
National Institute for Deaf
   Studies
LaTrobe University
Bundoora, Victoria, Australia

Karen Christie
Department of Cultural and
   Creative Studies
National Technical Institute for
   the Deaf
Rochester Institute
   of Technology
Rochester, New York

Karen Emmorey
The Salk Institute for
   Biological Studies
Laboratory for Cognitive
   Neuroscience
The Salk Institute
La Jolla, California

Brenda Falgier
The Salk Institute for
   Biological Studies
Laboratory for
   Cognitive Neuroscience
The Salk Institute
La Jolla, California

Sabina Fontana
Ente Nazionale Sordomuti
Ragusa, Italy

Meryl Glaser
Department of Logopaedics
University of Cape Town,
   South Africa

I Gede Marsaja
STKIP Singaraja
Singaraja, Bali, Indonesia

Betsy Hicks McDonald
Department of Cultural and
   Creative Studies
National Technical Institute for
   the Deaf
Rochester Institute of Technology
Rochester, New York

Melanie Metzger
Department of ASL, Linguistics,
   and Interpretation
Gallaudet University
Washington, D.C.

Don Miller
Department of Anthropology
Monash University
Melbourne, Victoria, Australia

Gary Morgan
Department of Linguistics
City University
London, United Kingdom

Cindy Neuroth-Gimbrone
The Center for Independent
   Scholarship, Teaching,
   and Research
Tucson, Arizona

Jennifer Rayman
Department of Communication
University of California-
   San Diego
La Jolla, California

Dorothy M. Wilkins
Department of Cultural and
   Creative Studies
National Technical Institute for
   the Deaf
Rochester Institute of Technology
Rochester, New York

# Introduction

*Storytelling and Conversation* focuses on discourse analysis. Discourse analysis looks at language in use, analyzing patterns beyond the level of the sentence, seeking to understand how language users build cooperative understanding through interaction. In this volume, contributors explore the context of communication, both from within and outside the discourse.

As a linguist, researcher, and interpreter, discourse analysis holds a special interest for me. As a linguist, I look at how discourse takes the study of language into the realm of practical applications; in other words, language in use. As a researcher, I know that discourse analysis of sign languages is still in its infancy compared to the longer histories of phonology, morphology, and syntax. As an interpreter, I study discourse analysis to learn the way each interpretation must be faced: from beginning to end, in context, using natural, real-world data to better understand the underlying meaning of each interaction. I hope this book is only the beginning of many more studies of discourse in sign languages.

In keeping with this series' goals, this volume presents an international perspective, including papers on the sign languages of Bali, Italy, England, and the United States. It is fascinating to see the intricate discourse patterns that have evolved in different languages. The papers explore two approaches to discourse: the analysis of the internal context of discourse and the analysis of the external context. An analysis of the internal context looks at the structures of language within a text that are used by signers to reflect their intended meaning. An analysis of the external context of discourse investigates the ways that languages influence and shape their communities and the ways those communities integrate and influence language use.

Focusing on the internal context of discourse, five authors investigate the ways that signers shape their messages, creating cohesion and coherence. Karen Emmorey and Brenda Falgier investigate signers' use of space for talking about space. Gary Morgan then analyzes the ways that signers package events, using space to accomplish complex narrative tasks. Jennifer Rayman focuses on the linguistic tools signers choose from to structure storytelling. Meryl Glaser then analyzes the internal context of text telephone conversations for strategies used to add affect, emphasis, and comment to these interactions.

Investigating the external context of language use, Jan Branson, Don Miller, and I Gede Marsaja discuss the integration of deaf people and sign language into the language communities of Bali—where the hearing populations integrate deafness and sign language into their religion and community life. Sabina Fontana describes the language mixing that results from the prolonged contact and interaction between deaf parents and hearing children.

The final two papers tie the internal and the external contexts together. Karen Christie, Dorothy M. Wilkins, Betsy Hicks McDonald, and Cindy Neuroth-Gimbrone discuss the application of internal text styles of ASL and English to teaching written English to Deaf students. These internal structures are explicitly taught as a means of improving written English, an important means of fitting into the external language communities in which Deaf people live. In the last paper, Melanie Metzger analyzes the language choices made by an interpreter who must shift footing in order to manage the "interpreter's paradox."

I am grateful to Ceil Lucas for the opportunity to be the guest editor for this volume, the fifth in the series, and am indebted to the patience of Ivey Pittle Wallace and Christina Findlay at Gallaudet University Press. The contributors have all worked with me to produce this volume, and I thank each of them for their valuable contributions.

Finally and most importantly, I express my gratitude and admiration for a special friend, June Zimmer. Her work in discourse analysis spurred my own interest, her support as a fellow researcher encouraged my work, and her friendship as a fellow student and colleague have continued to inspire me long after her death. This volume is dedicated to her memory.

# Storytelling and Conversation

# Part I **Internal Context**

# Talking about Space with Space:

## Describing Environments in ASL

*Karen Emmorey and Brenda Falgier*

Spatial discourse—talking about space—usually involves adopting a particular perspective on the scene or environment being described. For example, an addressee may be taken on a mental tour of an environment, as in this example from Linde and Labov's study of New Yorker's descriptions of their apartments: "As you open the door, you are in a small five-by-five room which is a small closet. When you get past there, you're in what we call the foyer. . . . If you keep walking in that same direction, you're confronted by two rooms in front of you . . . large living room which is about twelve by twenty on the left side. And on the right side, straight ahead of you again, is a dining room which is not too big" (1975, 929). Taylor and Tversky (1992, 1996) characterize this style of discourse as utilizing a *route perspective* in which landmarks and motion through the environment are described with respect to a viewer (usually "you" in English) using viewer-relational terms such as "left" and "right."

This type of perspective is contrasted with what Taylor and Tversky call a *survey perspective* in which the perspective is from above (a bird's-eye view); landmarks are described with respect to other landmarks, cardinal direction terms are used (e.g., north, south); and existential and stative verbs are used, rather than verbs of motion. The following is an excerpt from an apartment description from Linde and Labov that adopts

This work was supported by NSF grant SBR-9510963 awarded to Karen Emmorey, and NIH grants HD13249 and DC00201 awarded to Ursula Bellugi. We thank Holly Taylor and Barbara Tversky for the use of their methodology and for invaluable discussions concerning many of the issues addressed here. We thank Steve McCullough for his help in judging the ASL descriptions. We thank Bonita Ewan and Steve McCullough for their help in collecting the ASL data. Ed Klima provided crucial comments on an earlier draft of the article, but all errors remain our own.

a survey perspective: "The main entrance opens into a medium-sized foyer. Leading off the foyer is an archway to the living room which is the furthermost west room in the apartment. It's connected to a large dining room through double sliding doors. The dining room also connects with the foyer and main hall through two small arches. The rest of the rooms in the apartment all lead off this main hall which runs in an east-west direction" (1975, 927).

Do users of American Sign Language (ASL) describe environments using these same discourse styles? If so, do they make the same perspective choices that English speakers do? It is possible that language modality may influence perspective choice, given the different affordances of vision versus audition. Unlike spoken languages, ASL uses physical space to describe spatial relations. That is, locations within signing space can function topographically to represent locations within a real or imagined world. What are the consequences of this system for perspective choice? Does the nature of signing space change, depending on perspective choice? We investigate these questions by studying how ASL signers describe different types of environments.

To investigate the determinants of perspective choice for English speakers, Taylor and Tversky (1996) gave subjects maps of either a large-scale environment (a town) or a small-scale environment (a convention center). They asked the subjects to memorize the maps (see figure 1) and then write a description of the environment so that someone reading the description could find all of the landmarks. Taylor and Tversky found that English speakers more often adopted a survey perspective when describing the town, and a route perspective when describing the convention center. The following are excerpts from written English descriptions:

> Survey (town): North of town are the White Mtns. and east of town is the White River, which flows south from the White Mtns. The main road by town runs in the east-west directions and crosses the White River.
>
> Route (convention center): You enter from the southeast corner of the building. As you come in, turn right. To your right will be the "personal computers" room. Continue until you're forced to make a left. The "stereo components" room will be in front of you as you turn left. (Taylor and Tversky 1996, 379)

Taylor and Tversky proposed that choice of perspective is partially dependent upon the characteristics of the environment, with single paths

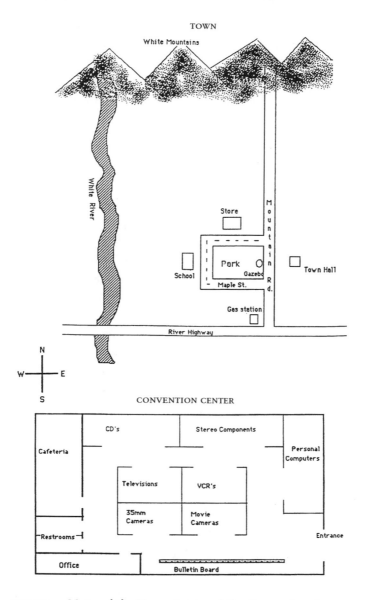

FIGURE 1. *Maps of the Town (top) and the Convention Center (bottom). Reprinted by permission of the publisher, from "Spatial mental models derived from survey and route descriptions," by Holly Taylor and Barbara Tversky (Journal of Memory and Languages, 1992) 31: 261–92.*

and size-equivalent landmarks encouraging a route rather than a survey perspective. To investigate whether ASL signers make similar perspective choices and to study the nature of these spatial descriptions in sign language, we presented ASL signers with the maps used by Taylor and Tversky and asked them to describe the environment shown on the map.

**METHOD**

Forty signers participated in the study (mean age = 25 years). Twenty-seven signers had deaf families and learned ASL from birth. Ten signers learned ASL prior to age seven, and three acquired ASL prior to age fourteen. Thirty-eight signers were deaf at birth or became deaf before one year of age, and two signers became deaf at or before age three. Signers participated in the study at Gallaudet University, the Salk Institute, California State University at Northridge, or at Deaf Community Services in San Diego.

Half of the subjects were given the map of the town, and half were given the map of the convention center (see figure 1). They were asked to study the map until they had memorized it. Signers were told to describe the environment so that if someone unfamiliar with the area were shown the videotape of their description, they would know what the environment (town or convention center) looked like and where all the landmarks were. The instructions were given in ASL by a Deaf native signer.

**RESULTS AND ANALYSIS**

We first examine the determinants of perspective choice for ASL signers compared to English speakers. We then compare spatial language in English and ASL, focusing on lexical spatial terms. Finally, we propose that ASL signers utilize one of two different spatial formats, depending on whether a route or a survey perspective is chosen.

**Perspective Choice**

Each description was judged as adopting either a route perspective, a survey perspective, or a mixed perspective. Two Deaf native signers were asked to decide if the description felt more like a "tour," a bird's-eye view description, or a mixture of both. They were also given examples of written English route and survey descriptions from Taylor and Tversky (1996). The ASL coders agreed on 88 percent of judgments; the English coders in the Taylor and Tversky study initially agreed on 83 percent of judgments. When disagreements occurred, the signers discussed the description and came to an agreement. The results are shown in table 1. The English data are from Taylor and Tversky (1996).

The results indicate that the perspectives adopted by ASL signers when describing these environments differed from those of English subjects.[1] ASL signers were significantly more likely to adopt a survey perspective when describing the convention center, whereas English subjects preferred a route perspective ($X^2 = 10.72$, $p < .01$). For the town, English and ASL subjects did not differ significantly in perspective choice (both preferring survey perspectives).

Why do ASL signers prefer to provide descriptions using a survey perspective? One possibility is that signers prefer survey perspectives in general, perhaps because signing space can be used so effectively to represent a map. That is, subjects can locate landmarks on a horizontal plane in signing space in a manner that is isomorphic to the locations of landmarks on a map (in fact, this is how signing space is utilized for survey perspectives). Another possibility is that ASL signers, but not English speakers, were strongly influenced by the nature of the task. The fact that signers studied a map may have influenced how they structured signing space within their description. A mental representation of the map may be more easily expressed using a horizontal plane in signing space with a fixed "bird's-eye view" vantage point, and this type of spatial format is more compatible with a survey perspective. English speakers were apparently not subject to such linguistic preferences.

However, ASL signers appear to choose either route or mixed descriptions when describing environments that they have actually experienced. In a pilot study, we asked eight ASL signers to describe their houses and five ASL signers to describe the locations of the dormitories on the Gallaudet campus. Only one person produced a description with a survey perspective. Thus, the difference between English speakers and ASL signers does not appear to be due to a general preference for ASL signers to adopt a survey perspective.

---

1. Evidence from spoken English descriptions collected by Taylor and Tversky indicates that the difference in the pattern of perspective choice still holds when English descriptions are spoken rather than written.

TABLE I. *Perspective Choice by ASL Signers and English Speakers*

|  | Route | Mixed | Survey | Total Number of Participants |
|---|---|---|---|---|
| Convention Center |  |  |  |  |
| English | 10 | 10 | 3 | 23 |
| ASL | 3 | 5 | 12 | 20 |
| Town |  |  |  |  |
| English | 2 | 10 | 10 | 22 |
| ASL | 7 | 4 | 9 | 20 |

Given that ASL signers and English speakers differ in perspective choice for the same environment, Taylor and Tversky's (1996) claim that the nature of the environment determines perspective choice must be qualified. The nature of the linguistic system may also influence which spatial perspective is chosen.

### Comparing ASL and English Language Use

It is possible that the differences between ASL and English regarding perspective choice are due to differences in linguistic judgment criteria used by the ASL judges and by Taylor and Tversky. To determine whether similar language was used by ASL and English subjects, we examined the use of motion verbs and spatial terms. Although ASL signers tended to rely on classifier constructions and the topographic use of signing space in their environment descriptions, signers did produce some lexical spatial terms. We compare the use of these terms with their English counterparts.

Taylor and Tversky found that English route descriptions contained significantly more "active" verbs (primarily motion verbs) and more terms that related a landmark to the viewer (e.g., *left/right*); whereas English survey descriptions contained more "stative" verbs (i.e., existential verbs) and more relational terms that related a landmark to the environment (e.g., *north, south*). Because stative verbs such as the copula (forms of *to be*) or verbs like *stand* or *lie* are rarely (if ever) used to express locative relations in ASL, we did not attempt to count these verb forms in ASL.

MOTION VERBS

ASL expresses motion with both classifier predicates and lexical verbs such as DRIVE, PASS, or WALK. We counted the occurrence of these verb types for each ASL description. Following the English pattern, ASL route descriptions contained significantly more motion verbs than survey descriptions ($t(30) = 4.4$, $p < .01$). The mean number of motion verbs for each discourse category is shown in table 2.

The most frequent motion verbs were DRIVE, VEHICLE-MOVE (using the ASL vehicle classifier), PASS, CROSS (as in "cross over the river"), and TURN-LEFT/RIGHT.[2] These verbs were most often used in route descriptions of the town. Motion verbs were rarely found in survey descriptions, but the verb ENTER was frequently used at the beginning of both route and survey descriptions of the convention center. The classifier predicate WALK (using either the 1 handshape or V handshape) was occasionally used in a mixed or route description of the convention center.

## USAGE OF THE LEXICAL RELATIONAL TERMS LEFT/RIGHT

Signers providing route descriptions of environments were significantly more likely to use the ASL signs LEFT/RIGHT (or LEFT-TURN/RIGHT-TURN) than signers producing survey descriptions ($t(30) = 4.01$, $p < .01$). The use of these terms was rare, however, even within route descriptions (see table 2). On average, ASL signers only used one lexical relational term per description ($x = 1.25$, s.d. $= 3.35$).[3] In contrast, English speakers used an average of 7.5 lexical relational terms per description (derived from table 3 in Tversky and Taylor 1996).

The citation forms of LEFT and RIGHT are shown in figure 2. The sign LEFT is unusual in that is articulated by the left hand when produced in isolation as a citation form. This may be the only sign in which handedness is specified within the lexicon. Within a discourse, the signs LEFT and RIGHT can be articulated with respect to distinct locations in the plane of signing space to indicate left or right from a particular vantage point. For example, some signers described the Maple Street "loop" of the town with a lexical relational term, but they articulated the sign with respect to a "loop" in signing space on their left side (matching the left-side location of the loop on the map (see figure 1a). Figure 3 illustrates such an example.[4] The sign RIGHT-TURN is actually articulated on the left side of

2. Underlining indicates an initialized sign.

3. Both native and near-native signers used these lexical spatial terms. None of the three late signers did.

4. Where possible, sign illustrations were taken directly from the subject's videotape (figures 3, 5a, 7, 8, 9, 10). In other cases, a model signer reproduced the subject's description for illustration (figures 5b, 6).

TABLE 2. *Mean Number of ASL Motion Verbs and Relational Terms per Discourse Type*

| | Route (N = 10) | Mixed (N = 8) | Survey (N = 22) |
|---|---|---|---|
| Motion verbs | 9.1 (8.0)[a] | 3.8 (2.8) | 1.5 (1.2)[b] |
| LEFT/RIGHT signs | 3.7 (4.2) | 1.3 (1.6) | 0.14 (0.35) |
| NORTH, SOUTH, EAST, WEST signs | 1.2 (2.1) | 0.75 (1.4) | 1.0 (1.8) |

[a] Standard deviations are given in parentheses.
[b] Significant difference between Route and Survey descriptions ($p < .01$).

signing space, and the movement is outward from the body, rather than toward the right (compare figure 2 with figure 3). Thus, the motion direction of lexical relational signs is not necessarily specified with respect to the signer's own left and right. Rather, the movement of the sign can specify a left or right direction from a particular vantage point indicated within the plane of signing space (in this case, the first corner of Maple Street). Such spatial manipulations of relational terms appear to be only possible when signing space performs a "diagrammatic" function and is not "viewer-centered" (see below).

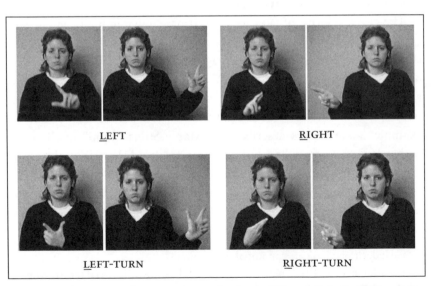

LEFT

RIGHT

LEFT-TURN

RIGHT-TURN

FIGURE 2. *Illustration of Citation Forms for Lexical Viewer-Relational Terms. For paired pictures, the picture on the left shows the beginning of the sign, and the picture on the right shows the end of the sign.*

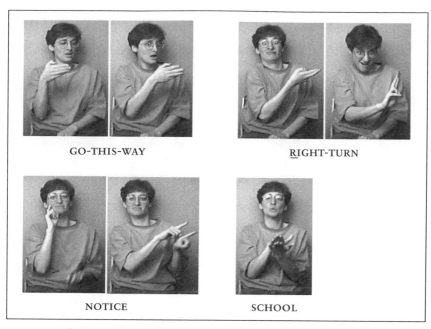

GO-THIS-WAY        RIGHT-TURN

NOTICE        SCHOOL

FIGURE 3. *Illustration of a Lexical Relational Term Articulated in Diagrammatic Space. English translation: "If you go this way and turn right, you will see a school . . . "*

USAGE OF N̲ORTH, S̲OUTH, E̲AST, W̲EST

Unlike their usage in English, ASL cardinal directions did not differ for survey and route descriptions, but this may be due to a floor effect, because signers produced so few cardinal direction signs. The citation forms are shown in figure 4. Like the relational signs in citation form, the cardinal direction signs appear to be specified in the lexicon with respect to the left-right body axis. For example, the sign W̲EST is specified as moving toward the left rather than toward the "nondominant side." For both left and right handers, the sign W̲EST moves toward the left, and the sign E̲AST moves toward the right. The direction of movement is fixed with respect to the signer's left and right, unlike other signs whose direction of motion changes depending upon the handedness of the signer.

As with the relational signs, signers can alter the direction of motion of cardinal direction signs to indicate direction with respect to locations mapped out in signing space. Figure 5 provides two examples. In both, the signers are describing the town. In example A, the signer is describing driving east on River Highway, and she produces the sign E̲AST away from

| NORTH | SOUTH | EAST | WEST |

FIGURE 4. *Illustration of the Citation Forms of Cardinal Direction Signs.*

her body indicating the direction of the road as it stretches in front of her. In example B, the signer is using space to map locations in the town on a horizontal plane. As in example A, the signer has "shifted" the orientation of the actual map (shown in figure 1a) with respect to signing space so that River Highway is described as a path traced outward and away from the signer (not shown in figure 5b). After describing the corner gas station, the signer traces the path of Mountain Road horizontally in signing space, and then articulates the sign NORTH along the same path (see figure 5b).

### Summary

Our analysis indicates that adopting a survey or route perspective when describing an environment leads to similar linguistic choices for ASL signers and English speakers. That is, for descriptions with a route perspective, both English speakers and ASL signers produce more motion verbs and more viewer-relational terms (e.g., *left* or *right*), compared to descriptions with a survey perspective. Thus, the *lexical* encoding of spatial perspective within a discourse is similar for both ASL and English. ASL signers can, however, "spatialize" relational terms by producing them at locations within signing space that represent positions in the environment being described (rather than positions relative to the signer herself). Furthermore, lexical encoding does not appear to be the primary mechanism for expressing spatial perspective (as attested by the relative rarity of these terms). Rather, signers structure signing space in various ways to convey a route or a survey perspective. We next examine this aspect of spatial language that is unique to signed languages.

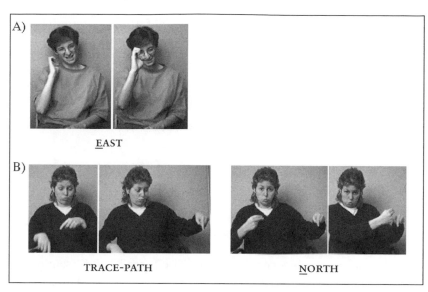

FIGURE 5. *Illustration of Cardinal Directional Terms in (A) Viewer Space and (B) Diagrammatic Space. English translation (A): "Go east." English translation (B): "(Mountain Road) stretches north along here."*

## PERSPECTIVE TYPE AND SPATIAL FORMAT

We use the term *spatial format* to mean the topographic structure of signing space used to express locations and spatial relations between objects. When a survey perspective was adopted, signers most often used a type of spatial format within signing space that we have termed *diagrammatic space:* 91 percent of landmarks within survey descriptions were located using diagrammatic space. When a route perspective was adopted, signers most often used a format that we have termed *viewer space:* 88 percent of landmarks within route descriptions were located using this format. Our analysis of the data revealed a number of properties associated with each spatial format, as shown in table 3.

Diagrammatic space is somewhat analogous to Liddell's (1994, 1995) notion of *token space* and to Schick's (1990) *model space.* Model space is characterized as "an abstract, model scale in which all objects are construed as miniatures of their actual referents" (Schick 1990, 32). Liddell (1995, 33) describes tokens as "conceptual entities given a manifestation in physical space," and states that "the space tokens inhabit is limited to the size of physical space ahead of the signer in which the hands may be located while signing." Diagrammatic space is also so limited, and under

TABLE 3. *Characteristics of Diagrammatic and Viewer Space*

| Diagrammatic Space | Viewer Space |
|---|---|
| Signing space represents a map-like model of the environment | Signing space reflects an individual's view of the environment at a particular point in time and space |
| Space can have either a 2-D "map" format or a 3-D "model" format | Signing space is 3-D (normal-sized scale) |
| The vantage point does not change (generally a bird's-eye view) | Vantage point can change (except for "gaze-tour" descriptions) |
| Relatively low horizontal signing space or a vertical plane | Relatively high horizontal signing space |

Liddell's analysis, signers could conceptualize tokens as representing objects and landmarks within a description of an environment. However, tokens are hypothesized to be three-dimensional entities, and our data contain some examples in which the spatial format is two-dimensional, representing a map with points and lines. For example, one signer used the vertical plane to trace a square representing the Maple Street loop, and the school, park, and store were located with points (see figure 6). This two-dimensional example contrasts with a similar three-dimensional example in which the signer uses the horizontal plane to trace the outline of the corridor in the convention center (see figure 7). At the beginning of this excerpt, the signer indicated that the plane in signing space was conceptualized as three dimensional by using B-handshape classifiers to specify the box-shape of the center group of rooms. The pointing signs then used by this signer indicated the locations of the entrances of four center rooms, rather than the location of the rooms themselves.

When a signer uses diagrammatic space within a stretch of discourse, the vantage point is fixed and represents a "bird's-eye view" of the horizontal signing space. For example, figure 8 shows the pointing signs used by one subject to indicate the locations of the outer rooms of the convention center. The locations within signing space map isomorphically to the locations of the rooms on the convention center map (figure 1b). This particular signer is unusual because she did not rotate the map. That is, most signers (80 percent) "shifted" the map so that the entrance was located at the chest and the bulletin board extended outward on the left of signing space. This pattern may reflect a convention for spatial descriptions of buildings (and rooms) in ASL: position a main entrance at the front of the body.

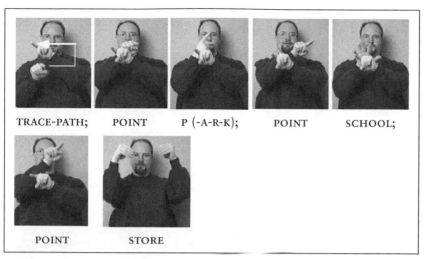

FIGURE 6. *Illustration of the Use of the Vertical Plane in Signing Space. English translation: "(The street) is like this. Here's a park; here's a school; and here's a store."*

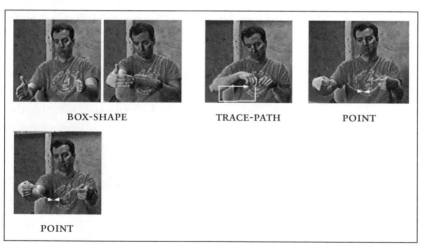

FIGURE 7. *Illustration of the Use of Horizontal Signing Space. English translation: "(The central rooms) form a box. (The corridor) is like this. (The room entrances) are here and here."*

Viewer space is similar to *surrogate space* described by Liddell (1994, 1995) and *real-world space* described by Schick (1990). We argue against the term real-world space because it implies the actual physical space surrounding the signer, rather than indicating a larger scale, as intended by Schick. It is important to distinguish between real space and

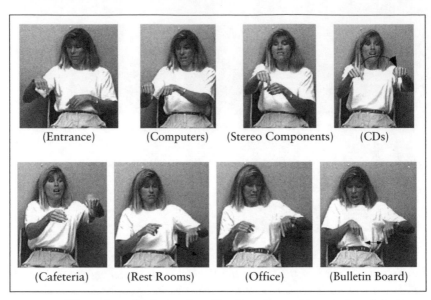

| (Entrance) | (Computers) | (Stereo Components) | (CDs) |

| (Cafeteria) | (Rest Rooms) | (Office) | (Bulletin Board) |

FIGURE 8. *Illustration of Pointing Signs Used in a Survey Description of the Outer Rooms of the Convention Center. The rooms associated with the pointing signs are given in parentheses. The intervening lexical signs are not shown, and the lexical and pointing signs for the inner rooms are also omitted.*

viewer space because in the first case the signer actually sees the environment being described, and in the second, the environment is conceptualized as present and observable. According to Liddell (1994), surrogates are characterized as invisible, normal-sized entities with body features (head to toe), and they are conceptualized as in the environment. When signers adopt a route perspective to describe an environment, the signer describes the environment as if he or she were actually moving through it. Under Liddell's analysis, the surrogate within this type of description coincides with the signer's body (i.e., it occupies the same physical space as the signer's body). We adopt the term viewer space rather than surrogate space because it is the environment, rather than a surrogate, which is conceptualized as present. Signers describe the environment as if they were viewing the landmarks and other elements within the scene. Signers know that their addressee cannot see the environment, and therefore the description is not the same as if both discourse participants were simultaneously observing the environment. Such a description would be quite different, and signers would utilize what we term *shared space* (Emmorey, Klima, and Hickok 1998), but this discourse situation will not be discussed here.

Figure 9 illustrates a route description of the convention center and shows the pointing and classifier signs used to indicate the locations of the outer rooms. In contrast to figure 8, the locations in signing space map to what the signer would observe as she describes moving along the corridor. The vantage point is not fixed, but changes with motion through space. For example, the signer indicates that the CD room would be in front of her (as she stands next to the cafeteria), but later she indicates that the personal computer room is in front of her because she has described going around the corner (refer to the convention center map in figure 1). The spatial meaning of signing space *changes* with the description. Now compare the location of these rooms as described by the signer in figure 8; in this case, signing space represents a model of the entire convention center, and the spatial relationship among locations does not change during the description.

Note also the relatively high signing plane used in the description shown in figure 9. Lucas and Valli (1990) hypothesized that signs articulated above the chest can engage a *perspective system,* and that the height of these signs has the meaning "from signer perspective." For example, they found that when the classifier construction glossed as SURFACE-PASS-UNDER-VEHICLE is signed at eye level versus mid-chest level, it does not indicate the relative height of the surface or vehicle being described. Rather, the height indicates whether the action is being described from the signer's perspective or whether the action is being described more generally, with no reference to the signer.[5] Our data support and elaborate the findings of Lucas and Valli (1990). When signers described environments as if they were moving through them, they articulated signs at a relatively high plane, thus indicating that the description reflected their own imagined view of the environment. For example, classifier constructions describing the location and contours of the town's White Mountains (e.g., a 5 handshape with fingers wiggling) were articulated at or above the forehead for route descriptions, but at the high-chest level for survey descriptions using the horizontal plane (the high-chest region contrasted with the mid- to low-chest region used to describe street locations in a three-dimensional spatial model).

5. Lucas and Valli (1990) note that the perspective is not necessarily that of the actual signer; rather, the signer may have signaled a referential shift (e.g., by a change in eye gaze), and the perspective is that of the character associated with the shift.

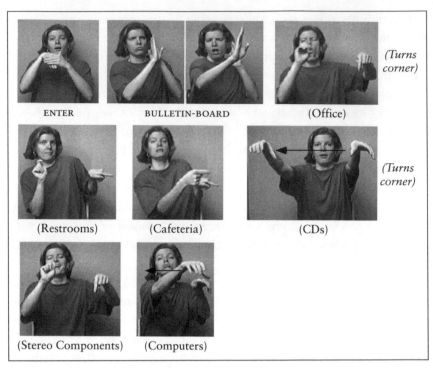

| | | | (Turns corner) |
|---|---|---|---|
| ENTER | BULLETIN-BOARD | (Office) | |

| | | (Turns corner) |
|---|---|---|
| (Restrooms) | (Cafeteria) | (CDs) |

| | |
|---|---|
| (Stereo Components) | (Computers) |

FIGURE 9. *Illustration of Pointing and Other Signs Used in a Route Description of the Outer Rooms of the Convention Center. The rooms associated with the pointing signs are given in parentheses. The intervening lexical signs for the rooms are not shown, and the lexical and pointing signs for the inner rooms are also omitted.*

## Shifting between Spatial Formats

The majority of descriptions with a survey perspective (62 percent) used a single spatial format: diagrammatic space. However, descriptions with either a route or a mixed perspective tended to shift at least once between diagrammatic space and viewer space: 80 and 89 percent of descriptions, respectively, contained at least one change of spatial format. Two route descriptions did not contain any spatial format changes, and both used viewer space, as would be expected. One signer produced a description with a mixed perspective that only used diagrammatic space. This description was judged as a mixed rather than as a pure survey perspective because the signer described part of the environment (the entire Maple Street loop) using LEFT-RIGHT relational terms articulated within diagrammatic space. That is, the signs were articulated with respect to a three-dimensional model within signing space, rather than with respect to the signer's own left and right (see figure 3 for an example). For route descriptions, signers often briefly summarized the boundaries of the town (or the corridor of the convention center) using diagrammatic space, while most of the route descriptions used viewer space to locate landmarks.

Signers did not appear to use explicit markers for shifting between diagrammatic and viewer space. For example, a break or change in eye gaze did not signal a shift in spatial format. In general, for both types of spatial format, signers maintained eye contact while identifying a landmark using a lexical or fingerspelled sign; then, their eye gaze shifted to the hands, as they described the location of landmarks using pointing signs or classifier constructions. Signers can shift very rapidly between these two spatial formats (even within the same sentence) with no overt cues to the shift. Similarly, English speakers do not overtly mark a shift from a route to survey description, for example, "Go left at the gas station, and then north to the White Mountains." For ASL, the lexical signs LEFT/RIGHT or the cardinal direction signs do not necessarily specify the use of a particular spatial format. Relational signs like LEFT or RIGHT can be used with either viewer space (as exemplified by the citation forms in figure 2) or with diagrammatic space (as shown in figure 3). Similarly, the cardinal direction signs can be used with either viewer space, as shown in figure 5a (note the higher plane used for the sign EAST), or with diagrammatic space, as shown in figure 5b.

### Gaze Tours

A gaze-tour description does not describe movement through space; rather, the environment is described from a fixed vantage point from which a signer or speaker views the environment (see Ehrich and Koster 1983). For example, English speakers may provide a gaze-tour description of a doll house by adopting a fixed point of view from the outside and describing the locations of furniture as "in front of" or "to the right" with respect to their outside view of the rooms, rather than as if moving through the rooms (Tversky and Taylor 1996).

For gaze tours in ASL, signers used viewer space, but with a fixed vantage point. For example, some signers began their description of the convention center by describing the location of the bulletin board and the first few rooms as if they were standing at the entrance looking down the hall. Often, but not always, these signers then switched to diagrammatic space for the remainder of the description. One signer's entire description of the convention center was a gaze tour from the entrance, even though all of the rooms could not actually be seen from this position. In his description, the signer used a relatively high signing plane, and his pointing signs were articulated as if he were pointing to room locations from the entrance. For example, figure 10 shows the classifier sign used to locate the cafeteria with respect to his position at the entrance; this construction could be glossed as OBJECT-LOCATED-ALL-THE-WAY-AT-THE-BACK. For the town, signers occasionally gave gaze-tour descriptions of the Maple Street loop, as if they were standing on the south corner or at the park.

### Horizontal versus Vertical Planes

Within diagrammatic space, signers used either a horizontal plane within signing space (as seen in figure 8) or a vertical plane (as illustrated in figure 6). Signers can shift back and forth from a horizontal to a vertical plane, either rapidly (e.g., between sentences) or slowly, for example, changing from the vertical plane to the horizontal plane across one or two sentences.

The horizontal plane can be a true two-dimensional plane, or it can represent a three-dimensional model of space (in which case it is not a true plane). In contrast, the vertical plane appears to be limited to two dimensions. It would be unacceptable to use the vehicle classifier within the vertical plane, for example, indicating that a car traveled around the Maple Street loop using the vertical plane. The vehicle classifier invokes

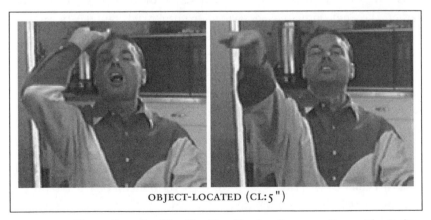

OBJECT-LOCATED (CL:5″)

FIGURE 10. *Illustration of a Classifier Sign Used to Locate a Room (the Cafeteria) in a Gaze Tour Description of the Convention Center.*

three-dimensional space because it refers to a three-dimensional object, and the classifier itself has three dimensions that can be referred to (e.g., another classifier handshape can be placed next to or below the vehicle classifier to indicate the location of another object with respect to the car). The vehicle classifier can be articulated with a vertical path in signing space, but such a construction would mean the car was traveling uphill.

Several subjects used the vertical plane to indicate the locations of different landmarks for the town (generally, either the Maple Street loop or the town boundaries: the river, White Mountains, and Mountain Road), and one subject's entire description used the vertical plane. However, *no* subject used this plane when describing the convention center. Neither the perimeter of the convention center nor the four inside rooms were described using a vertical plane. One possible explanation for this is that the rooms and the corridor of the convention center are not easily represented with points and lines, unlike the landmarks and streets of the Town. Furthermore, the sign ROOM was often articulated at various positions within the horizontal plane to specify the location of different rooms. This sign invokes three-dimensional space and cannot be used in the vertical plane. Thus, the fact that the vertical plane is limited to two dimensions may have restricted its use in convention center descriptions.

## FRAMES OF REFERENCE AND SPATIAL FORMATS

Sign linguists use the term *frame of reference* to refer to anaphoric reference within a discourse; for example, Lillo-Martin and Klima (1990) describe a fixed versus shifted referential framework (see also Engberg-Pedersen 1993). When describing spatial language, however, linguists and psychologists use "frame of reference" to refer to the spatial coordinate system invoked by a particular lexical item or sentence. Levinson (1996, 138–47) characterizes the three frames of reference that are linguistically distinguished as intrinsic, relative, and absolute.

An *intrinsic frame of reference* involves an object-centered coordinate system, where the coordinates are determined by the "inherent features," sidedness, or facets of the object to be used as the ground (the reference object). English examples: (1) "The man is in front of the house" (meaning at the house's front). In this example, the house is the ground, and the man is the figure (the located object). (2) "The ball is in front of me." In this example, the speaker is the ground and the ball is the figure.

A *relative frame of reference* presupposes a "viewpoint" (given by the location of a perceiver), and a figure and a ground that are both distinct from the viewpoint. Thus, there is a triangulation of three points (the viewpoint, the figure, and the ground), and the coordinates for assigning directions to the figure and ground are fixed on the viewpoint. English example: "The ball is to the left of the tree." In this example, the viewpoint is the speaker (the perceiver of the scene), the ball is the figure, and the tree is the ground.

An *absolute frame of reference* involves fixed bearings ("cardinal directions" or gravity), and the coordinate system is anchored to these fixed bearings with the origin on the ground object. English example: "The ball is to the north of the tree."

Spatial formats in ASL are clearly not the same as frames of reference. Rather they are specific ways of structuring signing space within a discourse. It appears that signers can adopt an intrinsic, a relative, or an absolute frame of reference when using either diagrammatic or viewer space. For example, using diagrammatic space, a signer could indicate that a man was in front of a car by positioning the classifier for upright humans (the 1 handshape) in front of the vehicle classifier (i.e., at the fingertips of the 3 handshape). Such an expression uses the intrinsic reference frame: the ground is the car, and the figure (the man) is located with respect to the features of the car. When viewer space is used with an intrinsic reference frame, the ground would always be the signer (or another character within the discourse if the expression was within a referential shift). For example, the signer could indicate that the car was in front of her, by positioning the vehicle classifier at eye level (see Lucas and Valli 1990); the English translation would be "the car is in front of me."

When viewer space is used within a relative frame of reference, the description is similar, but a figure and ground object are related to each other from the viewpoint of the signer (or other character if within a referential shift). For example, to express the equivalent of "the picture is to the right of the window" using viewer space, a signer would first describe the window on the left of signing space and then the picture on the right, both at eye level—the order of expression indicates which object is figure (described second) and which is ground (described first) (see Emmorey 1996). An example using diagrammatic space and a relative reference frame is shown in figure 11. In this example, the signer describes a man on a hill looking down on a house behind a lake. The viewpoint is that of the man (not the signer), the ground is the lake, and the figure is the house.

The signer is indicating that the house is behind the lake, from the man's viewpoint. The signer is not expressing his own view of the scene—that is, he is not indicating that the man is on his right and that the lake is in the center of view with the house to his left.

Finally, we have already seen examples in which signers specified an absolute frame of reference using cardinal direction signs with either viewer space (figure 5a) or diagrammatic space (figure 5b). However, signers rarely adopted an absolute frame of reference.

For route descriptions using viewer space, signers tended to adopt an intrinsic frame of reference with the signer (that is, the signer as imagined in the environment) as the origin of the coordinate system for locating a figure object. For survey descriptions using diagrammatic space, signers tended to also adopt an intrinsic frame of reference, but the origin of the coordinate system was centered on a ground object. What may be unique to signed languages is that a relative and an intrinsic frame of reference can be expressed *simultaneously* (see Emmorey 1996). For example, adopting a relative frame of reference, a signer could indicate that a car is behind a tree (from the signer's viewpoint). Now suppose that the signer indicates *in the same construction* that the car is facing away (such that the tree is at the car's back), by articulating the vehicle classifier with the palm facing sideways and the fingertips facing outward (away from the signer). In this expression, the intrinsic frame of reference is expressed via the intrinsic properties of the classifier handshape for vehicles (i.e., the fingertips represent the front of the vehicle). The fact that ASL can express two frames of reference simultaneously indicates that spatial reference frames are not mutually exclusive (see also Levinson 1996).

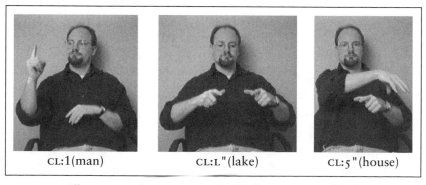

| CL:1(man) | CL:L"(lake) | CL:5"(house) |

FIGURE 11. *Illustration of Discourse with a Relative Frame of Reference Using Diagrammatic Space. The intervening lexical signs are not shown.*

It should also be clear that when a route perspective is adopted for an extended spatial description, it does not necessarily mean that a particular frame of reference has been adopted for that description. For example, motion is not a property of a particular reference frame, but it characterizes route descriptions. Using existential verbs and describing landmarks with respect to each other (rather than with respect to a viewer) characterize survey descriptions but are not properties of reference frames. Descriptions with a route perspective tend to use an intrinsic frame of reference, but are not defined by it. Survey descriptions in English may tend to adopt an absolute reference frame, but only when cardinal directions are used. In contrast, ASL descriptions that adopt a survey perspective rarely involve an absolute frame of reference because signers rarely use cardinal direction signs (see table 2). Instead, either an intrinsic or relative frame of reference is used, and the nature of signing space, as well as existential locative classifier constructions (rather than motion constructions), convey the survey perspective.

## SUMMARY

Our study found that ASL signers describe environments with the same discourse styles as English speakers, choosing either a route, survey, or mixed perspective. However, ASL signers did not make the same perspective choices as English speakers. The ASL signers were much more likely to adopt a survey perspective compared to English speakers. We hypothesized that signers were more affected than English speakers by the way the spatial information was acquired (i.e., via a map, rather than through navigation). Specifically, a mental representation of a map is more easily expressed using diagrammatic space because this spatial format is more compatible with a survey perspective. Thus, language modality does appear to have interesting ramifications for perspective choice and the nature of spatial descriptions.

With respect to lexical spatial terms and verbs of motion, English speakers and ASL signers make similar linguistic choices for route versus survey descriptions. However, ASL signers can "spatialize" both viewer-relational terms (LEFT/RIGHT) and cardinal directional terms (NORTH/SOUTH) to correspond with the particular spatial format adopted within a description. Within diagrammatic space, these terms can be articulated with respect to the map or model of the environment laid out on a horizontal or vertical plane. Within viewer space, viewer-relational terms are articulated with respect to the signer's body, and cardinal direction terms can be articulated at a higher plane to indicate that the signer (or character within a referential shift) is moving or facing in the direction specified.

Finally, we found that signers structure signing space differently depending on whether they adopt a route or survey perspective. For the viewer spatial format (preferred for route descriptions), signing space reflects a person's view of the environment, has a "normal-size" scale, a changing vantage point (except for gaze tours), and uses a relatively high signing plane. For the diagrammatic spatial format (preferred for survey descriptions), signing space represents a two- or three-dimensional model of the environment, the vantage point is fixed, and a relatively low horizontal or vertical signing plane is used. Spatial formats are independent of spatial frames of reference, and signers can adopt an intrinsic, a relative, or an absolute reference frame when using either diagrammatic or viewer space.

## REFERENCES

Ehrich, V., and C. Koster. 1983. Discourse organization and sentence form: The structure of room descriptions in Dutch. *Discourse Processes* 6:169–95.

Emmorey, K. 1996. The confluence of space and language in signed languages. In *Language and space,* ed. P. Bloom, M. Peterson, L. Nadel, and M. Garrett, 171–209. Cambridge, Mass.: MIT Press.

Emmorey, K., E. Klima, and G. Hickok, 1998. Mental rotation within linguistic and nonlinguistic domains in users of American Sign Language. *Cognition* 68:221–46.

Engberg-Pedersen, E. 1993. *Space in Danish Sign Language: The semantics and morphosyntax of the use of space in a visual language.* International Studies on Sign Language Research and Communication of the Deaf, vol. 19. Hamburg, Germany: Signum-Verlag.

Levinson, S. 1996. Frames of reference and Molyneux's question: Crosslinguistic evidence. In *Language and space,* ed. P. Bloom, M. Peterson, L. Nadel, and M. Garrett, 109–70. Cambridge, Mass.: MIT Press.

Liddell, S. 1994. Tokens and surrogates. In *Perspectives on sign language structure,* ed. I. Ahlgren, B. Bergman, and M. Brennan, 105–19. Durham, England: ISLA.

———. 1995. Real, surrogate, and token space: Grammatical consequences in ASL. In *Language, gesture, and space,* ed. K. Emmorey and J. Reilly, 19–41. Mahwah, N.J.: Lawrence Erlbaum Associates.

Lillo-Martin, D., and E. Klima. 1990. Pointing out differences: ASL pronouns in syntactic theory. In *Theoretical issues in sign language research,* vol. 1, ed. S. Fischer and P. Siple, 191–210. Chicago: University of Chicago Press.

Linde, C., and W. Labov. 1975. Spatial networks as a site for the study of language and thought. *Language* 51: 924–39.

Lucas, C., and C. Valli. 1990. Predicates of perceived motion in ASL. In *Theoretical issues in sign language research,* vol. 1, ed. S. Fischer and P. Siple, 153–66. Chicago: University of Chicago Press.

Schick, B. 1990. Classifier predicates in American Sign Language. *International Journal of Sign Linguistics* 1(1): 15–40.

Taylor, H., and B. Tversky. 1992. Spatial mental models derived from survey and route descriptions. *Journal of Memory and Language,* 31: 261–92.

———. 1996. Perspective in spatial descriptions. *Journal of Memory and Language* 35(3): 371–91.

# Event Packaging in British

## Sign Language Discourse

*Gary Morgan*

Sign languages are articulated in the space on and around the bodies of signers. The construction of extended discourse by native British Sign Language (BSL) signers calls on a rich reference system that exploits linguistic, as well as topographic, representational spaces. Describing ongoing scenes where two or more events are co-occurring requires sophisticated control of the laying out of events in sign space. Native signers exploit the various options available to them from within the BSL system to distinguish between referents and action. Focusing on event packaging, signers set up events in representational frameworks or use clear narrator information—articulated in narrator space—to guide the addressee through discourse by moving the narrative through a series of representational spaces. Packaging involves the activating of a series of spaces and the cohesive movement through these spaces.

Once speakers move on from the sentence and begin to construct extended monologue we can say that they are in the realm of discourse. Discourse in this sense is language beyond the sentence. Although discourse is a term used for many uses of language here it refers to "a large span of related spoken [*or signed*] utterances by one speaker" (Karmiloff-Smith 1985). In discourse, sentences need to be linked to other sentences in order to carry an idea or plot through a series of changes in events and temporal contexts. Constructing discourse is therefore about getting events and relations correct at the sentential level, as well as allowing relations to be encoded across the sentential boundary. One term used to express

This research was funded by ESR grant #R00429434231. I would like to acknowledge the support of Bencie Woll and the insightful comments on earlier versions by Neil Smith and comments by the panel of the Cognition and Deafness seminar, University of Plymouth, United Kingdom (April 1997).

discourse constraints is *cohesion.* Cohesion refers to relations of meaning that exist between sentences when the interpretation of some element in discourse is dependent on that of another (Halliday and Hasan 1976). Cohesion normally accompanies *coherence,* which refers to the overall intelligibility of the discourse or text. Users of language are constantly working within the requirements of making discourse cohesive and coherent. The linguistic labels chosen by speakers to mark cohesion reflects their attempt to manage information flow for themselves, as well as their addressees (Chafe 1987).

## SIGN DISCOURSE

Sign languages can be described as *discourse-sensitive* languages, that is, the face-to-face nature of interaction is coupled with nonliterate traditions of reporting events.[1] It is therefore valuable to describe the nature of discourse in this modality and how it differs from spoken language. This description focuses on three aspects of discourse in sign language: (1) the use of sign space for reference, (2) the representation of discourse in sign space, and (3) the nature of face-to-face communication. These aspects of sign language were first formalized in Friedman (1975) and have been explored since in several areas, for example, Ahlgren and Bergman (1992), Bahan and Petitto (1982), Gee and Kegl (1983), Poulin and Miller (1995), Roy (1989), and Winston (1995).

### The Use of Sign Space for Reference

Sign discourse exploits sign space for referring to protagonists in narrative.[2] Signers may use arbitrary locations assigned to areas of

1. Sign languages are no longer non-writable. Several sign languages have been recorded in the Sutton Sign-Writing system (e.g., Gangel-Vasquez 1997). The impact on BSL and the BSL-using community of recording experiences and history in a written form is an interesting sociological issue.

2. The sign space is a hemispheric zone extending from the signer's body in all possible directions of an arm's stretch. It is observed that reference will exploit space within a zone occupying a horizontal band between the waist and chest height as well as space on the signer's own body.

sign space to represent referents (e.g., Neidle, MacLaughlin, and Lee 1997). Another option is to represent the interaction of referents, as well as dialogue and action, through a shifting of reference from the narrator to another first person (e.g., Metzger 1994). This strategy is most akin to reported speech in spoken language discourse (e.g., Clark and Gerrig 1990). Signers construct discourse through the systematic use of reference to areas of sign space and through shifted reference.

## The Importance of the Shifted Referential Framework

The use of the shifted referential framework underlies the successful transition of reference through discourse and has not been the focus of the majority of comparative work in spoken language. Sign discourse has three overlapping referential frameworks. The specific markers of simultaneity are embedded into this three-tier framework. This relationship is schematized in figure 1.

These three schematized frameworks are used to carry information through narrative. Each space is devoted to different kinds of information marking, although there is interaction between the three (indicated by

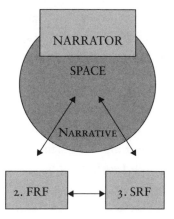

FIGURE 1. *Interaction and Use of Representational Spaces in Narrative.*

arrows from within the main area marked NARRATIVE). Each of the three representational spaces are described here in turn:

1. Using narrator space, the narrator describes information with a clear use of eye gaze toward the addressee, especially for scene setting, the first mentions of protagonists, plot motivations, and genre appropriate introductions. This space is used throughout the narrative for comprehension checks and narrative filling information. It may interact with both the fixed and shifted referential frameworks.
2. The fixed referential framework is used for scene setting involving topographic space, the movement of referents through proforms, and pronominal points toward spatial loci. Eye gaze toward hands marks the use of proforms. This space interacts with the shifted referential framework in discourse.
3. The shifted referential framework is mainly used to describe dialogue, actions, and thoughts of protagonists. Movement to the shifted referential framework is normally marked by eye-closes or nonmanual markers, which follow locations set up in topographic space set up in the fixed referential framework. There is often rapid interaction with the fixed referential framework.

### The Representation of Discourse

Sign language also exploits sign space to represent not only syntactic arguments but also topographic information. Spoken language makes large recourse to spatial language through arbitrary symbols. In English, spatial terms such as "back of, head of, mouth of, foot of," make reference to body coordinates while "under, over, in, next to," and so on are less iconic. There is a radical difference in sign language: signers may position units of language such as nouns and verbs in sign space in accordance with real-world spatial arrays. The interaction between syntactic and topographic space has been the subject of intensive sign language research in several different signing populations (see Emmorey, Corina, and Bellugi 1995).

### The Nature of Face-to-Face Communication

Sign languages are constrained in that the addressee must look at the person signing during interaction. Sign narrators use sign space on and around their own bodies to construct and represent discourse. Signers take into consideration their conversation partners' need to understand reference and uses of sign space. The patterns of sign discourse reflect this consideration. Signers monitor and adapt their discourse for conversation partners, normally representing discourse from their own perspective but marking the passage of events through discourse in various ways so as to allow full interpretation (Emmorey 1994; Morgan 1997). The discussion now turns to the use of reference forms in discourse.

## REFERENCE IN SIGN LANGUAGE

Previous work on reference in sign language has predominantly concentrated on an analysis of American Sign Language (ASL). Initial work focused on the sentential level of sign language and up until recently has even avoided tackling descriptions of longer stretches of sign language such as those observed in conversation or narrative (for a discussion of this see Neidle, McLaughlin, and Lee 1997). Work on BSL (Brennan 1986), as well as other European sign languages (e.g., Bos 1996; Engberg-Pedersen 1995; Pizzuto 1990) has made the general finding that morphosyntactic mechanisms are used within the space surrounding, as well as on, the signer's body.

### The Organization of Reference in BSL

Based on the previously cited early work, a preliminary investigation of discourse construction in British Sign Language (Morgan 1998) has described a system of reference forms that are employed by signers in several referential frameworks. The reference forms described here are noun phrase, pronominal points, proforms, verb agreement, verb agreement in the fixed referential framework, and verb agreement in the shifted referential framework.

#### NOUN PHRASE

In BSL, noun phrases have a similar referential function as in spoken language. They may constitute the name of a referent spelled out in the manual alphabet (for example, T-O-M, or a name sign for one of the characters (for example, FLAT-NOSE).[3] Indefinite and definite noun phrases are

3. For the use of conventional notation devices to record sign language, see appendix A.

distinguished by signers through nonmanual features (in particular a head nod or eye-gaze marker) or by using a strategy of ONE BOY to indicate an indefinite referent and BOY for a definite referent. Nominal reference in BSL is often, but not necessarily, accompanied by a point into signing space. Pronominal points (PRO) or nonmanual mechanisms directed at or from these areas maintain a referent in discourse focus:

EXAMPLE 1

<u>><          <<</u>

LITTLE-GIRL$_a$ PRO$_a$(index finger point right)

*the little girl*

The preceding overt reference followed by an index finger point (PRO) to the right functions to establish the referent "little girl" in this area of sign space for subsequent discourse functions.[4]

### PRONOMINAL POINTS

The referential partitioning of sign space through the use of pronominal points was described in ASL by Friedman (1975); it involves the grammatical use of points in sign space on and off the body to indicate locations for referent identities. It is argued that these referential locations are used as person or object referents; that they represent landmarks for the use of various morphosyntactic and discourse mechanisms; and that it is their successful control and manipulation which underlies one aspect of discourse. An index point for reference functions like a pronoun. When used, it simultaneously gives referent identity, as well as topographic information (if this is important in the discourse context).[5]

4. The use of semicircles to represent sign-space and arrows to represent the movement of signs toward specific locations, stems from a notation convention in van Hoek, Norman, and O'Grady-Batch (1987). Above the gloss, the vertical line indicates the extent of eye-gaze scope. In the example presented, the signer is looking at the addressee (><) up to the point of the pronominal point to the right, when eye gaze shifts to the right (<<). All eye-gaze notation is made from the signer's perspective. Accompanying the gloss are subscripted syntactic roles and an English translation (a full description of notation devices appears in appendix A).

Example 2

>< >>

THEN PRO$_a$

*then she*

The pronominal point in example 2 co-refers to the antecedent noun phrase. Points may indicate reference to objects, locations, or concepts, as well as people. Anaphora requires that the signer point, gaze, or face toward the previously established spatial locus. Subsequent discourse uses this referent establishment as a locus for future comment. What has been established is a fixed referential framework (van Hoek, Norman, and O'Grady-Batch 1987). The narrator needs to be consistent in the use of this framework for the narrative to be coherent. Any future additions to the spatial array—along with shifts in the narrative framework—need to be assimilated. In signed discourse, as in spoken language, the interpretation of these pointing forms depends upon the relational meanings that are understood by the addressee.

PROFORMS

Proforms (p.form) mark the semantic category or the size and shape of the referent noun. They are used for establishing referent identity as well as topographic information (if important in the current discourse context). A canonical person proform is articulated in BSL with a G handshape, alternatively the proform can be represented by an inverted V handshape denoting legs (handshape notation device from Stokoe 1960). Proforms may be moved around the signing space or may be manipulated into various positions such as SITTING, JUMPING, KNEELING. Pronominal points and directional verbs can also exploit proforms to convey complex morphosyntactic information. In example 3, a signer, after an overt

5. Traditionally, sign language description refers to these points as "index-finger points" because the signer uses the index finger. Subsequently signers are referred to as having "indexed" a referent. This is inherently confusing, as linguistic theory uses the term "index" to refer to a syntactic role in, for example, a verb agreement frame. Syntactic index and an index-finger point are not the same thing. Here an index-finger point functions as a pronoun form.

reference to a car, places a vehicle proform (flat B-hand) in the right side of the signing space and then signs BOY followed by a person proform (G-hand) that moves toward the stationary passive hand maintaining the car. These uses of referential spaces are used by adult signers to build cohesive discourse.

EXAMPLE 3

$$\frac{\text{—} \qquad \text{VV} \qquad \qquad \text{—} \qquad \text{VV}}{\text{CAR}_\text{a} \text{ CAR-p.form BOY}_\text{b} \text{ }_\text{b}\text{BOY-p.form-move-towards-car}_\text{a}}$$

*the boy approached the car from the left*

These pronominal forms are referred to as *manual* as they are articulated largely on the hands, although for their success as referential expressions they need to be produced at the same time as nonmanual information. For example, the use of a proform for PERSON-WALK would need accompanying nonmanual information (facial expression, body orientation, manner of movement) for its successful identification as an old man walking or as the boy in the story walking. Pronominal points often are accompanied by nonmanual information.

VERB AGREEMENT

In this description, verb agreement morphology is divided between two referential systems: the fixed and shifted referential frameworks.

*Verb Agreement in the Fixed Referential Framework*

Once signers have established referents through nominal reference, a range of linguistic devices exploits these areas of the sign space for building discourse. One of the more complex morphological devices used with these spatially arranged referent loci is verb agreement. The inflection of a verb across sign space between two already established referent locations is argued (e.g., in Janis 1995) to function in the same manner as in a pro-drop language such as Italian. In pro-drop languages the subject clause can be omitted and both subject and object can be incorporated into the verb stem (e.g., *voy* [I go] in Spanish, where *yo* [I] does not need to be expressed). A verb such as GIVE in BSL can move between two locations, representing referential antecedents, in order to convey the meaning, "John gave the book to Mary." Another directional verb in BSL LOOK, may remain static as the orientation of the handshape gives referent information. The location of the sign in sign space encodes the subject of the utterance; the orientation of the sign (which location the fingers are pointing toward) indicates the object of the verb (see example 4). The verb LOOK would be produced with alternate hands when reversing direction due to the phonological constraints of hand orientations (it is difficult to position the right hand with the fingers pointing towards the area close to the right elbow). The following utterances illustrate the use of verb agreement. The second sentence reverses the direction of the verb inflection, thus indicating a change in meaning.

EXAMPLE 4

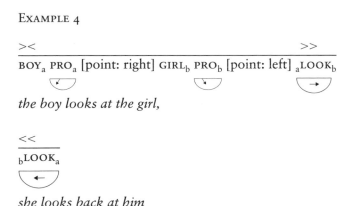

*the boy looks at the girl,*

*she looks back at him*

The use of directional verbs in the fixed referential framework may not be the most common reference strategy used in discourse. As described in the introduction, there is another discourse possibility that verb agreement can tie into, which is related to the change of perspective from speaker to shifted first person.

*Verb Agreement in the Shifted Referential Framework.*
In BSL, directional verbs inflect between referents that are present in the same way as they inflect between referential loci (representing nonpresent referents) in sign space.

In examples such as YOU-TELEPHONE-ME, YOU-GIVE-TO-HER, I-STAY-AT-YOUR-HOUSE, signers use similar verb-frame constructions between referents that are present, as in example 5 between the signer and a present second-person referent, and referents who are not present, as in example 6, between the signer and a nonpresent third-person referent.

EXAMPLE 5

signer
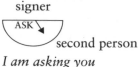
second person

*I am asking you*

EXAMPLE 6

signer
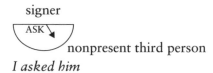
nonpresent third person

*I asked him*

The last two contexts refer to the fixed referential framework (FRF) in example 7 and the shifted referential framework (SRF) in example 8.[6]

EXAMPLE 7 (FRF)          EXAMPLE 8 (SRF)

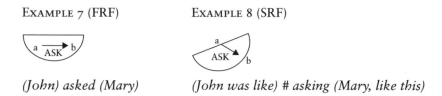

*(John) asked (Mary)*          *(John was like) # asking (Mary, like this)*

Once signers mark a movement from speaker to shifted first person, they report events from what has been referred to in the literature by terms such as *role shift* (Loew 1983), *referential shift* (Emmorey 1994), and *constructed action* (Metzger 1994), among others. This discourse option is equivalent in several ways to direct discourse or reported speech shifts in spoken language, but in sign language signers exploit this shift to report actions as well as words from another person's perspective. Examples 9, 10, and 11 illustrate the difference between the use of a fixed referential framework and a shifted referential framework in the utterance "the boy looks at the girl."

6. The notation # indicates the example is from within the shifted referential framework. This is characterized by accompanying nonmanual markers, such as an off-center orientation of the shoulders. An approximate translation attempts to capture this shifted diagram.

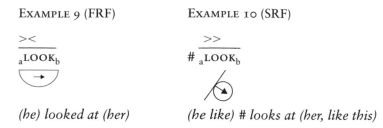

EXAMPLE 9 (FRF)    EXAMPLE 10 (SRF)

>< ̅ ̅ ̅ ̅ ̅ ̅          >> ̅ ̅ ̅ ̅ ̅ ̅
ₐLOOK_b        # ₐLOOK_b

*(he) looked at (her)*    *(he like) # looks at (her, like this)*

The signer in example 10 reports the action of "looking" from the shifted perspective of another first person. The body shifts toward the location of this referent; the eye gaze is directed at the second referent. The option of shifted perspective can also be taken while still in a marked narrator space, termed *mixed perspective* here, but possibly *role prominence* in other descriptions (e.g., Bahan 1996).

EXAMPLE 11 (mixed perspective)

>< ̅ ̅ ̅ ̅ ̅ ̅
ₐLOOK_b

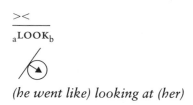

*(he went like) looking at (her)*

The salient aspects of these three distinctions are the different use of eye gaze between examples 10 and 11. Moving the body, as well as eye gaze, toward a referent's location is characteristic of a full shifted first-person device (coded as #). Hence signers not only make choices in the type of referential forms they use for person reference (pronoun, noun phrase, proform, verb agreement), they also make a discourse selection of perspective. The BSL reference system is exploited in a complex integration of the fixed referential framework and shifted referential framework in several discourse contexts. One of these contexts is now discussed.

### Event Packaging

One aspect of discourse that has received interest in the literature is the notion of simultaneity (e.g., Slobin 1996). In describing the encoding of simultaneity in discourse, terms such as *foregrounding* and *backgrounding of events* are used (e.g., Bamberg 1987; Hickmann 1994; Jisa and Kern 1997). Normally backgrounding is a continuing event against which a foreground event occurs. The use of temporal markings to distinguish background and foreground (ground) events in discourse is argued to guide attention flow for both speaker and addressee (Tomlin 1987). The use of markers to encode simultaneity relates to the speaker's intention to describe several different ongoing events as occurring within the same temporal boundary. In the semantics of English, these descriptions rely on the notion of main and subordinate events encoded as two clauses. These events describe moments of time and encode referent states, activities, or accomplishments. Moreover, the intervals defined in the two clauses may overlap or occur in succession (Slobin 1996). Thus speakers set up events along different "grounds," choosing to focus on one or the other.

In English it is common to use aspectual and temporal markings on verb morphology to mark background and foreground information, for example, "While he was sleeping the frog climbed out of the jar" (Berman and Slobin, chapter 1a).

The use of the aspectual marker "ing" marks the boy in background while the simple past "ed" marks the frog in foreground. The use of perspective marking is particularly salient in situations where two or more events happen at the same time, for example, "An owl came out and bammed him on the ground while the dog was running away from the bees" (Berman and Slobin 1994, chapter 1a).

Cross-linguistic work demonstrates that different languages have different options for encoding simultaneity. In Turkish, simultaneity may be encoded using case marking for causation on the verb for one referent and a topic particle "*de*" for the second (Slobin 1996, 74).

EXAMPLE 12

Baykus dusuruyor onu kopek de kaciyor
owl fall**causative** him dog **topic** run away
*the owl knocks him down and as for the dog he runs away*

Returning to English speakers, example 13 highlights the use of temporal connectives such as *while*. English speakers use connectives to join two or more events in discourse. Speakers also use these markers to overlap events along the temporal frame. But there are constraints on the extent to which different connective markers may encode overlap of events, illustrating their different semantic features. Comparing the temporal connectives *while* and *when* illustrates this point. "I am doing laundry while George is washing dishes," as opposed to "I am doing laundry when George is washing dishes!" which sounds strange (Silva 1991).

The use of connectives is related to the semantics of the event being described. In a comparison of the use of *while* and *as,* Silva (1991) found that the degree of interchangeability between the connectives depended on the event being described. Silva elicited sentences of a scene where a woman is using a vacuum cleaner inside a house and two children are watching her through a window from outside. Study participants used the connectives *while* and *as* equally as often to connect these two events:

She ends up cleaning up the living room as the kids watch through the window outside.

She's got a vacuum cleaner and is just tidying up very quickly while the little boy and girl are sort of watching her through the window.

Other scenes uniformly elicited only the temporal connective *as* from subjects. When two events are embedded in each other (e.g., walking and thinking) and have the same subject, the marker *as* carries more appropriate semantic information than other connectives. In English, Silva proposes the conjunction markers *when, while,* and *as* make up a continuum of simultaneity. *When* is the least specific as to the exact temporal relationship it encodes between events and at the same time the least constrained as to what predicates it can connect. *As* is the most specific and the most constrained and *while* is in the middle of the continuum. In terms of the role, temporal connectives perform in the construction of discourse. Silva cites Chafe's (1984, 445–50) statement that these markers "serve as guideposts to information flow, signaling a path or orientation in terms of which the following information is to be understood."

## Encoding Simultaneous Events in Sign Language Discourse

Although discourse has been explored in analysis of several sign languages, the strategies for encoding simultaneous events has received less attention. The analysis of simultaneity in terms of event packaging in extended discourse differs from the analysis of simultaneously articulated signs (e.g., Miller 1994), in that whole events involving several referents are happening simultaneously rather than description of signs involving two hands.

Previous descriptions of sign language discourse have described the use of representational spaces that appear to function as spatiotemporal connectives in spoken language, such as, *when, while,* and *as* in English. The nature of these uses of representational space needs to be explored further to understand how simultaneity is described in connected extended discourses. Looking at recent analysis of sign discourse, Winston (1995) describes ASL signers' use of what she terms "comparative frames" for establishing nominal reference in space. At the discourse level, spatial reference is an integral feature of at least three types of discourse frame: comparisons, performatives, and time mapping. Winston describes the use of the third type of discourse frame, time mapping spatial devices, as a discourse strategy whereby spatial comparisons are used to establish and maintain the major theme of the signer throughout the text. The device is also used to juxtapose current and past events, that is, a cohesion device for allowing simultaneous events to be packaged.

Within these discourse frames, time references are traced through a specific section of text by the initial establishment of a referent at a location in space and by subsequent co-references to that entity at that location. Abstract concepts, such as temporal frames, may be assigned locations in the spatial array and subsequent reference to these "reactivates" that temporal frame. These ideas can be traced at least as far back as Friedman (1975) and Padden (1983). Signers use temporal referencing in several ways:

1. the signer directs eye gaze toward the marked space as referring to the marked temporal frame;
2. the signer points to the space;
3. the articulation of a sign for a referent is moved from neutral to marked space indicating another temporal frame;
4. the signer rotates the torso/head towards the space;
5. the signer indicates a shift in time by physically stepping into the space and producing the signs; and
6. the signer switches hands (from dominant to nondominant) in order to articulate the signs with the hand on the side nearest the established temporal frame in space.

Mechanisms 1 through 3 can be seen in the previous description of pronominalization. Mechanisms 4 and 5 can be seen in the description of the shifted referential framework provided earlier. Mechanisms 1 through 5 may be ordered along a hierarchy of explicitness, from the most reduced (1), to the most overt (5). Signers make pragmatic judgments as to the extent of explicitness required in order to shift reference (Morgan 1997).

In an echo of Chafe and the "guideposts" notion just presented, Winston (1995) argues that these repeated references to temporal frames in space provide the watcher with cues for interpreting the signer's intended meaning; this analysis is extended in Mather and Winston (1996). Different spatial scenes and markers of movement evoke conceptual referents in the mind of the audience. The use of space in sign language thus extends to the marking and distinguishing of temporal events, as well as referential functions. Signers, in attempting to describe different events, may devote locations or areas of representational space to refer to events and move back and forward from these locations to package events.

Emmorey (1992) has related this use of space to encode surface relations in sign languages to the elaboration of cognitive models of language such as those in Fauconnier (1985). Fauconnier writes that communication through language works to the extent that communication partners "build up similar space configurations" from the linguistic and pragmatic data. Building a scene in sign space, which perhaps reflects an internal "mental discourse map" (Tyler 1983), is one of the most exciting aspects of sign language analysis at the discourse level. Understanding the mechanisms of sign space and referential frameworks that signers work with, in their construction of online complex discourse, is an important area to be described and assimilated into the field of general discourse analysis. The preceding description of a rich referential system in BSL suggests signers are disposed to report events in a dramatically different surface form to speakers of spoken languages. The present study reports on the use of sign space for the reporting of simultaneously occurring events in freestanding monologue narratives.

## DESCRIPTION OF THE PRESENT STUDY

The data presented here come from a larger study, which describes discourse cohesion and its development in young deaf children (Morgan 1998). The data centering on the packaging of events formed one part of this investigation.

### Method

PROCEDURE

Signers familiarized themselves with stimulus material. They then retold the story to the author, who is a fluent BSL signer, after being requested to "tell the whole story in as much detail as possible to me." The picture book was not present as the participants retold the story. The narrative was recorded on a video camera positioned next to the addressee. The study participants were two deaf native BSL signers, one male and one female, both in their early forties.

MATERIAL

The data discussed here forms part of a picture book narrative, *Frog Where Are You?* (Mayer 1969), henceforth referred to as FS (for Frog Story). This material was first used in descriptions of narrative production in Bamberg (1986); it is rich in opportunities for the encoding of temporal distinctions, sequencing, simultaneity, prospection, and retrospection. Recently a major cross-linguistic comparison of narrative production using FS has been reported (Berman and Slobin 1994). This analysis included ASL data (Galvan 1988). The story is depicted by nontext pictures showing the adventures of a young boy, his dog, and a lost frog. The boy and dog characters appear in twenty-three of the twenty-four pictures. The data described here are taken from the middle section of the narrative, where a complex scene depicts the simultaneous actions of the boy and the dog searching for the frog. The stimulus material used to elicit this part of the narratives are reproduced in figures 2 and 3 on p. 43.

MEASURING THE EXTENT OF EVENT PACKAGING

The analysis involves a qualitative description of three aspects of discourse in sign space:

1.  Scene setting. This aspect refers to the use of the surface of sign space for the division of background and foreground events, i.e., the actions of the dog and the actions of the boy, as well as the placement of "narrative props" such as trees, holes, beehives, and so on.
2.  Movement between representational spaces. This aspect describes the switching between events through the use of spatial means. These means focus on the use of the BSL reference system (described previously), and the signaling of these shifts through narrator information to the addressee.
3.  Temporal devices. This category focuses on the use of temporal strategies for the combination of events, the switching between events, and the tying of events together across discourse.

FIGURE 2. *The First Picture from* Frog, Where Are You?

FIGURE 3. *The Second Picture from* Frog, Where Are You?

### Results

The following data are taken from the overall FS narratives of two deaf native BSL signers. The analysis focuses on one section of these elicited narratives. This part of the narrative involves the encoding of two simultaneous events. In figure 2 (on the left side of the scene), the dog who has been pushing at a tree, where a beehive is hanging, stands looking at the beehive, which has fallen to the ground with the first bees beginning to come out of the hive. On the right side of the scene, the boy has found a large tree with a hole in the trunk and is investigating inside. In the next picture (figure 3) we see the dog running across the foreground, pursued by a long swarm of bees. The boy in the meantime has discovered that the hole is the nest for a large owl, which is seen angrily emerging from the hole, while the boy falls from the tree in shock. In relation to the discussion of the grounding of discourse, it is important to mention that in the type of discourse elicited in this study, the inherent foreground and background of events are not given by the pictures themselves but are constructed by the narrator (Slobin 1996). The action of the dog pushing at the beehive could be foregrounded in the main clause with an active verb and the actions of the bees backgrounded in a subordinate clause: for example, "the dog runs away as the bees follow him." The available options to encode events are diverse. The speaker can choose between marking the dog as focus and the bees by a passive tense, for example, "the dog is being chased by the bees;" or encode the action of the dog in a subordinate clause that represents the next plotline in the scene, for example, "all the bees start chasing the dog, who runs away." The organization of experience in narrative, as following the available options in a given language has been labeled "thinking for speaking" by Slobin (1996). First the glossed version of these events is first presented for Signer 1. The second signer's narrative will then be described before attempting to draw commonalities between the two pieces of signed discourse.

EXAMPLE 13

Signer 1: Frog Story

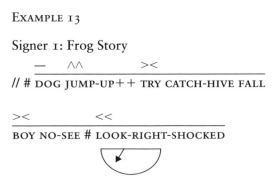

//  # DOG JUMP-UP++ TRY CATCH-HIVE FALL

BOY NO-SEE # LOOK-RIGHT-SHOCKED

>< -                              (squint--------

―――――――――――――――――――――――――――――――――――――――――――
TREE WIDE TRUNK HAVE HOLE # BOY THINK

――――――――――――――――――――――) <<                    θθ

―――――――――――――――――――――――――――――――――――――――――――
PRO-THERE MAYBE LOOK-IN-HOLE ++ SHOCK

><                 ∧∧
―――――――――――――――――――――――――――――――――――――――――――
WHAT OWL # FLAP-WINGS PECK-ANGRILY

θθ                              ><                    -
―――――――――――――――――――――――――――――――――――――――――――
BOY FALL-DOWN    // SAME-TIME PRO-THERE BEE

                                        <<
―――――――――――――――――――――――――――――――――――――――――――
HIVE-FALL PRO-THERE BEE-pl ANGRY LEAVE

><
―――――――――――――――――――――――――――――――――――――――――――
SWARM-FLY FLY LONG-THIN-TRAIL p.form-SWARM //

*The dog is like jumping up and down again and again, trying to get the hive hanging from the tree when it falls onto the ground, the boy as he didn't see what happened like turns around and is like shocked. There is this big wide tree with a hole in the side of the trunk. The boy thinks to himself 'in there maybe.' He like looks into the hole, really looking around inside and gets a real shock as there is this big nasty owl like flapping away and pecking angrily, the boy falls from the tree, just as the bee-hive falls over to the left, the bees come flying past from the hive, the whole swarm of bees comes flying and buzzing away out of the hive and in a huge cloud they come flying toward the boy.*

The preceding excerpt is an extremely rich piece of signed discourse. The complexity is only hinted at by the selective glosses of signs, movements, and eye-gaze behavior. The following section discusses the presence of the three aspects crucial for packaging events across discourse in this narrative excerpt.

*Scene Setting*

The signer begins with a description of events coming directly from the dog's perspective. She marks the shift of perspective through a break from mutual eye gaze with the addressee and a series of nonmanual characterizations of the dog, including eye gaze directed toward a representation of the tree and beehive. The information of why the dog is jumping up, TRY CATCH-HIVE FALL, is accompanied by eye gaze at the addressee (><).

The signer using the shifted referential framework constructs a direct report of actions, rather than using pronominal and agreement forms between spatial locations on the surface of sign space within the fixed referential framework (see previous discussion of pronominal points, proforms, and verb agreement in shifted referential framework). Next, the signer reintroduces the boy through an overt noun phrase: BOY NO-SEE. This is the same type of narrator "aside" to the addressee, as the TRY CATCH-HIVE FALL comment in the previous utterance. An aside to the addressee is characterized by mutual eye gaze (><) and is used for clarification, filling information, and marking the subsequent information as important—something like "now pay attention to the next bit, as it's important to the story."

A shift to a different referent is marked through the break in eye gaze, which is interpreted as the subject of the previous utterance: the boy. This perspective shift sets up the first division of signing space between the boy and the dog. The boy looks to his right to see the dog's actions, and is shocked to see what is happening. This brief mention of orientation creates a scene where the boy is to the left of the dog. The signer chooses to mark this orientation from the point of view as mirroring the left/right distinction in the stimulus material. This scene is still reported as a shifted representation of events at this point. The signer continues from the boy's perspective as he faces a large tree, while switching to narrator information marked by >< to describe the scene. The signer sets up a representation of a hole in front of her at face level: TREE WIDE TRUNK HAVE HOLE. The owl emerges from the hole and has a marked upward eye gaze contrasting with the boy's level eye gaze. The use of different eye-gaze levels creates the impression of a height difference, thus allowing shifts in perspective between the boy and the owl to be accomplished in the same representational space. These shifts involve a 180-degree rotation of perspective.

There is a change in the use of sign space, as the signer describes the boy falling from the tree with a V proform moving away from her own body, accompanied by nonmanual characterizations of the boy falling through space using facial expression and body orientation appropriate to the boy's experience. A new scene is set up through a marked look to the addressee and the transition: SAME-TIME PRO-THERE BEEHIVE-FALL PRO-THERE. The location of the fallen hive is articulated twice with a point to her left and with the finishing point of the falling hive also on the left side. The signer takes the boy's new perspective on events as the scene rotates 180 degrees, with the boy now lying on the floor. The dog had previously been located by LOOK-RIGHT-SHOCKED in the right side of signing space from the signer's point of view, but the dog's actions are now located toward the signer's left sign space. This rotation of both the fixed referential framework and shifted referential framework is a complex construction both in terms of the spatial locations of referents and objects that need to be integrated with linguistic devices, as well as in terms of the representation of this new scene at the cognitive level.

*Movement Between Representational Spaces*

The signer shifts between representing action on her own body through the shifted referential framework to representing events in the signing space through the fixed referential framework. There is also a frequent movement to a narrator perspective to give "filling" information, to mark changes in referent perspective, to mark structural units of the discourse, and to monitor addressee comprehension. Movement between these three representational spaces (fixed referential framework, shifted referential framework, and narrator) involves setting up locations in sign space as well as signaling movement through these spaces. The signer "moves" between a series of spaces. The sequence begins with space devoted to the actions of the dog, which moves cohesively into a space occupied by the boy. The two spaces replace each other in terms of where they articulated. The signer does not physically move from one area to another, but in terms of representation she is in one space when she represents the dog and another space when she represents the boy.

The movement between these two representational spaces is signaled first through a break in shifted reference and a comment on the dog's actions (TRY CATCH-HIVE FALL) to a narrator comment on the boy's actions (BOY NO-SEE). Once focus has moved from the dog to the boy, the signer signals another shift in reference, this time to the boy's perspective on events. Thus the movement between these spaces appears entirely cohesive. The signer goes further than this and marks an intermediate movement between the two spaces, signing LOOK-RIGHT-SHOCKED. This implies that the dog has now moved from the signing space to somewhere to the right of the boy. Following this shift is information from narrator perspective and then a shift back to the boy. Rather than solely action, this shift reports the boy's internal thoughts: # BOY THINK PRO-THERE MAYBE. The space set up by the tree and the hole in the tree are extensions of the space representing the boy. When the boy looks in the hole, the signer moves her hands to depict the hole moving toward her own face rather than moving her face toward the hole, emphasizing the representational nature of these descriptions. Pointing toward the hole is consistent with the boy's new point of view, facing the tree rather than looking down onto the ground.

The next movement in space is between the owl and the boy. As in the exchange in the use of the same signing space between the boy and the dog in the earlier part of the narrative, the signer now represents the owl's actions in the same space the boy had occupied, marking the shift in reference with an intermediate narrator comment (WHAT OWL) and mutual eye gaze. The new referent to be represented in this space uses eye gaze up to the boy as a signal of the new perspective. Again, rather than a full jump to another perspective, this allows only a shift from boy as primary focus to boy as secondary focus, or from agent to patient.

### Temporal Devices

In this part of the narrative there is a complex problem to solve concerning the laying out in discourse of the two events, which are occurring simultaneously. The signer uses a sequence of event descriptions to describe both the dog's and boy's actions, ordering events as first the dog then the boy. The dog's actions terminate at the moment the beehive falls. The middle part of the description focuses on the boy's actions and the dog's are assumed to be occurring off the main focus. When the boy falls from the tree the signer uses the temporal marker SAME-TIME and reintroduces the dog into the discourse. The reintroduction begins with the beehive falling, although the last mention of the beehive had suggested it had already fallen. The signer uses a "flashback" and depicts the fall once more.

The analysis now moves onto the same event described by the second signer. The description follows the same organization, revolving around the three aspects of event packaging.

EXAMPLE 14

Signer 2: Frog Story

<pre>
     >>                      ><
// #LOOK-ACROSS-LEFT LOOK TERRIBLE
</pre>

<pre>
        ^> ><              ^>        ><
// DOG # SEE BEE HIVE    // # LOOK-UP TERRIBLE SWARM
</pre>

<pre>
   θθ>>                    -              ><
// # LOOK-ACROSS-LEFT BAD WALK-AWAY    // SEE THERE
</pre>

<pre>
              -
TREE HOLE POSSIBLE CHECK INSIDE WHAT LOOK-IN THERE HOLE
</pre>

<pre>
                                      ><
HEAD-IN-HOLE//p.form-HEAD-EMERGE-QUICK OWL SHARP-BEAK
</pre>

<pre>
PUFFED-OUT LIKE SAY PISS-OFF INSIDE WHAT NOT-ALLOWED
</pre>

<pre>
          >>   ∧∧           ><     θθ   ><
TREE    // # DOG JUMP-BACK BOY RUN ESCAPE RUN WALK-AWAY
</pre>

*He looks over at the dog who is looking up at the beehive. That is terrible!*
*The bees are all swarming out. He like looks over, that is bad, then walks*
*away from there. He sees a hole in a tree in front of him, 'Maybe I should*
*check and see what's in there.' He like looks into right into the hole, like*
*puts his head right into the hole looking around like that. With that an*
*owl comes shooting out of the hole, all puffed up feathers a big sharp beak*
*like to say, 'piss-off out of here, this is my house in here, you're not al-*
*lowed in this tree.' The dog suddenly jumps back frightened and runs off*
*with the boy escaping away from the scene. . . .*

*Scene Setting*

As in the first signer's story, the second signer begins with a dominant perspective on the scene, the relative positions of the referents are indicated from the boy's perspective. The signer marks a shift to the boy and indicates that the dog is some way off to his left: # LOOK-ACROSS-LEFT LOOK TERRIBLE. Very quickly the signer moves across to the location previously designated as the area to the left of the boy. This shift of reference to the dog is very rapid. The position of the beehive, as well as activity of the bees, are described from the dog's perspective: DOG # SEE BEEHIVE // # LOOK-UP TERRIBLE SWARM. The narrator comment that breaks this description includes the use of two proforms representing the swarm of bees that move toward the narrator's body. Abruptly, the signer signals a change in perspective and moves the description back to the boy positioned to the right of the dog. There is a lexical repetition that increases the predictability of this reduced shift through: LOOK-ACROSS-LEFT.

Now that the relative locations are set up, the signer moves the boy through the signing space with a person proform. The next part of the description involves a narrator point, a description of the tree and the tree hole: SEE THERE TREE HOLE POSSIBLE CHECK INSIDE WHAT LOOK-IN THERE HOLE HEAD-IN-HOLE. This description uses mixed shifted-narrator perspective. The two referents are brought together abruptly for the escape.

## Comparing the Two Signers

MOVEMENT BETWEEN REPRESENTATIONAL SPACES

Both signers adopt a similar strategy in setting out a clear perspective on events at the beginning of this complex scene. In the second signer's story, the boy's actions are represented in a shifted referential framework in the first utterance. The movement to the dog is marked by a look to the left side of sign space, indicating that some distance off there is something terrible happening. A noun phrase reintroduces the representational space of the dog. This example illustrates that representational space is "cleared" and "reused" through the signaling of a new perspective by an overt reference form: DOG # SEE BEEHIVE. The signer blends representational spaces at points, allowing the dog's actions to move into narrator comments: # LOOK-UP TERRIBLE SWARM.

In contrast with the intermediate "stepping-stone" narrator comments of the first signer, which seemed to facilitate transition between representational spaces, the second signer chooses to move back to the boy solely through lexical repetitions involving perceptual verbs to locations: LOOK-LEFT, LOOK-UP. There is movement between different levels of referential space by the proform BOY-WALK-AWAY, followed by the narrator comment SEE THERE. The narrator comment serves to switch attention from the movement of the boy to the description of a new scene. The description of the tree and tree hole are thus linked to the previous scene through the perceptual verb SEE, as was the previous transition between the dog and the boy actions through LOOK.

Signers exploit these perceptual verbs (e.g., LOOK, SEE, GLANCE) to move discourse between areas of representational space in similar ways to temporal links such as "earlier, next, and later," and metaphorical spatiotemporal terms such as "after, back, behind, and before." For the owl's entrance into the scene the signer uses an A handshape as a head proform, thus describing both the action of the owl leaving the hole as well as the reaction of the boy looking at this event. This is an example of a simultaneous event being encoded by the signer using different parts of his own body to represent different referents. The subsequent narrator marked comments are from a mixed perspective, contrasting the indignant owl and the narrator reporting what happened: p.form-HEAD-EMERGE-QUICK OWL SHARP-BEAK PUFFED-OUT LIKE SAY PISS-OFF INSIDE WHAT NOT-ALLOWED TREE. The final part of this excerpt involves the bringing together of both referents.

The first signer used a complex construction that involved setting up a new "thematic perspective" through the boy's new position on the ground as well as a "flashback" construction of the beehive falling. The second signer manages this through moving from the narrator-owl comments to a representation of the shocked dog. The addressee perhaps has to make more of an intuitive leap here, as there is no description of the falling hive. As the boy is the dominant perspective, the signer concentrates on describing the boy's actions, leaving the dog as a secondary character that follows the boy out of the scene.

TEMPORAL DEVICES

The second signer marks the two events in a similar right/left representation. Although there is less emphasis on the dog's actions, the signer concentrates on the description of the boy's movements as well as the dialogue with the owl. This emphasizes the point that signers and speakers are selective in which events are described and which take precedence over others in encoding complex scenes in discourse. The first signer concentrates on the two characters' actions while the second signer focuses more on the boy. The jumps between two simultaneous events are made by the second signer through rapid shifts in reference signaled through noun phrases for the dog and lexical or semantic repetitions for the boy.

## Discussion

Both adults construct a series of events that are cohesively linked through a reference system that exploits different levels of representational spaces. The preceding description has highlighted several salient aspects of these spaces and how they are used in discourse. The creation of cohesive discourse through the use of the mechanisms discussed above is complex. In the comparison of the two narratives, it is clear that although the constraint of being cohesive in the use of spatial devices to mark and shift between perspectives on events is being adhered to, individuals vary in how these perspective shifts are marked. Pragmatic judgments are made by signers as to how explicit or reduced reference forms are to be used in specific discourse contexts. In the description of the packaging of events through simultaneity and perspective, an observation was made concerning the signer's use of a *thematic perspective*. A thematic perspective on an event refers to the signers' use of a main or dominant perspective to report events, as contrasted with a secondary perspective. Signers set up a thematic perspective when narrating, thus allowing reduced reference to be used in keeping this perspective in discourse focus. The *secondary perspective* is activated through overt reference forms. Thus, in the context of event packaging, two perspectives can be used on events without having to label both overtly.

The use of spatial devices in BSL narrative is constrained in terms of the number of active referents a signer can report on at any one time. The use of multiple perspectives on events seems to be constrained by factors dealing with processing rapidly changing spatial information. Signers focus early on in their discourses on scene setting. Much time is spent setting up scenes and spatial relations between protagonists. These foundations are used for subsequent rapid transitions between events and referents. Signers divide sign space up at several levels, both by assigning different areas of sign space to different events and by overlaying different events in the same sign space. The divisions of space refer to the use of the fixed referential framework and the shifted referential framework respectively. Sign space can be cleared for new events, if marked by appropriate eye gaze. Signers switch between different sign spaces through marked eye-closes, as well as looks to the addressee to signal shifts, as well as to check for comprehension. Often these changes in sign space are rapid.

The movement between simultaneous events is complex. There are many examples of narrator asides, which surround shifts and frequent checks for comprehension. Thus narrators often use mutual eye gaze or a comment directly to the addressee before and after a shift. There is a system of three steps to shift between two events. There is an intermediate stepping-stone that retains partial semantics of the first events while signaling the new event as primary. There is also a high proportion of perceptual verbs especially involving vision, which are used to link different representational spaces cohesively. Signers also use temporal devices such as flashbacks to link two events separated by a third. The overlaying of temporal frameworks is at the core of achieving cohesion in these constructions. In describing these shifts signers combine different representational spaces. The shifted referential framework and the fixed referential framework are linked through simultaneous perspectives such as proform and referential shift. Often signers mix their report of events by remaining narrators while also representing thoughts, emotional states and physical actions of narrative protagonists.

## CONCLUSIONS

Referential forms in BSL are multifunctional. Signers use reference to track protagonists through discourse as well as to organize discourse into episodes, themes, and hierarchies. For example, the use of eye gaze can be seen as syntactic and discourse relevant. Adult signers thus make choices based on both local and global discourse constraints. The use of sign space is pervasive at all levels of sign discourse. Sign space is made up of several subsystems. To set up referents and maintain them through transitions in representation space, signers use the shifted and fixed referential frameworks. The creation of overlaid representational spaces is used to encode simultaneously occurring events. Adult signers effortlessly rotate sign space for discourse purposes, in particular, to switch perspectives on events. Adult signers choose to construct discourse from a shifted perspective, setting up referential loci on their own bodies rather than in the spatial array in front of them. A series of shifted verbs are used to mark perspective as well as maintain reference. The complexity of this framework is only hinted at in the preceding analysis of simultaneity and serial verb usage. This motivation has consequences for discourse strategies adopted by adult signers in narrative. Signers combine overt reference forms with shifted reference to report language, action, and thought. (This may be a motivation stemming from the nature of face-to-face communication rather than discourse based on a literate tradition.) This has been a preliminary attempt to capture the richness and complexity of this use of sign language. Further work should elaborate the use of representational spaces for describing other discourse contexts, as well suggesting possible existing underlying constraints.

## REFERENCES

Ahlgren, L., and B. Bergman. 1992. Reference in narratives. In *Fifth international symposium on sign language research,* ed. I. Algren, B. Bergman, and M. Brennan. Salamanca, Spain: ISLA.

Bahan, B. 1996. *Non-manual realization of agreement in American Sign Language.* Ph.D. dissertation, Boston University, Boston.

Bahan, B., and L. Petitto. 1982. Aspects of rules for character establishment and reference in ASL. San Diego: Salk Institute University of San Diego. Duplicated.

Bamberg, M. 1987. A functional approach to the acquisition of anaphoric relationships. *Linguistics* 24: 227–84.

Berman, R., and Slobin, D. 1994. *Different ways of relating events in narrative: A cross-linguistic developmental study.* Hillsdale, N.J.: Lawrence Erlbaum Associates.

Bos, H. 1996. Serial verb constructions in Sign Language of the Netherlands. Paper presented at the Fifth International Conference on Theoretical Issues in Sign Language Research. Montreal, Canada.

Brennan, M. 1986. *Productive morphology in British Sign Language: Focus on the role of metaphors.* Edinburgh: Moray House College of Education.

Chafe, W. 1987. Cognitive constraints on information flow. In *Coherence and grounding in discourse,* vol. 11 of *Typological studies in discourse,* ed. W. Chafe. Amsterdam: John Benjamins.

Clark, H., and R. Gerrig. 1990. Quotations as demonstrations. *Language* 66:764.

Emmorey, K. 1992. Processing topographic vs. arbitrary space in ASL. Poster presented at the Fourth International Conference on Sign Language Research. San Diego.

———. 1994. The confluence of language and space in sign language. In *Language and space,* ed. P. Bloom. Cambridge, Mass.: MIT Press.

Emmorey, K., D. Corina, and U. Bellugi. 1995. Differential processing of topographic and referential functions of space. In *Language, gesture, and space,* ed. K. Emmorey and J. Reilly. Cambridge, Mass.: Lawrence Erlbaum Associates.

Engberg-Pederson, E. 1995. Point of view expressed through shifters. In *Language, gesture and space,* ed. K. Emmorey and J. Reilly. Cambridge, Mass.: Lawrence Erlbaum Associates.

Fauconnier, G. 1985. *Mental spaces.* Cambridge, Mass.: MIT Press.

Friedman, L. 1975. Space, time, and person reference in American Sign Language. *Language* 51:940–61.

Galvan, D. 1988. A sensitive period for the acquisition of complex morphology in American Sign Language. *Papers and Reports on Child Language Development* 28:107–14.

Gangel-Vasquez, J. 1997. *Literacy in Nicaraguan Sign Language: Assessing word recognition skills at the Escuelita de Bluefields.* N.p.: California State University. Duplicated.

Gee, J., and J. Kegl. 1983. Narrative/story structure, pausing, and American Sign Language. *Discourse Processes* 6:243–58.

Halliday, M., and R. Hasan. 1976. *Cohesion in English.* London: Longman.

Hickmann, M. 1994. Discourse organisation and the development of reference to person, space and time. In *The handbook of child language,* ed. P. Fletcher and B. MacWhinney. Oxford: Blackwell.

Janis, W. 1995. A cross-linguistic perspective on ASL verb agreement. In *Language, gesture, and space,* ed. K. Emmorey and J. Reilly. Cambridge, Mass.: Lawrence Erlbaum Associates.

Jisa, H., and S. Kern. 1997. *Discourse organisation in French children's narratives.* Working paper, Centre de Reserches Linguistiques, Universiteré Lumière, Lyon, France.

Karmiloff-Smith, A. 1985. Language and cognitive processes from a developmental perspective. *Language and Cognitive Processes* 1:61–85.

Loew, R. 1983. *Roles and reference in American Sign Language: A developmental perspective.* Ph.D. dissertation, University of Minnesota.

Mather, S., and E. Winston. 1996. Comparative frames and ASL discourse. Paper presented at the Fifth International Conference on Theoretical Issues in Sign Language Research. Montreal, Canada.

Mayer, M. 1969. *Frog where are you?* New York: Dial Press.

Metzger, M. 1994. Constructed dialogue and constructed action in American Sign Language. In *Sociolinguistics in deaf communities,* ed. C. Lucas. Washington, D.C.: Gallaudet University Press.

Miller, C. 1994. Simultaneous constructions and complex signs in Quebec Sign Language. In *Perspectives on sign language usage,* ed. I. Ahlgren, B. Berman, and M. Brennan. Durham, England: ISLA.

Morgan, G. 1997. Discourse in British Sign Language. In *Discourse analysis,* ed. E. Pedro. Lisbon: Colibri.

———. 1998. *The development of discourse cohesion in British Sign Language.* Ph.D. dissertation, University of Bristol, Bristol, U.K.

Neidle, C., D. MacLaughlin, and R. Lee. 1997. *Syntactic structure and discourse function: an examination of two constructions in American Sign Language.* Report No. 4. Boston: American Sign Language Linguistic Research Project, Boston University.

Padden, C. 1983. *Inflection of morphology and syntax in American Sign Language.* Ph.D. dissertation, University of California, San Diego.

Pizzuto, E., E. Giuranna, and G. Gambino. 1990. Manual and nonmanual morphology in Italian Sign Language: Grammatical constraints and discourse processes. In *Sign language research: Theoretical issues,* ed. C. Lucas. Washington, D.C.: Gallaudet University Press.

Poulin, C., and C. Miller. 1995. On narrative discourse and point of view in Quebec Sign Language. In *Language, gesture, and space,* ed. K. Emmorey and J. Reilly. Cambridge: Lawrence Erlbaum Associates.

Roy, C. 1989. *Features of discourse in an American Sign Language lecture.* In *The sociolinguistics of the deaf community,* ed. C. Lucas. San Diego: Academic Press.

Silva, M. 1991. Simultaneity in children's narratives: The case of when, while, and as. *Journal of Child Language* 18:641–62.

Slobin, D. 1996. From "thought to language" to "thinking for speaking." In *Rethinking linguistic relativity: Studies in the social and cultural foundations of language,* vol. 17, ed. J. Gumperz and S. Levinson. Cambridge, England: Cambridge University Press.

Tomlin, R. 1987. Linguistic reflections of cognitive events. In *Coherence and grounding in discourse,* ed. R. Tomlin. Amsterdam: Benjamins.

Tyler, L. 1983. The development of discourse mapping processes. The on-line interpretation of anaphoric expressions. *Cognition* 3:309–41.

van Hoek, K., F. Norman, and L. O'Grady-Batch. 1987. *Development of spatial and non-spatial referential cohesion.* Working paper, Salk Institute, San Diego.

Winston, E. 1995. Spatial mapping in comparative discourse frames. In *Language, gesture, and space,* ed. K. Emmorey and J. Reilly. Cambridge, Mass.: Lawrence Erlbaum Associates.

**Transcription Conventions**

| Example | Explanation |
| --- | --- |
| Gloss | |
| LITTLE-GIRL | Approximate English gloss of signs. Where more than one English word is required this is indicated through a hyphenated gloss. |
| T-O-M | Fingerspelling indicated through small caps separated by hyphens. |
| Location/ pronominalization | |
| PRO  (x) | Point or localization in front of signer at x |
| Verb Morphology | |
| (↘ left arrow) | Left |
| (↗ arrow) | From right |
| (→ arrow) | Across body |
| (↑ arrow) | Towards body |
| (↗ arrow) | Right + up |
| (↘ arrow) | Left + down |
| Eye Gaze | |
| SEARCH | Scope of eye gaze marked by line across top of gloss |
| >< | Mutual |
| — | Neutral |
| << | Right |
| >> | Left |
| ∨∨ | Down |
| ∧∧ | Up |
| θθ | Closed |
| — | Squint |

*Event Packaging in British Sign Language Discourse* : 57

| | |
|---|---|
| <ᵛ | Right + down |
| ^> | Up + left |
| Discourse Markers | |
| // | Pause |
| # | Shifted first person |
| ++ | Repeated sign for grammatical purposes |
| p.form- | Proform sign |
| pl- | Pluralization marker |
| abc | Syntactic indices |

# Storytelling in the Visual Mode:

## A Comparison of ASL and English

*Jennifer Rayman*

This paper is an investigation into the tools of language and how these tools influence the structure of the symbol system. Past studies of American Sign Language (ASL) storytelling have focused on how features of storytelling—such as pauses, eye gaze, and other nonmanual behaviors—create patterns of poetic organization (Gee and Kegl 1983; Bahan and Supalla 1995; Wilson 1996). In addition, Wilson (1996), using Labov's (1972) theory of story structure, has analyzed how evaluative content in ASL is portrayed through nonlexical features such as pantomime, facial expression, and role-shifting. But none of these studies has ventured into the realm of how linguistic tools themselves shape the stories that ASL signers tell.

Discussions of ASL have often remarked on its unique ability to depict spatial and visual elements (Liddell 1996; Emmorey and Casey 1995; Taub 1997). If in fact the resources that allow ASL to represent spatial and visual events are unique to the language, then this should be evident in how ASL users depict events in the stories that they tell, compared to similar stories that speakers of English tell.

In his work on comparative storytelling structure, Slobin (1996a) avoids an exaggerated version of Whorf's (1956) hypothesis that language form governs the representation of the world. Instead, he argues that language provides its users with a range of resources that entails a

This research was funded by a grant from the U.S. Department of Education, #HO23T30006, awarded to Carol Padden and Claire Ramsey. My appreciation goes to Sharon Allen, Darline Clark, and Francine MacDougall for research assistance and language consultation on the data reported here. I also want to thank Carol Padden for crucial comments and suggestions that have greatly contributed to the development of this paper.

certain type of "thinking for speaking" but that language does not necessarily limit or determine thought. Rather, the dynamic interplay between thought and language, particularly thought that is aimed at speaking, yields tendencies toward particular patterns of attention and representation in language.

Slobin argues that different languages offer different portraits of the world. With their different grammatical properties, languages provide their users with a multitude of representational tools. Slobin views narration as a task in which not all of the details of an event are actually encoded linguistically in the storytelling. Instead, language users select details based on the perspectives they take in relation to the events and the linguistic options available to them. Thus the process of encoding events into language is filtered through the perspective chosen and the linguistic resources available within a particular language. Information is then packaged in ways that organize the events in time and space in a manner typical for the linguistic options available in that particular language (Berman and Slobin 1994).

In Slobin's (1996b) comparison of Spanish and English, he focuses particularly on the description of motion events in elicited narratives as their form and content are shaped by different language typologies. He supports Leonard Talmy's (1985) characterization that language typologies, being either satellite-framed or verb-framed, can account for differences in storytellers' narrative choices. Determining which typology involves analyzing whether the core schema is mapped onto the verb or the satellite. In the case of Slobin's study the schema analyzed is that of motion. Using Talmy's example of a bottle floating out of a cave, Slobin (1996b) shows that English is a satellite-framed language. In the sentence, "the bottle floated out of the cave," the core information of the path of motion is mapped onto the satellite "out." In Spanish, a verb-framed language, the core information of motion path is mapped onto the verb, as in *la botella salio flotando*—"the bottle exited floating." Slobin found that English relies on verb particles in order to convey paths of motion, whereas languages like Spanish rely more on the verb itself to convey such information. English also has a richer availability of verbs of motion than does Spanish. By analyzing the different rhetorical styles of stories retold by native English speakers and native Spanish speakers, Slobin concludes that different language speakers devote different attention to the dynamics of motion because of the greater or lesser availability of verbs of motion that are easily associated with satellites in the particular language. The stories of English speakers proved to more richly describe the paths of motion in the story than did the stories of Spanish speakers because of the diversity of verb satellite pairings available in English (Slobin 1996b, 195–206).

In Slobin's cross-linguistic analysis of storytelling, he focuses on the details of verb typology and on motion and path. In analyzing ASL storytelling, this paper looks to other aspects of narrative as well: character, space, motion, and manner of movement. Moving outside of the realm of analyzing verbs in themselves as they relate to paths of movement, this paper will look at other resources within language, particularly those involved with representing the manner of motion, spatial relationships, and the portrayal of characters, to show that these resources do in fact shape the way stories are told.

## THE TASK

In this study stories were elicited using a silent cartoon (Disney 1935; Supalla et al. in press). The cartoon is about two minutes long and provides a rendition of the well-known Aesop's fable of the race between the tortoise and the hare. The events depicted in the cartoon invite a rich array of spatial relations, character descriptions, and expressions of manner of movement as the characters line up in particular ways at the starting line and maintain different spatial relationships as they pass each other in the race. The fable is commonly referred to as "The Tortoise and the Hare," but in the Deaf community it is known as "RABBIT TURTLE STORY." Throughout the paper, I refer to most references to the story as "The Rabbit and Turtle Story," and reserve the more formal title for the original folktale. I refer to the characters as the rabbit and the turtle unless directly quoting another usage by a narrator.

Five adult native users of ASL and five adult native speakers of English were individually shown the cartoon and then asked to retell the story to a researcher as they were videotaped. A native user of ASL elicited the ASL stories and a native speaker of English elicited the English stories. The adults across each language group were matched to the extent possible for gender, age, and educational background. For example, when we found that one of our Deaf participants had an extensive theater background, we found a hearing actress to perform the story in English for comparison. Though all participants viewed the same cartoon stimulus, each expressed different linguistic and narrative content. All storytellers from both language groups included the bare minimum of the basic plot, but Deaf storytellers included far more details, not only of visual character development but of supporting actions that move the plot along.

In the cartoon, both the rabbit and the turtle emerge from their hovels to the cheers of the onlooking crowd and are summoned to the starting line by the raccoon officiating the race. As the two characters line up at the starting line, the turtle faces the wrong way. When the raccoon starts the race by firing his gun into the air, the turtle spins around in the wake of the rabbit's speedy take off and begins plodding along the path. En route the rabbit notices that the turtle is far behind him and sees a tree to lie down against and take a nap. When the turtle comes upon the rabbit sleeping he tiptoes past the rabbit and then rushes toward the finish line. The rabbit wakes up and chases after the turtle, but he is too late as the turtle crosses the finish line by stretching his neck forward and tearing through the finish line with his mouth. Meanwhile, the rabbit, in hot pursuit, trips and falls. By the time he sits up, he looks on with surprise to see that he has lost the race. For the grand finale, the turtle is uplifted by the crowd in a grand hurrah and tossed into the air landing upside down with his hat on his tail.

## ENGLISH AND ASL: DRAWING ON DIFFERENT RESOURCES

Users from ASL and English draw on the linguistic resources provided by their respective languages differently in order to relate the story of the turtle and the rabbit. Certain aspects of the story, such as manner and path of motion, take a more prominent place in the ASL stories than they do in the English stories. This may be due to the ease with which ASL users can represent both the manner and path of motion, and the linguistic labor necessary for representing these aspects in spoken English.

Perhaps we could imagine two piles of linguistic resources within a language. In one pile we have commonly used structures that have become the preferred rhetoric; in the other pile we have those resources that are called upon less frequently, but can be drawn upon with more practice. For example, the hearing actress's theater training had undoubtedly given her more practice telling elaborate and fascinating stories in order to maintain an audience's attention. Thus it is not surprising that she was able, to a certain extent, to accomplish a certain type of role-playing and vivid description of motion that most of the average ASL users accomplished as a matter of habit.

Our Deaf and hearing actresses, Samantha and Brenda,[1] told the most elaborate and entertaining stories, which is not surprising given the craft they have honed in order to work in the theater. What is interesting, however, is that when we compare the hearing group as a whole to the Deaf group, the ASL users included much more detail depicting the actions of the rabbit and the turtle. The Deaf storytellers reliably characterized the rabbit and the turtle as cocky and humble, respectively, and maintained this characterization through use of role-shifting throughout the story. Deaf storytellers also showed the spatial relationships of the runners as they came to the starting line and indicated the precise manner of motion as the characters ran the race. Typically, the English speakers did not enter into the role of either of the characters. At the beginning of the story, their only mention of characterization is that the rabbit was confident, leaving out any descriptions of the character's actual visual demeanor. English speakers often left characterization to be inferred throughout the plot and concluded with evaluative comments about the characters' emotional states. They often failed to elaborate on the manner of movement that is iconically represented in ASL. Instead they merely stated that the turtle was slower.

ASL has a different pool of linguistic resources available, due in part to the primary mode of transmitting information through a visual-gestural system rather than an aural-oral system. Rather than using the linguistic features of tense and gender that are prevalent in English, ASL relies heavily on space to represent these concepts. In facing the problem of tense, ASL relies on its tools of spatial relationships to represent time, locating the past behind the signer and the future in front of the signer. Where English uses gender in pronouns such as *he* and *she* to refer to people, ASL uses gender neutral indexing. In addition, ASL uses the flexible systems of classifiers and role-shifting to depict both manner and path of movement along with depicting aspects of the character's personality. English relies on different resources using verbs that conflate manner with motion, often relying on extra-linguistic resources, such as vocal inflection and gestures, to elaborate characterizations and indicate spatial aspects of representation.

1. Pseudonyms are used for participants in the study.

Analysis of stories reveals distinct contrast in rhetorical style between English and ASL. The reason ASL users devoted more narrative attention to dynamics of character, manner of movement, and spatial features may be because of the availability and flexibility of the linguistic resources of the classifier and role-shifting systems within ASL. In contrast, English speakers devoted less narrative attention to these dynamics, in part perhaps because of the paucity of resources within the language or because of different cultural values surrounding the act and practice of storytelling.

## DEPLOYING ASL RESOURCES

Role-shifting can be characterized by a shift in body position, facial expression, and eye gaze during a sequence, thereby shifting into the role of a character in a narrative (Padden 1986; Poulin and Miller 1995; Engberg-Pederson 1995). The shift in body position can contrast by either shifting the body right and left or shifting the body forward and backward. Shifts can also take place without shifting the body by simply changing the eye gaze and facial expression. ASL allows for very rapid shifts between the characters to maintain a dynamic sense of movement and plot. In the rabbit and turtle story, the Deaf signers relayed much of the story while shifting between the roles of the rabbit or the turtle.

Sign language linguists (Padden 1986; Poulin and Miller 1995; Engberg-Pederson 1995; Lillo-Martin 1995; Emmorey and Reilly 1998) have been concerned with distinguishing role-shifting as a linguistic resource in ASL from role-taking or play-acting as a storytelling resource available in all languages.[2] How much of ASL role-shifting could be due to skills in play-acting? Though the English speakers in our subject pool had play-acting available to them as a resource, only the woman trained as an actress used it to any extent and even then her use was limited; whereas almost of all the ASL storytellers used role-shifting adeptly. This could be due to the fact that role-shifting for Deaf people is not simply a theatrical resource but a typical linguistic resource that has been shown to follow conventional rules of grammar.

2. Poulin and Miller (1995) and Emmorey and Reilly (1998) prefer to use the term referential shift rather than role shift in order to make this distinction less ambiguous.

The performance of these stories illustrates that not only is role-shifting used for indicating reported speech or quotations of speech, it is also adeptly used to report action, or, in a sense, to quote action (see Emmorey and Reilly 1998). It is the classifier system that allows for a rich variety of representational options for depicting action and describing characters. The classifier system provides a range of categorical representations that reveal the size and shape of an object, the semantic category of an object, the bodily animation of a character, the body parts of a character, or how an instrument is manipulated (Supalla 1985). By using the rich range of ASL classifiers to show exactly what happens in what manner and in what spatial relationship, storytellers are able to create a vivid picture. As is evident in the rabbit and turtle story, both role-shifting and classifiers are used in tandem to depict the characters as having distinct personalities and abilities.

### DEPLOYING ENGLISH RESOURCES

Regarding representations of movement in space, as pointed out by Slobin (1996b), English verbs often conflate manner with movement but do not indicate direction or path. In the story we therefore could use a variety of verbs that indicate manner of locomotion: *strut, stride, run, spin, zoom, hike, skid,* and *fall.* Verbs that do not indicate manner are verbs like *come, go,* and *get,* which do not indicate the speed or style of locomotion. Though all of these verbs do not indicate the direction or path of motion, some latinate verbs such as *proceed* do indicate the direction as forward or continuing ahead. These types of verbs were less likely to be used in the rabbit and turtle story. Most commonly, verbs of motion were combined in various ways with verb particles to indicate the directionality and path: *stride out, strut around, come from, come out, go in, zoom on down, head off, lean back, hike up, look up, look around, look out, lift into, get up,* and *fall onto.* This sample indicates the great variation of both verbs and verb particle combinations that allow the English language to specify direction. *Look up, look out,* and *look around* all indicate the same action but different directions of that action. Verbs such as *run* and *tiptoe* specify the manner of locomotion more precisely than the simple verbs of *come* and *go.* In describing spatial relations, English must rely on prepositional phrases that place the characters in relation to one another or in relation to the setting such as *on, below, behind,* and *in.*

Directly quoting the character's speech would be the equivalent of role-shifting in ASL. In a quotation, an English speaker can adapt the vocal qualities of the character being represented and speak from the perspective of that character constructing or reenacting a dialogue. Though not analyzed in depth here, vocal inflections can add meaning and emphasis to the linguistic content in subtle ways.

Also, English speakers have the option of complementing their speech with gestures to clarify spatial relationships. McNeill (1992) argues that with spoken languages, gestural and linguistic resources form a holistic communicative system. Thus, where spoken languages lack certain ways to express spatial or path relationships, they complete their ideas by accompanying their words with appropriate gestures.

In the following sections, I look in depth at two examples of storytelling, the stories told by our two actresses. These stories are of particular interest in order to examine more rigorously the extent to which the varying tools in each language shape the stories. In each performance we can see the rich potentials and possibilities for representation in each of the languages. Looking at examples of stories that exploit linguistic resources to the fullest, we can truly examine the differences in storytelling in the visual mode and how these impact the form and content of the stories.

### ASL Storytelling: Samantha

At the beginning of the story, Samantha establishes the opening scene as the rabbit and then the turtle make their entrance onto the scene and the crowd cheers them on. She makes rich use of the classifier system and the role-shifting system available to her in ASL to both describe the setting and to portray the characters. Though Samantha's is the most elaborate story of those told by the Deaf subjects, the resources that she uses are commonly used in their stories.

She first sets up the scene by defining the cartoon's banner stretched in midair. Extending both the index and middle fingers on both hands into the letter U hand shape, she sweeps the air above her head in an arcing motion starting at a midpoint and extending outward and upward in opposite directions with each hand, mimicking the way the banner hangs between two points suspended in the air. Then indicating the writing on the banner, she returns to the virtual space of the banner that she just created above her head, and fingerspells H-A-R-E off to her left side with her left hand then signs CHALLENGE with both hands in a central location, and fingerspells T-O-R-T-O-I-S-E with her right hand in the space to her right. She spatially represents that the cartoon banner says, "Hare vs. Tortoise." Explaining that this is a race between the rabbit and the turtle, Samantha has prepared the context for the ensuing story. She immediately shifts from her role as narrator into her role as the crowd, indicated by her change in facial expression as her hands depict (CL:5) the enthusiastic crowd rising to their feet and cheering.[3]

Samantha smoothly moves in and out of narrator mode and between the different characters, sometimes so rapidly that the boundaries between narrator and character roles become nearly blurred. When clearly in her role as narrator she makes eye contact with the viewer and removes any character facial expressions from her face. She reserves her role as narrator to only a few functions within the story, emerging briefly as she pops out of character to describe some aspect of the setting or make some evaluative commentary about the characters. Often as narrator she briefly names the character as a means of identifying which character will be appearing next and then quickly shifts into the character role by adapting the prototypical facial expression and mannerism of the character. This naming or introduction of the character by the narrator eases the work of the audience in making transitions between characters, especially because there is no body shift accompanying the transition and the role shift is indicated only by shifts in facial expression and bodily deportment. Here, the role of narrator functions primarily to introduce the transitions between roles and to relay evaluative commentary about the story or characters. In addition, while in narrator mode Samantha relays certain descriptions of the characters' spatial relationships to each other or to the environment that would not be appropriately portrayed through the role of one of the characters.

After introducing the context of the story and the crowd cheering on, Samantha moves briefly into narrator mode to introduce the rabbit by naming him and then quickly takes on a distinctive facial expression to indicate the cocky demeanor of the rabbit who enters the scene wearing

---

3. For those familiar with the ASL classifier system, I have encoded a common transcription scheme (Humphries and Padden 1992) for representing more precisely the classifiers used in particular instances. "CL" stands for classifier. Immediately following that is the common handshape used in making the classifier: "5," which has all five fingers extended out from the hand. Sometimes, I describe the handshape more specifically as "fist" or "bent-v."

a robe and swaggering out with his hands uplifted and clasped in a self-congratulatory motion. Here, Samantha alternates between the use of classifiers that are in proportion with her body or life-size classifiers (what Supalla 1985 might call body classifiers) and those that are miniaturized, with the hand as representing the entire body. While maintaining the cocky expression of the rabbit to provide an anchor on her body for the descriptive classifiers, she clasps her hands above her head and shows the rabbit wearing a robe by indicating the collar of the robe with her hands as if she were putting it on her own body and tying it around her waist. She repeats the hand clasp above her head and then with both hands at either side of her head, using her index and middle finger extended together (CL:U) imitating the shape of the rabbits ears, she swaggers them back and forth. All of the previous classifiers that are anchored to her body in a description of the rabbit are of the life-size variety signed in proportion with her body. Now she alternates to Lilliputian size, reducing the rabbit's body to her index finger as she shows his entire body walking out confidently.

Before switching characters to the turtle, Samantha slips into narrator mode and rapidly describes the action of the turtle tumbling out of a hole in a tree. Then she repeats the account from the point of view of the turtle by immediately assuming the character of the turtle and using a complex of small-scale classifiers, depicting the turtle with the person classifier of a bent index and middle finger configuration (CL: BENT-V) and the hole in the tree with the shape classifier of the entire hand curved into the shape of a C (CL:C). Maintaining the prototypical turtle face, she shifts to life-size classifiers with her hands in position at her sides, indicating the outline of the shell as if the shell were attached to her own body. She depicts the turtle with his appearance wearing a small hat and a tie. She then interjects the turtle's thoughts, talking to himself, "Am I really ready for this race? I just don't know about that." Continuing in character as the turtle, she depicts the action of the turtle walking up to the starting line. Using life-size classifiers she indicates legs by extending the index finger on each of her hands downward and alternately moving them forward to imitate the turtle's slow awkward walk.[4] Then she leans her body and her hands

4. In finer distinctions of the proportionality of classifiers as they relate to the body, this could be labeled a midsize classifier. These in-between classifiers use the body as an anchor but move as extensions of that anchor—as with CL:clenched-fist acting as head leaning forward or with CL:1 acting as legs extended from the

forward as if kneeling down at the starting line. Fluctuating between the different scales of classifiers creates a more dynamic story with detailed images of the appearance as well as the behaviors of the characters.

Quickly, Samantha switches into narrator mode by changing her facial expression to that of a serious narrator, removing all trace of the dopey turtle smile. She comments on the fact that the turtle is facing the opposite direction as the rabbit. Using her index finger extended horizontally (CL:1) on both hands, she points one facing the viewer (representing the rabbit) and one facing her own body (representing the turtle). Still in narrator mode, she comments on how ridiculous this is by using a variant of the sign SICK. Then she leads into the turtle role shift by signing TURTLE, thus naming him. This leads into the role shift and indicates that her comment relates to the turtle's behavior of facing the wrong way.

She repeats the scene of each character at the starting line by using life-size classifiers representing the characters through her body, first taking on the character of the turtle awkwardly leaning forward with his hard shell and then switching to the rabbit confidently leaning forward in racer formation. Here, she shifts to using small scale classifiers (CL:1) to repeat again the fact that the characters are facing opposite directions.

Still as a narrator, she indicates the beginning of the race by dropping her right hand as would someone starting a race; in the meantime her left hand maintains the fact that the turtle is facing the wrong way. She introduces the raccoon as officiator of the race by naming him and then immediately takes on his character by looking around with her hand raised in the shape of a gun and then fires it while mouthing "bam!"

At this point Samantha switches back and forth between representing the rabbit and the turtle. In typical fashion she introduces them in turn by naming them and then taking on the character by using particular facial expressions. When interjecting commentary she pops out of character mode and into narrator mode. As she switches back and forth she sometimes drops the narrator introduction of a character and simply transitions between characters by showing both a prototypical face and a prototypical way of running for each character: speedy and intense for the rabbit, slow and plodding for the turtle. Samantha spends considerably more time than hearing narrators developing the characters' dispositions by alternately showing their manner of running along the path.

---

body. These enable the signer to move body parts that would be awkward to move while recounting a story from a stationary position.

The story now shifts to the next key plot as the rabbit notices a tree and decides to take a nap. Samantha first relates the fact that the rabbit is running very fast in comparison with the turtle. Then, maintaining her role in rabbit mode, she turns her head to her right as if looking to see where the turtle is behind her. In the rabbit's "voice" Samantha comments on the fact that the turtle is far behind, and noticing a tree, decides to take a nap. Here she uses life-size classifiers or miming to imitate the cartoon rabbit's gestures as he extends his legs, crosses them and stretches his arms behind his head and she follows suit by extending her index fingers in imitation of legs and simultaneously crossing her fingers and her legs and then stretching her hands behind her head and then indicates that the rabbit is fast asleep by signing SHUT-EYES.[5] She uncrosses her legs before she reintroduces the turtle. Thus the crossing and uncrossing of her own legs is part of the story, not just a shift in sitting positions. The act of uncrossing her legs is part of the referential shift from rabbit to narrator.

In the next episode of the story, the turtle, running as fast as he can, comes upon the rabbit snoozing and tiptoes carefully past him. Then the turtle picks up speed and continues plodding along in the race. Samantha shifts quickly and easily between the two roles. She embodies the characters in her face. This is clearly evident in the transition from the turtle running along to the key moment when he sees the rabbit ahead asleep under the tree. As she names the turtle, she has already attached his facial traits to her own face. She reveals uncertainty in her eyes and strain in her mouth, with her lips stretched across her teeth and downturned as she imitates the turtle gasping for breath while he runs. Samantha uses her leg classifier hands to slow down the running to a slow motion tiptoe and immediately drops the straining face into a face of sudden realization and shifts her eye gaze to the right, the location of the rabbit. While in narrator mode, she indicates that the turtle sees the rabbit and shifts momentarily to imitating rabbit's posture with her arms extended briefly behind her head and leaning back with her torso. She reenacts the turtle's aside to the cartoon audience by looking off to her left, as the turtle had, at an imaginary audience. Placing her finger to her lips, she indicates that the audience is complicit in the turtle's attempts to quietly sneak past the rabbit. Then she simultaneously lifts her imaginary shell and extends her classifier legs (CL:1) and her real legs, mimicking the turtle's careful tip-

5. This sign is similar to CLOSE-WINDOW but represents the eyes closing into a deep sleep and is made with the head nodding down and the eyes closing.

toe. In addition she scrunches up her face to indicate the concentrated effort and concern that the turtle has in maintaining silence as he passes the rabbit. Then she shows the turtle speeding up once more as he once again lifts his shell and plods along. She projects the turtle's thoughts, commenting that he has to hurry up because he doesn't want the rabbit to hear him and wake up.

Samantha's modulated use of leg classifiers illustrates the flexibility with which ASL permits the language user to indicate the manner of movement. This is best seen when contrasting the leg movements of the rabbit and the turtle, and looking when the narrator shows the turtle's run slowing to a tiptoe. All of these factors—facial expression, head and body tilts, and classifier use—work in tandem to create the image of the turtle.

Now clearly shifting into the mode of narrator she states that the rabbit unexpectedly wakes up. In this instance she acts as narrator only for the evaluative sign WRONG. She then fluidly morphs into the rabbit waking up and seeing the turtle far ahead of him, then spinning his legs in a frantic attempt to catch up.

Without even naming the turtle she slips into his character clearly with a distinct shift in facial expression and manner of locomotion. Before switching to the crowd role, however, she introduces the crowd into the scene by mentioning PEOPLE briefly as narrator and then, in the mode of the people, indicates them cheering and jumping.

She then switches into narrator mode for evaluative purposes. Indicating a surprising turn of events she signs WRONG RABBIT LOSE CONTROL. Using a complicated string of classifiers (CL:V-rabbit flipping over, CL:1-rabbit's neck twisting, CL:fist-rabbit's head coming upright) she indicates that the rabbit trips and flips over flat on his face and then lifts his head to see that he has lost the race. Then in narrator mode she comments that the turtle had already won the race.

Once again she introduces the characters by name and then shifts into their role; mentioning the crowd once again she shows them carrying and tossing the turtle in the air. Then she nearly makes a mistake by starting to introduce the rabbit and quickly corrects herself when she really means the turtle. After introducing the turtle by name she slips into the turtle's role with a goofy yet cheerful face and uses her entire body to represent the turtle's body with arms raised in the air and upper torso bouncing as if bouncing on the arms of the crowd. Shifting to narrator she signs REAL TURTLE FEEL . . . , then takes on the turtle's body once again to portray him as exhausted. She contorts her face into an expression of awkward exhaustion, as if it had not really sunk in that he, the turtle, had really won and leans her head forward in a typical turtle-like gesture as his head extends from his shell. She even indicates the shell by placing her hands to her sides as an outline of the turtle's shell. Now without foregrounding her shifts she moves from turtle to crowd to turtle, indicating with a complex of different classifiers the crowd tossing the turtle in the air (CL:5-hands tossing imaginary turtle) and the turtle flipping in the air (CL:V-turtle flipping in the air). Then as the turtle lands upside down, she creatively shows his head represented by her fist as being jostled around in different directions inside his shell and finally emerging below. In the final lines of the story she returns to narrator mode and shows the hat represented by her index finger and thumb curving into the C-shape of the rim of the hat landing on the turtle's tail represented by an upright index finger on her nondominant hand. She closes the story with the sign COOL either commenting on the funny final image of the story or on the story as a whole.

### English Storytelling: Brenda

At the beginning of the story, Brenda prefaces her narrative as the story of the tortoise and the hare. Unlike the majority of hearing storytellers in our subject pool, Brenda uses gestures to complement her storytelling, emphasizing key points or supplementing her descriptions of the characters and the ensuing action. In addition, the level of detail brought to bear through her varied use of vocabulary and sentence structure brings the story to life in ways that the other hearing narrators were not able to accomplish. As stated before, part of Brenda's skill in this area may derive from her experience as a performer on the stage, where the goal of any performance is to entertain an audience. The other hearing narrators presented more condensed versions of the story, relying perhaps on the common knowledge of their audience to supply the details.

Brenda next frames the story as a competition by stating that it was the day of the big race. She then moves into describing the main characters not by simply mentioning that the rabbit was confident and the turtle slow, as many of the other hearing narrators do, but by providing descriptive details of their appearance and locomotion: "And the hare in his great jacket came striding out fast from his, ah, his little little hovel to the crowd, to the cheering crowd, and he was very proud of himself—strutting around." As she relates this she mimes putting on a jacket and punctuates the rabbit's striding by extending her right fist in a punch at the air. She also indicates spatial relations and direction of movement with her gestures. As she begins to mention the hovel she puts her hand in a somewhat clawed formation into the gestural space in front of her body, seeming to indicate the location of the hovel. She then extends her right hand again in the hovel shape and then moves it forward and downward as if indicating the rabbit's path of motion down a hill. In addition to using gestures, Brenda uses her facial expression and head movements to convey the rabbit's cocky nature by mimicking a subtle strutting motion with her shoulders as her nose is slightly upturned and head erect. These body gestures accompany her statement that the rabbit was very proud of himself, and is strutting around. Though she uses more facial expression than any other hearing narrator, her expressions are still more subtle than most of the Deaf narrators, perhaps because she is able to convey the tone of the story and the characters through her vocal inflections.

Turning her attention to the character of the tortoise she describes his physical appearance and demeanor: "And from the other side comes the little Mr. Tortoise in his little shell with his little hat. He was much slooower as he came out." Here Brenda uses her voice to add textures of meaning to the words little and slower. As she says "little" her voice becomes higher pitched and she extends the vowel "i," she also does this with "slower" by extending the "o." In addition, she contrasts the turtle and the rabbit with her head movements by leaning her head down in a gesture of the turtle's shyness and lack of confidence.

Returning to the plot, she begins the race as the turtle and the rabbit approach the starting line. "The raccoon *blew* his whistle for everyone to take their marks at the beginning of the race. The crowd was cheering wildly in anticipation. As it turned out the tortoise was pointed in sort of the *opposite direction* of the direction of the race and the *hare* was, of course, was *in the direction* of where he should be going." (Words in italics indicate moments accompanied by key gestures.)

She punctuates the word "blew" by leaning forward and raising her right fist in an upward motion toward her mouth, mimicking the raccoon bringing the whistle to his mouth. Then in a complicated spatial navigation of the English language, Brenda shows the rabbit and the turtle facing opposite directions at the starting line. She complements her words with gestures indicating the direction of motion of each of the characters. Emphasizing the word "opposite," she lilts her voice and extends the "o" sound while tilting her head to her right. On the word "direction," indicating how the turtle was facing the opposite direction, she gestures with her left hand palm perpendicular to the ground and turned inward toward her body as if her hand represented the turtle at the starting line. This gestural representation appears again in the next line of her story. As she mentions the "hare," she brings both palm hands into the gestural space with the left hand again pointed towards her body and the right hand pointed and moving away from her body. This small, complex set of gestures captures the spatial relationship of the rabbit and the turtle in ways that the English language less easily captures. Her gestures not only provide emphasis by punctuating her words, they clarify paths of movement and spatial relationships. Though most of the other hearing narrators did not use gesture in this way to complement their stories, Brenda's story illustrates that English speakers can elaborate their stories by drawing on gestural resources.

As the race begins and the rabbit and the turtle take off down the path, Brenda draws on metaphors of guns and arrows in her speech and gesture. She accompanies the next phrase with a gesture of pulling back her hand and then releasing it as if she has released a javelin to soar through the air. "The raccoon blows the whistle and *off like a shot* goes the hare, which of course spins Mr. Tortoise around *completely.*"

When the turtle has spun around she lifts her right hand up emphasizing the word "completely" and possibly the cessation of the turtle's spinning motion. She also shakes her head to imitate the turtle's apparent disorientation. "And he stands up, looks around, sees that he's not going in the right direction and heads off to the direction following the hare."

All of the verbs used in the preceding phrasing are modified by particles found in phrases such as "stands *up*, looks *around*, going *in*, heads *off*," to specify the direction and path of motion. In this segment of the story and throughout motion path descriptions, Brenda relies heavily on the verb structures that Slobin notes are typical of English, conjoining strings of verb particles that specify the path of motion. She uses a rich variety of verbs and verb particle combinations.

Unlike ASL, English does not have an easily adaptable system of mapping spatial relations in language iconically; in relying more heavily on a different means of representation with the resources available, it leaves the visualization up to the audience rather than the performer. In addition to these verbal representations the linguistic resources can be supplemented with gestural resources. However, most hearing storytellers did not exploit the gestural possibilities available to them; this may have been due to cultural constraints on the uses of gesture or other performance factors.

As the story continues we reach the pivotal point when the rabbit decides to take a nap. Brenda begins taking on the role of the rabbit in a constructed self-dialogue by looking over her shoulder as she relates that the rabbit "looks around and sees a nice tree." In one of the rare moments in all of the English retellings of the story, Brenda directly takes on the role of the rabbit by quoting his imaginary speech, "Hmm, well, I think I'll just stop here." In taking on the character she puts a mischievous look on her face and inflects her voice to reflect the rabbit's cocky and confident nature. She also quotes imagined gestures that the rabbit might have used in such situations, putting her index finger to her mouth in contemplation as she says, "He stops and thinks." Once the rabbit has decided to rest under the tree, she literally copies the actions of the rabbit from the cartoon by stretching her arms up in the air as she states that very fact. This gesture was imitated by nearly all of the Deaf narrators, but Brenda was the only hearing narrator who did so.

"So he stretches his arms up as far as he can, leans back on the tree and decides to take a little snooze, knowing of course that he is far ahead of Mr. Tortoise." As she switches her focus onto the turtle's actions, she mimics his behaviors as well. She mimes the turtle lifting up his shell by placing her hands out at her sides as if grasping the edge of an invisible shell and lifting it up, clenching her hands into fists and making arm motions as if jogging. The extent to which Brenda mimes is unusual in comparison with all of the hearing narrators.

She continues, "And the tortoise is running as fast as he can, hiking his shell up as far as he can, of course he's running on just two legs, his little hat is popping up into the air and holding it onto his head as best he can. And he's sweating, and he's sweating, going as fast as he can." She also accompanies her description of the hat popping in the air with a gesture that indicates the path motion of the hat by moving her index finger up in the air in a circular motion to indicate the spinning of the hat. She then clenches her hand into a fist and motions it towards the top of her head to indicate the turtle holding onto the hat as best he can. During much of this description of the turtle she leans her head forward in imitation of the turtle's posture.

At this juncture, the turtle discovers the rabbit napping and quietly passes him. Brenda's face quickly changes expression with eyes widened, indicating the surprise of the turtle upon seeing the rabbit resting by the tree. "He soon approaches the hare and notices that the hare is asleep in the tree. He looks out at us, makes a little quiet sound, so that we don't wake up the hare. He lifts his hat into place and tiptoes past Mr. Hare." As she indicates verbally that the turtle makes a quiet sound, she puts her index finger to her lips to mimic the turtle's gesture in the cartoon. She again mimes adjusting the hat into place with her clenched fist, and modulates her voice to a slower pace to emphasize the careful tiptoeing past the hare.

As the turtle actually passes the sleeping rabbit Brenda's voice speeds up and becomes louder, matching the intensity of the turtle's efforts. She also uses more gestures to complement her representations of the turtle's efforts, by mimicking the turtle lifting his shell.

"Then hikes his shell up and runs as fast as he can he even hikes his shell up higher and stretches his legs out longer so that he can run. He is sweating hard, but he is running as fast as he can." Brenda also emphasizes the turtle's speed by using her javelin-throwing fist to punch forward in the air. On each repeated mention of hiking the shell up, she repeats her gesture of lifting the imaginary shell up. She uses her voice, extending the vowels on "loooonger" and "hiiiiigher" to emphasize the efforts made by the turtle. At this point she simultaneously represents the turtle by running through her jogging motions even before she explicitly mentions the turtle running. She continues her jogging gesture, or at least alludes to it, by maintaining clenched fists throughout her description of his sweating and running. The moment that she switches focus to the rabbit she unclenches her fists.

Brenda now modulates her voice to convey the rabbit's cocky self-assured and nonchalant character. "Well, of course, the hare has seen that Mr. Tortoise has run past him. He opens one eye, looks up and gets up and proceeds in the race. As she relays the part about the rabbit getting up and proceeding in the race she lifts her right fist and slightly punches it forward in the air.

"The tortoise looks backs and sees that, of course, Mr. Hare, whose legs are just going as a buzz saw, is coming in right in behind him. However, the tortoise has quite a lead on Mr. Hare and we see the finish line up ahead, the cheering crowd." When describing the rabbit's locomotion she scrunches up her face to reflect the intensity of the movement and also, almost in a quasi-classifier use, she places both hands with index fingers extended into the gestural space and moves her index fingers in alternating circular motions indicating the spinning of the rabbit's legs.

"And Mr. Tortoise is sweating, he's hiking his shell up as high as he can. His legs are stretching as long as he can and he's running as fast as he can, he's sweating bullets. And he's ahead, but the hare is right behind him." In this repeated scene she uses the same gestural and vocal resources, extending the vowels of "high," "can," and "long," and miming the lifting of the shell and the jogging. On the description of the turtle stretching his legs out she releases her fists slowly and extends her fingers. Scrunching up her face into an intense expression and clenching her fists again, she illustrates the extreme effort of the turtle and may even be representing the stretching of the legs by the stretching out of her fingers from a clenched fist.

Transitioning to the final denouement of the climax where the turtle wins the race, she widens her eyes in surprise and lifts her right index finger slightly into the air to draw attention to the unexpected turn of events. "But what should happen? At the very end of the race, we can't see that it is quite tight, but the tortoise hits the finish line, grabs the ribbon in his mouth and wins the race. Mr. Hare is right behind him, skids into the dirt face first and comes up around, his head is completely screwed around, zooms back around and he doesn't know what hit him. He's fully suspected, I think, that he was going to win."

As she recounts the fact that the turtle and the hare are very close in the race she bounces her two palm flat hands back and forth alternating in the air, as if one hand represents the turtle and the other represents the rabbit as they vie for first place. With her left palm hand she extends forward as the tortoise hits the finish line and then she extends her hand to grab an imaginary finishing ribbon clenching her hand into a fist and then pulling it back and punching forward into the air as the turtle wins the race.

Illustrating her verbal description of the rabbit's demise with her right palm hand representing the motion of the rabbit, she makes a motion of sliding forward in space and into the dirt. As he comes up, she points her right index finger up into the air and moves it in a quick circular motion spinning first one way and then the other way, revealing how the rabbit's neck unwinds. She does this all while bobbing her head in imitation of the rabbit's head spinning. She negatively shakes her head as if emphasizing the fact that the rabbit doesn't know what hit him and lowers her voice when she makes a personal evaluation indicating her own thoughts about the rabbit. "Well, the tortoise is grabbed by the crowd, onto their shoulders turned upside down, his poor little head is sticking out below, his shell's turned around, his hat falls onto his tail and he is the winner, much to the chagrin of the hare. And that's the end."

At the conclusion of the story she continues her pantomime. She indicates the turtle being turned upside down by quickly moving her index fingers in one round of circular motion as they are pointed towards each other and then she also indicates his head sticking out of his shell from below by tracing the movement with her right index finger in the air to the right. She shows his legs turned around by flipping both palm hands up off to the left (the hands representing his feet). In the grand finale she shows the hat falling onto the tail by using a classifier-like hand shape of a clawed hand falling from above and landing on an imaginary tail in space. She then gestures with her palms up in a shrug, indicating the end of the story.

## Discussion

In comparing the stories of Samantha and Brenda it is clear that vivid descriptions are possible in both languages. The detailed content of Samantha's and Brenda's stories were nearly equivalent, yet there were significant differences. One notable difference is in the perspectives taken throughout the stories. Brenda told the majority of her story in narrator mode, and Samantha told the majority of her story in character mode. When comparing the entire set of ASL stories and English stories, more distinctions arise on the level of narrative attention paid to visual detail. ASL users provided more visual and spatial details. They spent more time introducing the characters as they came onto the scene and illustrated the characters' facial expressions and physical demeanor on their own bodies.

All of the Deaf narrators imitated the rabbit in some way, most by mimicking characteristic gestures or showing the manner of walking, but only two hearing narrators managed to capture the rabbit's manner of walking using elaborate vocabulary such as "striding out." The ASL users used the multiple channels available in the visual-gestural modality to use role-shifting to represent the characters' personalities and behaviors through facial expressions, attitudes, and body movements. In contrast, the hearing narrators rarely used facial expression to depict characters or a means comparable to role-shifting because it is not a practice readily available in their language system. Only Brenda, the actress, used facial expression to any extent. Even though she exploited this paralinguistic feature far more than any of her hearing peers, she did not come close to the ways in which the Deaf storytellers embodied the facial expressions of the characters in their role shifts.

Differences in English and ASL storytelling were further revealed in the plot line where the rabbit and the turtle come to the starting line. For the Deaf narrators, the process of the characters approaching the line was an important character-building event, regardless of whether the narrator noticed that the rabbit and the turtle were facing opposite directions. It seems almost obligatory when discussing a race in ASL to show the contestants at the starting line. While all of the ASL users represented the starting line approach, this aspect of the race did not appear to be very salient to English speakers. For the hearing narrators the approach and sometimes even the fact of being at the starting line was left to be inferred by the audience.

In addition to omitting the characters' approach to the starting line, the majority of the hearing narrators did not represent the actual start of the race. Only two hearing narrators indicated how the race begins and only one of those indicated that a gun is shot in the air in order to start the race. The ASL narrators easily depicted the action of the raccoon starting the race by raising their hand in the shape of a gun and recoiling it quickly, mimicking a gun shot. The hearing narrators often skipped over this detail saying "the official begins the race," or "they took off from the starting line," or "when the race starts." Though they all indicated in some manner that the race has started, only one included the detail of the gun.

With its visual resources, ASL easily indicates precise manner of movement and the spatial relationship of the runners as they pursue their goal. In watching the narrators, one could actually see the action depicted almost as if it were directly quoted. This difference was clear at two points in the story that ASL users elaborated, but English users left somewhat undeveloped. For example, at the point where the rabbit awoke from his nap and takes off in hot pursuit of the turtle, the ASL users are able to show the manner of running by alternately spinning their extended index fingers in a running motion.

We can clearly see a difference in the resources that each language relies on to create the relationship between the two characters. ASL uses alternating role shifts and classifiers to show the manner and relationship of the two runners. The ASL users placed each character into the signing space and illustrated the relationship of the runners catching up and falling behind with the spatial relationship shown between their two hands, whereas the English speakers used words such as *behind, after,* and *in front of,* to indicate the spatial relationship. So, where the listener to the English version of the story has to imagine how close the rabbit is to the turtle, the ASL listener can see proportionally what the relationship is whether he is far behind or gaining on the turtle.

The question arises: Why did the Deaf people in this sample pay more narrative attention to these details? Perhaps certain details in the story appear to be less salient to English speakers; it is not entirely due to the fact that the resources are not there in English (for it is simple enough to add that the official shot the gun). But in the case of English speakers certain details may be superfluous. ASL's visual modality may, in effect, facilitate the performance of more visual detail from average storytellers, not just from trained actors.

In part, these phenomena are due to the linguistic resources readily available to language users and the way those resources shape the rhetoric of storytelling. This does not mean that an English speaker cannot convey the level of detail that the average ASL user does. Nor does it mean that every ASL user will rely heavily on the tools available in a spatial grammar.[6] What it does mean is that linguistic resources can constrain and shape the possibilities of narration. Language does not demand certain storytelling styles, but it does lead to certain tendencies in patterned discourse.

What determines what was important or salient in the cartoon may have some roots in the grammatical structure of the language that in turn shapes the rhetoric. Although questions of culture and ontology (cultural practices and physical experiences) certainly must enter into the picture when we consider cognitive salience, grammar is also a factor.

Deaf people may be more visually oriented because of the way they experience the world. With limited access to meaningful sound, they must rely on flashing lights and approaching shadows rather than sirens and footfalls. Their ability to adapt to the world around them depends more heavily on their sight, on their perception of the world through their eyes rather than ears. This visual orientation to the world shapes their culture and the modality of their language that may in turn promote the value of vivid depictions in storytelling.

In some sense the stories we tell shape our identity, our cognitive development, and our world view (see Ochs and Capps 1996). Underlying

6. One of our Deaf participants departs from the general pattern of the ASL stories by telling the story primarily in narrator mode and using less classifiers creating a more linear style of storytelling. As with Brenda, this indicates the range of potential language use within each language.

all of the inquiry in this paper is the fundamental question of whether language determines thought. In the final analysis a strong version of Whorf's hypothesis does not hold up. Despite the limitations or tendencies of a specific linguistic system, the possibilities within the communicative system are vast. With a little extra labor the strictures of a particular linguistic system can be overcome through use of elaborate forms or extra-linguistic means. Though the linguistic resources may not directly determine thought, they remain an intricate thread in the complex web of cultural and social practices. This thread wends and weaves its way into shaping how we think and live through language.

## REFERENCES

Bahan, B. J., and S. J. Supalla. 1995. Line segmentation and narrative structure: A study of eyegaze behavior in American Sign Language. In *Language, gesture, and space*, ed. K. Emmorey and J. Reilly. Hillsdale, N.J.: Lawrence Erlbaum Associates.

Berman, R. A., and D. I. Slobin. 1994. *Relating events in narrative: A cross-linguistic developmental study.* Hillsdale, N.J.: Lawrence Erlbaum Associates.

Disney, W. 1935. *The Tortoise and the Hare.* Cartoon, directed by Wilfred Jackson.

Emmorey, K., and S. Casey. 1995. A comparison of spatial language in English and American Sign Language. *Sign Language Studies* 88:255–87.

Emmorey, K., and J. Reilly. 1998. The development of quotation and reported action: Conveying perspective in ASL. In *Proceedings of the twenty-ninth annual Stanford child language research forum,* ed. E. Clark, 81–90. Stanford: CSLI Publications.

Engberg-Pedersen, E. 1995. Point of view expressed through shifters. In *Language, gesture, and space,* ed. K. Emmorey and J. Reilly. Hillsdale, N.J.: Lawrence Erlbaum Associates.

Gee, J., and J. Kegl. 1983. Narrative/story structure, pausing, and American Sign Language. *Discourse processes* 6:243–58.

Humphries, T., and C. Padden. 1992. *Learning American Sign Language.* Englewood Cliffs, N.J.: Prentice Hall.

Labov, W. 1972. The transformation of experience in narrative syntax. In *Language in the inner city: Studies in the Black English vernacular.* Philadelphia: University of Pennsylvania Press.

Liddell, S. K. 1996. Spatial representations in discourse: Comparing spoken and signed language. *Lingua* 98:145–67.

Lillo-Martin, D. 1995. The point of view predicate in American Sign Language. In *Language, gesture, and space,* ed. K. Emmorey and J. Reilly. Hillsdale, N.J.: Lawrence Erlbaum Associates.

McNeill, D. 1992. *Hand and mind: What gestures reveal about thought.* Chicago: University of Chicago Press.

Ochs, E., and L. Capps. 1996. Narrating the self. *Annual Review in Anthropology* 25:19–43.

Padden, C. 1986. Verbs and role-shifting in American Sign Language. In *Proceedings of the fourth national symposium on sign language research and teaching,* ed. C. Padden. Silver Spring, Md.: National Association of the Deaf.

Poulin, C., and C. Miller. 1995. On narrative discourse and point of view in Quebec Sign Language. In *Language, gesture, and space,* ed. K. Emmorey and J. Reilly. Hillsdale, N.J.: Lawrence Erlbaum Associates.

Slobin, D. I. 1996a. From "thought and language" to "thinking for speaking." In *Rethinking linguistic relativity,* ed. J. J. Gumperz and S. C. Levinson. Cambridge: Cambridge University Press.

———. 1996b. Two ways to travel: Verbs of motion in English and Spanish. In *Grammatical constructions: Their form and meaning,* ed. M. Shibatani and S. A. Thompson. Oxford: Oxford University Press.

Supalla, T. 1985. The classifier system in American Sign Language. In *Noun classification and categorization,* ed. C. Craig. Philadelphia: Benjamins North America.

Supalla, T., J. Singleton, E. Newport, S. Supalla, G. Coulter, and D. Metlay. In press. *Test battery for American Sign language morphology and syntax.* San Diego: Dawn Sign Press.

Taub, S. 1997. *Language in the body: Iconicity and metaphor in American Sign Language.* Ph.D. dissertation, University of California, Berkeley.

Vygotsky, L. S. 1986. *Thought and language,* ed. A. Kozulin. Cambridge, Mass.: MIT Press.

Wallin, L. 1994. *Polysynthetic signs in Swedish Sign Language,* trans. D. Miller. Edsbruk: Akademitryck AB.

Whorf, B. 1956 [1939]. The relation of habitual thought and behavior to language. In *Language, thought, and reality: Selected writings of Benjamin Lee Whorf,* ed. J. B. Carroll. Cambridge, Mass.: MIT Press.

Wilson, J. 1996. The tobacco story: Narrative structure in an American Sign Language story. In *Multicultural aspects of sociolinguistics in Deaf communities,* ed. C. Lucas, 152–80. Washington, D.C.: Gallaudet University Press.

# Affect, Emphasis, and Comment in

## Text Telephone Conversations

*Meryl Glaser*

This paper reports on an application of the principles of conversation analysis (CA) to a deaf person's text telephone conversation with both deaf and hearing coparticipants. It is assumed that such conversations are examples of natural everyday talk.[1] The following questions are addressed: How are conversations on the text telephone (Minicom) successfully accomplished given the constraints of the medium and the technology? How do form and function impact on one another? How is the talk interactionally organized in this different mode? How does the text become "talk-like," incorporate openings in the absence of "voice recognition tests," and display affect, tone, and register, pausing, overlap and turn-taking, facilitating repair, and coordinated closings? Does the "talk" resemble that accomplished interactionally by speaking partners or is it a series of separate events?

The telephone is a central feature in the communicative lives of people in modern society. It has been described as the "primary electronic medium for interpersonal communication" (Hopper 1992, xi). Since the late 1970s, text telecommunication technology has allowed access to remote (non face-to-face), real time communication for deaf people.[2]

This is one aspect of a larger study conducted as a master's thesis examining several aspects of text telecommunication including openings and closings, turn-taking, repair, errors, and methods by which transmission rate is increased. I would like to thank Bencie Woll for her supervision of this study and Debra Aarons for reviewing the drafts of this paper.

1. The point of the research is not to study disability or incompetence, but to examine the organization of conversation in a different mode. See McIlvenny (1995) for similar assertions regarding CA and Sign Language.

2. TDD, TTY, and TT have been used at various times in the U.S. and Canada to refer to Telephone Device for the Deaf, Teletypewriter, and Text Telephone,

The communication exchange on Minicom calls displays the fundamental characteristics of conversation. It involves turns at talk, the size, content, and allocation of which vary in the same manner as spoken face-to-face and telephone conversation. The turn allocation is similar to a conversation involving only two participants where selection of the next speaker is necessitated by virtue of the situation (Sacks, Schegloff, and Jefferson 1974).[3] Text telephone calls also clearly exhibit those same features that differentiate spoken telephone calls from face-to-face conversation. However, there are additional differences that are largely due to the constraints placed upon the communication by the technology used to transmit and receive the participants' contributions (Nash and Nash 1982).

Similarities between the two modes of telephone calls include the fact that the communication is dyadic, involving an exchange between two speakers or parties: a caller and the person called.[4] Minicom calls display definite beginnings with a summons by a visual signal, which may interrupt ongoing activity in the same way as a telephone ring.

Caller hegemony inherent in spoken telephone calls results in the same asymmetry in text exchanges, such that the called is obliged to speak first, thereby identifying self to an as-yet-unidentified caller and the caller gets first chance to make inquiries and to introduce the first topic (Sacks

---

respectively. In the United Kingdom, the equipment is referred to as the Minicom, stemming from the introduction of Britain's first purpose-built product. Minicom is thus the generic term used for text telephones in the United Kingdom and this term will be used throughout this paper when referring to this specific technology.

3. Although there are now facilities that allow for more than two parties (e.g., conference lines), most telephone talk remains an interaction between two participants or one dyad.

4. The terminology used in relation to conversation, be it spoken, typed, or signed, will be speaker, listener, talk, and the like, as this is the language that the Deaf themselves use to describe their communication (McIlvenny 1995). It is in keeping with American Sign Language (ASL) usage, that is, signs for "talk," "told," etc., are made in the area of the mouth (Baker 1977), and highlights language-rich interaction. British Sign Language (BSL) has modality specific signs for signed and spoken.

1972; Schegloff 1979; Hopper 1992) with the same proviso for modern technology.[5]

Differences between spoken and text telephone conversations primarily concern the restriction of the conversation to text, although both are similarly split from visual copresence. Text telephones provide access to neither vocal (suprasegmental aspects of speech—intonation, stress, volume) nor nonvocal behaviors (signs, lip patterns, facial expressions, gaze, or gesture) (Nash and Nash 1982). For text calls, a printout copy of the text interaction, as opposed to an audio tape-recording (Schegloff 1986), displays what the participants make available to one another at the time of the call.

The turn-taking mechanism inherent in text interaction is different and may be viewed as a form of situated adaptation. It exhibits features specific to the constraints of receiving and sending text at discrete times, as the technology cannot accurately transmit and receive messages in overlap. The turn-taking system is managed locally by the current speaker with the convention GA (go ahead) to relinquish the turn. The current speaker selects the next speaker, and has almost complete control in holding the conversational "space" as there is little opportunity for self-selection, interruption, or overlap (cf. Sacks, Schegloff, and Jefferson 1974). Interruptions can be facilitated by simultaneous transmission to alert the other party to difficulty, such as transmission errors (Cagle and Cagle 1991).

The identification and recognition of participants cannot occur vocally or from text greeting alone; both parties need to be explicit to facilitate identification. In spoken telephone conversations, the first greeting token, hello, is often used concurrently for identification and recognition of the speaker (Schegloff 1986). According to Nash and Nash (1982), within a small group of TTY users there is an ability to associate a person with a "type of typing," including speed and rhythm.

Finally, the technology relies on literacy skills (reading comprehension and encoding by type), which are not required for spoken telephone calls. This communication mode also imposes cost and time restraints on the

5. This may be less salient nowadays with announcing answering machines and "caller display" facility on modern telephones, whereby answerers can screen calls, having the information about the identity of the caller before they answer the call.

conversations: it takes longer to type than to speak or sign (Nash and Nash 1982).

## CA AND ITS APPLICATION TO TEXT TELEPHONE CONVERSATIONS

The organization of conversation is thought to be context free, that is, not usefully described by reference to the identities, characteristics, or social background of the parties at talk. CA researchers believe that what is important is how the parties make relevant features apparent to their conversational partners. The aim is to describe "how conversational machinery operates independently of the characteristics of particular identities" (Lee 1987, 48). Whichever characteristics of the conversational partners are relevant to the exchange will be revealed by the talk itself.

The interaction that occurs on the text telephones shares many of the properties of organization of spoken telephone conversations reported extensively in the CA literature (Sacks 1972; Schegloff 1979; Hopper 1992, among others). Most interactional tasks apply similarly to both mediums. Calls need to be opened; topics need introduction, maintenance, and termination; the reason for the call must be identified; and calls need to be brought to a close. These tasks need to be accomplished in a sequential, turn-by-turn manner involving coordinated participation from both parties to the conversation. Minicom conversations happen in real time, they are unrehearsed, and the fundamental characteristics of conversation are free to vary as they do in spoken telephone conversations. The constraints of the technology used may well impact on the organization of conversation. Situational adaptation may be necessary to adapt to the local situation of typed turns and the lack of vocal cues to interaction. There is no intelligible overlap; turn-taking is regulated by a self-selected relinquishing of current turn to the other participant by a stylized code (GA). Pausing, either within or between turns, cannot be recognized as such unless the party doing the pausing marks this with tapping of the space-bar or fills the space or time with dots. These adapted features of text telephone conversations may be regarded as an appropriate response to a particular context or setting.

Nash and Nash (1982) conducted a study of teletypewriter (TTY) conversations in the United States, investigating the content and organization of text telephone conversations. The authors describe both features of the conversations and the remarkably wide range of exchanges that are accomplished by TTY users. They compare aspects of TTY and voice-to-voice telephone conversations. They highlight three factors that restrain TTY communication: the absence of "vocal" and gestural cues suggesting that TTY messages may be telegrammatic and nonexpressive, the general literacy level of the deaf as a group, and the time limitations on typed communication. Despite these restraints, the inspection of the large corpus of data collected from a single household of TTY users led the authors to conclude that "a means of communication that on the face of it seems to be quite restricted and linear becomes, upon close inspection, a channel capable of carrying multiple meanings and of performing wide ranging functions" (Nash and Nash 1982, 211).

## METHODOLOGY

The research employed inductive analysis driven by the nature of the data. A sample of naturally occurring interaction was collected. The principles of CA were used to investigate the nature of the organization of talk and the devices used to achieve this organization.

The conversations were collected by installing an external printer to the Minicom of a regular and experienced user. The printer allowed all calls received by or transmitted from that Minicom to be recorded in sequence. The printout recorded both participants' contributions to the conversations. It also recorded all calls that are relayed via the operator service "Typetalk" and all messages that were left on the answering machine when the Minicom was not answered.[6] In a 1981 study by Wiemann (as cited by Hopper 1992) it was found that being recorded did not necessarily induce artificiality and that people quickly forgot they were being recorded.

Conversations were recorded from a single subject's Minicom. These conversations incorporated fifteen other participants (a number of these on more than one occasion). Printouts of Minicom exchanges provide a full record of all the conversational information available to each party "at

6. Typetalk is the United Kingdom's telephone relay service provided jointly by the Royal National Institute for the Deaf (RNID) and British Telecom (BT), which enables telecommunication between text telephone users and users of regular telephones by operator mediation between text and voice.

talk" at the time of the talk. They are thus analogous to the tape recordings and transcripts which form the basis of the CA tradition (Lee 1987).

The primary subject of the study was a deaf adult who was employed at a national deaf organization. Conversations included personal calls with deaf and hearing family and friends, business calls, calls relayed by the Typetalk operator, and messages left on the Minicom answering machine. As is the case with many deaf people, the subject is bilingual, using code mixing of British Sign Language (BSL), Sign Supported English (SSE), and written English as the situation demands.

### Procedure

The subject agreed to connect the external printer to her Minicom VII for a month of recording. The resulting printout was collected in two batches, one mid-month and the other at the end of the recording period. As well as being assured of anonymity in the corpus of data, the subject was told that the printer could be switched off manually when she thought that the conversations were of a confidential nature. All quoted sections were to be reviewed by the subject before publication.

### Data Corpus

The printed data collected consisted of a corpus of 28 conversations, comprising 22 direct back-to-back Minicom conversations, 2 answering machine messages, and 4 conversations that were conducted via Typetalk, that is, a third-party mediated conversation. For the purposes of this study, the mediated conversations were omitted from the data as this introduces variables other than those present in the back-to-back two-party conversations, but the two answering machine messages were included. The corpus is classifiable into personal and business-type calls; 16 calls were of a personal nature and 6 were business calls. The subject to whose Minicom the printer was attached was the caller in half of the personal calls and the called in the other half. In the business calls, she was the caller in four and the called party in two of the calls. The answering machine messages consisted of one personal call and another for which the type of call is unknown, although it is a business telephone message.

### Transcription of the Data

A printed record of a text telephone conversation yields a transcript that runs from margin to margin, that is, taking up full lines. It is single-line spaced and thus very dense to read. This was felt to be unsuitable for analysis and the printed record was reformatted, while remaining faithful to the original in content. The revised format adopted a playscript layout with each new turn starting at the beginning of a new line in the alternate lettercase. This is in line with data transcription convention in the CA literature (devised by Jefferson, as outlined in Atkinson and Heritage 1984).

Insert spaces have been retained as closely as possible from the original, which was printed in a font that allows accurate counting of spaces manually inserted using the space bar. However, multiple spaces have been condensed due to the restrictions of reproducing the conversations in this book. Additionally, although spacing may indeed contribute considerable meaning to text conversations, this paper focuses instead on other methods for displaying affect, emphasis, and comment. For example, orthographic characters and punctuation marks have been reproduced exactly from the printout, including all repetitions, spelling and typographic errors, abbreviations, and omissions. All transmission "junk" is reproduced verbatim.

Each conversation has been numbered chronologically and the lines of text within each conversation have been numbered in the left-hand margin. Fragments of transcripts presented in the text will preserve the line numbering that existed for the entire transcript. Above each fragment presented, square brackets enclose numbers indicating the conversation from which it was taken.

Anonymity in the data corpus has been established by changing the names of people, places, organizations, activities, telephone numbers, and some of the dates. Items were changed if they were judged sufficiently specific to allow identification of the person to whom they referred. All substitutions were such that the conversation remained comprehensible and the style unchanged. Thus, the original form was followed closely with abbreviations, and maintaining format of name (e.g., first only, initial plus surname, first and surname, nicknames, gender, and morphology).

## ANALYSIS

The analysis presented in this paper is of the "talk-like" features, that is, the establishment of affect, emphasis, and comment. Spoken languages use prosodic features such as stress and intonation to carry some of their meaning. These are not available in text with the Minicom technology and may be compensated for by the use of (repeated) punctuation marks (!, ?, ", and . . . ), explicit cuing in words, *smile,* and inserted laughter, *haha* (as well as other representations of speech), to convey the emotional content of the proffered talk. These features are of the kind that may be found in written English that portrays dialogue, that is, sections of text in quotation marks or text that represents direct speech. These additional features bring the text to life, giving it an "intonational signature." Restricted by medium and technology, the only resource text telephone users have to mark this aspect of conversation is the Minicom keyboard. The letters, punctuation marks, and numbers on the keyboard are their tools to display the intonation overlay or affect of their talk. The creative use of these features results in repetition of letters and punctuation marks, the insertion of explicit cues to the emotional intent of the message, the use of colloquialisms commonly associated with spoken rather than written communication, and the exclamations and reactions by which the recipient can clearly see the speaker's response. A wide range of these devices operating together creates the connotative meaning of the text utterances, thus many of the fragments presented will illustrate more than one feature.

It can sometimes be difficult to locate whether the next speaker's reaction to the connoted meaning of the previous turn is explicitly displayed in their next turn. Most often the "on-topic" talk simply continues, which does display to the coparticipant, and thus the analyst, that the reaction was seen to be appropriate, and talk continues. This does, however, mean that some of the judgments of intended meaning may well be those of the analyst and not those intended by the speaker.

Nash and Nash (1982) describe a variety of "ingenious adaptations" to compensate for the linearity of the written form and the time taken to type a message. They include in their description plays on words, humor, and idiom. They assert that these devices add fluency to the messages and lighten the task of both reader and typist. These devices also save time, allowing parties to read through one another's messages to get intent. In their TTY manual, Cagle and Cagle (1991) advise users that it can be difficult to sense what the other person is feeling because of lack of accessibility to their facial expression or tone of voice and suggest that speakers should display emotion by using explicit cues for laughter, repetition of letters, punctuation for emphasis, and other speech-related devices. The lack of facial expressions may be particularly pertinent as it is by means of these, occurring simultaneously with signs, that mark intonation in BSL (Kyle and Woll 1985) and other sign languages.

Question marks used for affect tend to be double or multiple markings, which alert the listener to more than the presence of a question and carry some other affective meaning. This may be for emphasis or comment, or to mark uncertainty, sarcasm, or humor. Many turns throughout the corpus contain examples of this feature. A similar pattern is seen in the use of exclamation marks. Word elongation by letter repetition is particularly visible in the openings and closings of calls, but is also used regularly for emphasis, exclamation, and to show emotional content.

Terms of endearment, too, are often found in the opening and closing sections of the conversations. They appear to be used in the openings to re-establish acquaintanceship and intimacy and to display the speaker's perception of the relationship between the two parties. They are either an endearment together with a name (C6/4 "pen lovy"), or stand as a substitute for the other's name (C1/3 "darling").

Inserted laughter is evident and it appears to function in different ways to mark sarcasm (C26/53–55 GUESS WHAT I WAS THE FIRST TT LEAVE THE WINEBAR TO CATCH THE TRAIN LIKE I GOOD LITTLE GIRL HA! GA good for u !), appreciation of a joke in the previous turn (C4/5–7 GOOD WHERE HAVE U BEEN TOGET A COLD DIDNT RU FAST ENUFF GA ha ha ha wish i coukld !!! think it change in weather !!!), linked to a joke in the same turn (C5/32–34 "so no peace for the wicked so maybe me and mark been awful bad when we wwere kids !! ha ha oh well !!"), irony (C18/8–10 WAS ALMOST ON ROAD TO RECOVERY WHEN I HHHAD THAT ACCIDENT!!!! SO ITS BEEN ONE STEP FORWARD, TWO BACK! HAHAHA . . .) or facilitating repair (C18/26–29 OK . . . AND DO U KNOW HHOWW LONG IT S TO LAST ? GA u mean the jump or bus journey ! ga NMEITHER!! ! HAHAHA, THE JUMP? ).

Sound effects are used to indicate cold (C4/68 BRRR) and silence (C4/91–92 "but sssh u making me hungry"). Use of slang and dialectal items, as well as idiomatic language and colloquialisms give the text a flavor that is personal and reflects the characteristics of the speakers. Many responses to previous turns show exclamations (C1/19 BRILL, C7/4 "nah!!", C19/5 SUPER), phrases of affirmation (C7/35 "aye me too") and the agreement or alignment of one speaker with the other (C4/53 "too true!," C7/13 YES SNAP).

Fragments of text have been selected here to display a variety of features, the first being an entire conversation (with the exception of the end, which has not printed). This short conversation, C17, is an invitation to meet.

C17

1  evening ga
2  EVENING THIS IS ROBIN PIKE HERE HOW R U Q GA
3  hgi love i am fine thanks just doing a report !! horrible thing abt me trying to get interps
4  for my hosp appts ha ha what a joke ga
5  DO U WANT A BREAK . SAYY MEET ME UP AT THE ACTON TUBE QQ GA
6  sure that lovely i can prog the video and let all hell get lose ! ga
7  WOW !!! WHAT TIME MEET U AT TUBE Q GA
8  have u eaten ? ga
9  NO GA
10  do i wanna put a face on !! ha ha so how abt 7.30 ? ga
11  FINE LOVELYY SEE U IN 50 MINS THEN SEE U LATER DEAR BIIIII FOR NOW
12  XXXC GA
13  ta for calli-

The caller self-identifies in a formal way providing both a first and surname (line 2), but the greeting from the called is informal and affectionate in register using a "hgi" and a term of endearment (line 3). This is the tone displayed by both speakers for the rest of the conversation. There are three examples of double or triple exclamation marks; the first incidence is (line 3), a description of having to write a report, and the comment that these marks provide is strengthened by the next comment, "horrible thing." This turn carries other affect with the inserted laughter (line 4), marking its irony accompanied by "what a joke." The response DO U WANT A BREAK (line 5) in the following turn acknowledges the intent of the previous speaker, as being involved in an undesirable task. In the following turn the offer is accepted and an idiomatic expression, "and let all hell lose" (line 6) is included, displaying enthusiasm for the invitation. This receives an exclamation, WOW!!!, with the second example of multiple punctuation (line 7). A different kind of inserted laughter is seen in a later turn (line 10) to mark a joke, and the first terminal item is encoded with repetitions of the letters BIIIII as well as a term of endearment DEAR (line 11). This short conversation serves as a good example of how a simple interactional task viz. an invitation, contains many features that enrich the text and carry much affectional meaning.

The next extract shows the use of letter repetition and consequent word elongation. This feature is most often seen in the opening and closing sections of the calls (see C17), but also appears elsewhere in the conversations to mark emphasis.

C6
4   pen lovy can i call u back i was in the bath !! gza
5   SURE ILL WAIT TIL LATERV-THEN BI FOR NOW GA
6   i call u back sooooooooonn cheers love sksksk
7   OK BI KIS-KISSSSSKKSK
8   sksks

C6 shows an elongation of "soon" (line 6) for emphasis. This links up with the request to delay this call until later as the called was in the bath. It serves to counteract the inconvenience or rejection that may arise from postponing talk. This gets an affirmative response in the next turn OK (line 7) and the intimacy of the relationship, first displayed by the term of endearment attached to the caller's name, "lovy" (line 4) is reciprocated in the terminal item from the caller, which is a transformation of the SK code into OK BI KIS-KISSSSSKKSK (line 7).[7]

An example of letter repetition in an opening section of a conversation follows.

C10
1   F BLO HA GA
2   Hello lyn bloomberg here for sharon ga
3   HIIIIIII LYN. . . . .ME SHARON HERE HOW ARE U KEEPING GA
4   me fine tks !!! i done application form !! and i used your ideas for letter to cover
5   many thanks will show u copy Sunday u helped me a lot ! ga

Here (line 3), the letter repetition registers delight at receiving the call, in addition to serving as a greeting and displaying recognition of the caller. The use of multiple exclamation marks in the following turn (line 4) is interesting in that they give a bland response to HOW ARE U KEEPING, "fine," an additional contour, the reason for which is given immediately

7. SK is the abbreviated form of "stop keying." It is the stylized code used to signal the end of a conversation. Most often this code appears in adjacent turns as the terminal item.

thereafter and is again followed by the double exclamation marks. The pleasure and relief of having done the application form is evident. The nuances that intonation gives a bland spoken word are replicated in type with the use of multiple punctuation.

The following extract shows letter repetition within the body of a call to create a feeling of empathy.

C4

32  oh no poor dad .. what will happen next time he had two explorations so next

33  wwhat ? ga

34  WELL SEEMS TO BE A COLONSCOPE TOUGHT IT WAS GOING TO

35  BE THETOP END BUT EVIDENTLY NOT GA

36  he has my sympathy coddle him for me i know he dont likee it but say i thinking of

37  him ga

38  YEP WILL DO I GO TO EYE CLINIC TOMORROW FOR A FIELD TEST

39  SUPPOSED TO BE TO JUDGE IF I HAVE GLAUCOMA COMING GA

40  good luck to u too mum that would be tooooooo much as well so i will keep in

41  touch so i know what going on . . . ga

In this conversation (which continues on to line 110), the use of repeated letters affords the speaker the ability to emphasize both her empathy and the awfulness of the possibility that, in addition to her father's medical problems, which they had been discussing, her mother may have glaucoma

The use of colloquialisms and inserted laughter (mentioned previously in C17) can also be seen in the following extract.

C1

26  GOOD OK THEN WELL I AM UP TO EYES !! AND LEAVING AT 2.00

27  ISH !! SO I BEST SAY BIIIEEEE HAVE GOOD WKEND GA

28  yes tks cant wait to work with bl tmw hahah ok let u go now once again tks for putting up

29  with me see u soon and dont overrdo things ok t

There is evidence of two colloquialisms (lines 26 and 27) and a word elongation in the lead up to closing. The next turn responds to HAVE GOOD WKEND with "tks" and adds a comment that is sarcastic, marked by the inserted laughter (line 28), but would appear very differently if the text were read literally. The corpus contains many other examples of colloquial language use, both phrases in common spoken use and short-cuts such as "-ish" (C7/107 "free ish").

Another example of a sarcastic intent is shown in C10, which uses the double "??" to display the speaker's doubtfulness at enjoying the weekend given what has to be done; without this marking the intent would be lost.

C10
27  fine ok then i aim for 3pm ish and let u know Sunday ok so im let u go . . . enjoy day off
28  me ?? do c.v. ! ga

A reading of line 28, had it not contained the punctuation marks, might well suggest spending a day off preparing a curriculum vitae to be an enjoyable venture. This is shown clearly not to be the case. The rhetorical question here is particularly interesting in that it mirrors the structure of sign language.

In C25, the multiple question marks emphasize the text they follow.

C25
3  hi there !! great to hear from u !!! i am ?????? not sure re myself this cold flu really
4  knocked me out regarding my eyes but getting that sorted how are u ?? things ok
5  managed to get sandy tv sorted ? ga

The marks (line 3) highlight the hesitancy of "not sure" in response to a "how are you" in the previous turn. They clearly convey to the listener that something is not quite right.

The question marks in C7, which follows, not only mark a question, but strengthen it in conjunction with the choice of wording.

C7
34  RIGHT OK ILL KEEP MY FINGERS CROSSED FOR YOU! GA
35  aye me too so how work same demonic mad race ?? any better or worst ? ga

The comment, "demonic mad race" (line 35) attached to the question about work displays the speaker's strength of feeling. The force of this lexical choice is further emphasized by the question marks.

The next fragment picks up a conversation where the uppercase speaker has phoned to tell the other about passing a sign language examination.

C23
14  brill well done congrats u deserve it ! ga
15  MANY THKS! IDIDNT THINK I DID WELL COZ I COULDNT RELAY ONE PART
16  OF THE VIDEO . . . PERHAPS IT WAS MARKED DOWN AS A POSITIVE

17 RESPONSE THAT I WOULDNT MAKE IT UP, JUST BEING HONEST??!! GA

18 desnt matter u dit it u got it !! well done i saaw ur mum last mon ! ga

19 SHE DID SAY WHEN SHE CAME ON THURS.. SHE SAID IT WAS GOOD TO SEE

20 U.. SHE ENJOYED HERSELF THAT EVE GA

21 i did too !! and mp s. lang !! did sign the reading me jake and jayne all gobsmackedga

22 I MET SAM LANG, HE DIDNT STRIKE ME THAT WAY?!!!! GOOD! GA

23 well maybe the ukcod and the usher conf convinced him !!! no one ekse signed ! ga

24 SO HE STUCK OUT AND BEING MINNISTER FOR DISABLED, HE SHOWED

25 EM . . . MAKE PEOPLE THINK EH? GA

26 sure did !!! ha ha oh well so how are u overall now got over your aches pains? ga

27 SO AND SO!!!! THE ACCIDENT . . . (turn continues)

The recipient of the good news affirms this with four comments in the same turn (line 14). At the end of the next turn the punctuation marks emphasize a query or doubt (line 17), which is dismissed in the following turn with "desnt matter u dit it u got it !! well done" and a further congratulations (line 18). The marks are used again later (line 22) to show the speaker's doubt about the information in the previous turn. Also note the response "sure did," exclamations to emphasize agreement, and the inserted laughter which shows appreciation of the previous speaker's comment (line 26).

In the following conversation about a visit to an eye hospital, the receiver responds to the irony of the inserted laughter and then gives an explanation for its presence.

C26

129 re moorfiled i just wait and see i am ok in home but outside in traffic it is awful i nearly

130 got knocked down yesterday plus work is weird too been like it since last weds bit

131 worrying but moorfield seem sympathetic my eyes work independently very well both

132 very good but at moment they refuse to work together !! ha ha ga

133 DUNNO WHY U LAUGHINGK! I KNOW U TRYING TO LE POSITIVE . . .

The listener's response (line 133) acknowledges that the inserted laughter is ironic and that the situation in which the speaker finds herself is not actually funny, but rather distressing.

An especially creative use of punctuation is shown in the following turn.

C25
78  i was """"dragged""""" screaming then remebered that . . . (turn continues)

The multiple quotation marks denote the license with which the inserted word is used. It is doubtful that the speaker was either dragged or screaming, but her sentiment about the situation is poignantly portrayed.

The corpus is replete with examples of these speech-related text features that superimpose tone onto the typed text: every turn is marked in some way that differentiates it from a formal written missive. The small sample provided hardly does justice to the wide range of nuances displayed by the creative use of the keyboard.

An interesting feature (in addition to the other representations of speech) that recurs in the data is the fact that there are many auditory or speech-related references in the talk. The speakers use vocabulary variations of *say, tell, hear,* and *listen* to describe their interactions with other parties. This usage is resonant with the work of McIlvenny (1996) who asserts that the Deaf participants in his study on CA and sign language used the terminology of speech to describe their interaction.[8]

C5
14  ITS GOOD TO HEAR THAT YOU ARE BACK ON YOUR FEET ONCE
15  AGAIN AND I MYSELF HAVE GOT SOME BACK ACHES (turn continues)
C26
 9  i ring to say (turn continues)
C7
46  DID YOU SAY WELL TR UNWELL IT CAME OVER WELL BUT DIDNT
47  QUITE FIT WITH WHAT YOU TYPED GA
48  u talking abt stan or your job ? ga
49  STAN GA
50  stan ok he was in nottingham yestterday too ga
C7
81  RIGHT ITS SAD NEWSIBAND WELL BEFORE TIME FOR SARAH GA
82  yes but apart from sarah i was interested in the way u put it . . . but i talk to u
83  another time abt that ga
84  WELL . . . I ONLY DID IT HOW I FELT WAS BEST GA

Many other examples can be found; see C22/21–22 and C5/110, later in the paper.

8. In these and other extracts in this chapter, underlines have been added to highlight words and phrases usually associated with speech and hearing activities.

There are also pieces in the corpus that root these conversations firmly within Deaf culture. In the following extracts C4 and C5, the spoken English expression "keep your ears open" when listening out for something is transformed into "keeping eyes open," "ears and eyes," and even more pointedly "eyes and fingers." Both conversations involve, in part, job hunting by the caller and the called's husband.

C4

88  YEP WE HAD SIMILAR LAST WEEK IT WAS EVEN BETTERE THEN
89  ITS LOVELY COLD AND MAKES GOOD SANDWICHES BUT A BIT
90  PRICEY GA
91  oops but if dad can eat it then in consideration not so dear !! but sssh u mak- ing me
92  hungry !!! so not got much news really just on toes looking for another job and
93  keeping eyes open it may not happen but one never knowws ga
94  YEP SPOSE U NEED TO KEEP EYES OPEN BY WAY PETE THINKS HE
95  HAS SOLD HHOUSE (turn continues)

C5

34  oh well !! how did the aromotherpay go ? ga
35  WELL THE FIRST DAY WENT OK BUT THE TEACHER WAS
36  TERRIBLE AND NERVOUS AS IT WAS HER FIRST WEEKEND COURSE
37  WITH STUDENTS BUT SHE HAS A VERY QUIET VOICE AND I HAVE
38  ASKED HER MANY A TIME TO LOOK STRAIGHT AND INSTEAD SHE
39  FACED DOWN AND POTTERED WITH HER PAPERS AS IT WAS A
40  RIGHT TOTAL MESS ACCORDING TO EVERYONE THERE SO I DID
41  NOT GO BACK NEXT DAY AS I DECIDED ITS BEST FOR ME TO SPEND
42  THE DAY WITH JOHN ASIT WAS HIS BIRTHDAY SO WE ALL HAD A
43  GRAND DAY AND I AM NOT SORRY FOR NOT GOING BACK TO
44  AROMATHERAPY BUT I HAVE WRITTEN AWAY TO MANY PLACES
45  GAKY COURSES BUT THE NEAREST IS ABOUT TWO HOURS RUN TO
46  GET THERE AND HOME AGAIN AND BACK AGAIN THE NEXT DAY OR
47  I WILL HAVE TO GET B/B NEAR VBUT I AM THINKING HARD ABOUT
48  IT AS I AM KEEN TO TRY AND ITS VERY COSTLY AND THE B/B IS SO
49  QUIET JUST NOW AT THE MO I HAVE A NORWEGIAN GIRL/LADY
50  STAYING WITH ME GAKY FOUR NIGHTS AS HER MUM IS IN
51  HOSPITAL ACROSS THE ROAD FROM HERE SO ITS WAS HANDY AND
52  AFTER THAT I MAY HAVE TO SIGN ON THE DOLE GA
53  well first i am sorry that aroma. . . . .was not good for u pls check out abt interpreter
54  next time or even lipspeaker if i see anything in london i pass onto u maybe u can
55  book apex fare and stay with sally or even here but will keep eyes open and glad
56  u not yet give up !!! seconnd re norwegian girl glad u got compnay eben though it

57   an ill wind brings bad ?? or what ever the saying is. . . . so hope all goes well but

58   any time or if u want more info abt anything lemme know ok ga

59   YEAH THANKS LYN THAT WILL BE SUPER AND I DO APPRECIATE
60   THAT HELP YES I DIG ENQUIRE ABOUT THE INTERPRETAR BUT
61   THE BOOKING WAS MADE OVER THE PHONE AND THE PERSON AT
62   THE OTHER END TOLD ME I SHOULD MANAGE IT BUT I WISH I
63   SHOULD HAD A HOLD OF HER NAME THAT I SHOULD COMPLAIN TO
64   HER AS I DID SAY TO THE TEACHER ABOUT IT AND I DO NEED AN
65   INTERPRETER FOR THE COURSE AND THE TEACHER SAID THAT
66   WOULD BE WONDERFUL SO I AM GLAD THAT BIT IS BY VAND I
67   WILL KEEP AWARE OF THINGS FROM NOW ON AND HOW IS YOUR
68   JOB GA

69   i hope u write and say how u couldnt follow the course and how the person taking

70   your booking advised u didnt need interpreer so u should write and say summat

71   for future if someone esle maybe need isnt there someone in scotlanmd who

72   already done aromoatherpay i think i saw tv prog sign on someone do it ?? but i

73   know deaf blind woman in london is qual armoatherapy massage so <u>wwill keep</u>

74   <u>eyes and fingers open !!!!!</u> me job yup service closes feb 96 i have till April to

75   wind up with reports etc then either i re deploy or look for another job not easy

76   but will see what i can do. . . . so how mark get on wwith job seeking ? ga

77   V I AM SORRY ABOUT YOUR JOBVBUT HOPEFULLY SOMEONE
78   WILL SNAP YOU UP AND YOU HAVE DONE A GREAT JOB DOWN
79   THERE ACCORDING TO WHAT YOU HAVE TOLD US RECENTLY AND
80   OARK HAS NOT FOUND ANYTHING SUITABLE YET AND
81   THEHQO WAS SUMMAT FROM DAVID JOHNSON A WEE WHILE
82   BACK ASKING MARK IF HE WOULD LIKE TO GET INVOLVE WITH HIS
83   COUNSELLING INRESEARCH AS THERE WAS A TENDER.
84   SOMEWHERE IN SCOTLAND BUT CARDIFF UNIVERSITY HAS
85   BEATEN DAVID JOHNSON SO MARK WAS KINDA DISAPPOINTED IT
86   WOULD BE INTERESTING SO HE WILL HAVE TO TRY AND <u>KEEP UPB</u>
87   <u>EARS AND EYES OPEN</u> VITS NOT EASY AS YOU SAY (turn continues)

Previously mentioned features are apparent in the previous two extracts. In C4, there is evidence of the use of sound effects (line 91) and idiomatic use of language (line 92), which is seen again in C5 (line 40) and (line 57), making the text seem more like talk.

The two examples that follow show that text telephones are in the realm of the everyday lives of deaf people. They show the visual nature of the alerting mechanism such that a call can be missed if one is not in the room, and that by switching off the lights one can avoid being alerted at all. The first example, C20, is a complete interaction between a caller and an answering machine and is followed by a second call, C22, where the answering machine activates but is then interrupted by the called.

C20
1 SORRY NO ONE IS ABLE TO ANSWER UR CALL NOW, PLS LEAVE UR
2 NAME AND NOS AND WILL CALL U BACK THKS BI SK
3 hello stan lyn bloomberg here wanna call chk abt tonite i am home till 10:00am
4 then out shopping will call again bibikssksk

C22
1 SORRY NO. . . . HELLO WHO IS IT GA
2 hello stan it lyn bloomberg got u at last how are u? g-a
3 HIYA THERE, I JUST MISSED UR CALL THIS AM, AS I WAS JUST
4 ENTERING INTO LIVVING ROOM FROM KITCHEN WITH A NICE
5 CUPCA A ANYWAY NTO TOO BAD REALY, BUT OTJHERWISE IA M
6 IN ONE PIECE AND WOT ABT U? GA
7 i am ok just get over a cold ga
8 RIGHTO, ANYWAY ABT UR MESS THIS AM, PLS EXPLAIN IN MORE
9 SPEIFIC WHAT I U R TRYING TO ASK ME ? GA
10 jayne white say summat abt u and me join jayne and pen for drink tonight they at
11 visotria victoria wine bar ?? but really i canna afford i just went mad xmas
12 shopoping ! ga
13 OH REALLY WHAT A STRANGE AS I SAW PEN LAST NIGHT AT 66
14 CLUB XMAS PARTY AND SHE SAID SHE COULDSN T MAKE IT ??? GA
15 oh well maybe jayne got mix up? ga
16 SO PEREHAPS WE CAN RE-SCHEDULE ARRNAGEMENT ? GAS
17 sure jayne say u want meet me and her soon before xmas ? ga
18 YEAH, BUT DUNNO DAY BEST FOR US ALLL AS I UND ALL BEING
19 BUSY WITH PRE XMAS GA
20 aye for me best mon or tues ga
21 ERM . . . I DUNNO MYSELF SO CAN WE DISCUSST OVER MINICOM AT
22 WORK ? GA
23 sure i can ring abt 3.00pm on Monday busy before then but i ring u mon ok u at
24 scd? ga
25 LOVELY AND YEAH GA
26 ok then thats fine !!!! so call u Monday and hope all ok with u and u happy in new
27 home ga
28 ITS STILL AN EARLY TO SAY YET GA
29 i unerdtstand !! ok i hooooopppppeeee to see u soooooon so i call on Monday ! ga
30 YEAH NO PLM, ITS JUST UNPACKING THAT I COULDNT CON-CENTRATE

31  U CAN IMAGINE IT OTHERWISE ALL IS OK WITH ME ATHERE GA

32  good that progress !!! ok then i let u go i goinmg shopping for food now $!!! mad

33  i am !! take care <u>talk sign type</u> mon !!! biiiee love h

The final extract reveals the visual method of avoiding telephone calls.

C5

105  ANYWAY I WILL PASS THE MESSAGE TO HIM AND THANKS FOR

106  RINING LYN AND YOU TAKE GREAT CARE OF YOURSELF GA

107  i wwill but u must too !!!! so hope u can take a bath with lavender !! and some

108  candles and relax i am just gonna jump in bath with all that and switch off my

109  mind and lights so no phones can distb me !!!! so hope u mark john and kathy

110  all fit well and i will be back !!! ok take care thanks for the cchat be in touch

111  again biiiiiieeeeeee for now cheers smile !! sksksksk

112  THANKS A LOT LYN AND FOR PHONING AS WELL . . . (turn continues)

What is evident from all the extracts and the entire corpus of data from which they are drawn is that they are interactive, creative, and expressive. They resemble conversations conducted via the spoken-auditory channel in both their construction and their function. The form they are obliged to take does not seem to detract from the participants' ability to express a wide range of affect nor to achieve interactional success. Despite the restriction of these conversations to text, they do not resemble a series of typed notes, but rather a conversation, as each turn shows a hinge onto the last and serves as a starting point for the next.

**DISCUSSION**

The description and analysis of the conversations in the data corpus have unearthed a rich diversity and complexity of interaction. The conversations span a range of interactional types, including business calls, those that are purely social, and many that involve the setting up of arrangements. They reflect very clearly the different social relationships between the parties.

During analysis of the selected features an overriding theme became evident. Two conflicting processes appear to be at work: the constraints of a text-based technology and the demands of natural conversation. This is a case of form in interaction with function. In order for conversation to proceed in real time with the local management inherent to its nature, function must overcome the limitations of form. The intent of participants to engage in natural conversation overrides the form. They overcome the text and system restraints and conduct conversation in a way similar to that which they might do in either signed or spoken face-to-face interaction. This was evidenced throughout the analysis. The technology constraints do not permit interruption or intelligible overlap and make the turn-taking system more stylized than occurs in natural spoken or signed conversation. The openings of text-telephone calls need to take special account of the demand to both self- and other-identify before the business of the call can proceed. This has to be achieved with little secondary information.

Conversation by its very nature—and this is what differentiates it from other speech exchange systems—allows most of its parameters to vary freely. In spite of the constraints, however, the turn-taking mechanisms, procedures for repair, openings and closings, turn size, turn allocation, and turn content are locally managed in a turn-by-turn fashion by the participants. For the most part, text telephones allow these parameters to vary similarly, but aspects of turn-taking, turn allocation, opening, and closings need to show "situational adaptation" to meet the demands of the system. There is a classic case of human-machine interface in successfully conducting conversation in this mode. The effectiveness of a particular configuration depends upon its adaptation to, and acceptance by, the persons who will operate it (Schein and Hamilton 1980). Knowledge of the operation of Minicom alone will not result in successful conversation. Although the medium of transmission may at first glance be thought to be "voiceless," "expressionless," and linear, this is revealed not to be the case. The range of subtleties displaying humor, irony, anger, surprise, and confusion is striking. The suprasegmental aspects of speech that are clearly unavailable to parties on text telephones are substituted for by a wide range of text features that appear "speech like." The creative use of punctuation, spelling, regional "dialects," slang, and exclamation together create the impression of a spoken or signed face-to-face interaction. The participants manage well to overcome the constraints set up by the technology to display a wide range of affect to their conversational partners.

These affects run parallel with the literal content of the text in much the same way as the content of a spoken message is interwoven with the intonational meaning conveyed. If a party to the talk wishes to move the coldness of text into a display of affect this needs to be encoded volitionally in order to supersede the linearity and anonymity of moving text. Speakers need to imprint this text with their own "intonational signature" to stamp their emotional response, their personality, and their worldview on the conversation. They cannot rely on the cadences of voice inherent in spoken interaction nor facial expression in signed interaction, but instead need to map these explicitly. Their success in this endeavor is shown throughout the corpus; it pervades every conversation regardless of speakers or type of call. Although the business calls in the corpus show different features from the personal calls, they are, nevertheless, not a series of messages transported back and forth between two people, but clearly display the parties' orientation to one another in a collaborative pursuit. Elements of this "recipient design" are evident throughout the corpus. Speakers design their turns with the other in mind, adjusting register, abbreviation use, slang, and punctuation for different listeners. The information provided also displays this feature such that it is specific to that particular participant.

A good example of this design is evidenced in two successive conversations (C25 and C26), where the lowercase speaker is describing trouble she is having with her eyes. In the first of the two conversations she talks about "my squint" and in the second she describes this in more detail: "years ago I had a squint." Both others respond to this information with very similar empathic comments SORRY TO HEAR ABT. . . . Patently, the first call was to a friend who knew about this squint and the second friend needed the background information.

The conversations evidenced in the data show coordinated, collaborative organization. The aspects of overall organization, that is, the openings and closings of the encounters, are particularly adapted for this medium, but these show successful resolution within a small number of turns. The ensuing conversation is sequential in nature, with each party's turn linking firmly with the previous turn and providing a stepping-stone for the next speaker on which to build their own turn.

Conventions have been adapted and created by Minicom users to facilitate just those parameters that define conversation, in order to allow them to vary as freely as is possible. Thus, the GA code that governs all turn transfers (Nash and Nash 1982) smooths the turn allocation and transfer mechanisms. This ensures that each party transmits successively and that little overlap in transmission occurs. Similarly, the SK code is collaboratively used to ensure that closing down of conversations happens only once both parties have agreed that this is what they want. The extended sequence of SK turns shows this orientation of speakers to one another. There are opportunities for either speaker to pursue the conversation or simply to add in another comment or a last greeting. Problems with poor transmission result in what has been called transmission "junk." This is a by-product of this technology and something that needs to be accommodated so that it does not impinge on the meaningful interaction. All occurrences of these strings of numbers, letters, and punctuation marks appear to be ignored by the parties at talk who concentrate on the content of the message but seem less perturbed by the form. This is similarly evidenced in the high tolerance for typographic and orthographic errors that pervade the corpus. On a small number of occasions these give rise to repair procedures, but largely they are ignored or the intended meaning is extracted from the text. Whenever this does detract from a party's understanding of the other's previous turn, a repair sequence is initiated. This is another indication of the participants' alignment to each another and their commitment to ensure that conversation proceeds with mutual understanding.

The cost of Minicom charges is a factor that manifests in a particular style of interaction. There is an attempt to increase the communication rate as much as possible, but not enough to make the interaction incomprehensible. Again the community of regular Minicom users have adapted to this necessity by using a large group of formalized abbreviations.

## CONVERSATION ANALYSIS OF TEXT INTERACTION

The use of CA on text interaction yields a wealth of information that would not be apparent if the analysis were restricted to a syntactic or checklist paradigm. The discipline of rooting each utterance within the context of the previous, as well as the successive, turn allows the rich nature of the data to emerge. It demonstrates the parties' orientation to each other, and their display from turn to turn of understanding of the other's turn. Although performance errors abound, the salient feature of these conversations is the extent to which speakers achieve mutual comprehension. If turns were evaluated out of their sequential context and in relation only to their syntax, punctuation, and spacing, this feature would be swamped. Although the analysis needs to take into account the differences inherent in spoken and text telephone calls, the methodology employed is a useful route to uncovering the successful achievement of conversational interaction.

The CA literature looks predominantly at spoken data in U.S. and British English and some European languages. The early work is all from the U.S. and cultural differences are beginning to emerge in the work being done in other countries. Differences may well be reflected in the current data, which is a product of a culture separate from that of hearing, speaking society. Cultural variations may well contribute to the management of interactional tasks necessary for coordinated conversation, such that both local and cultural aspects resolve themselves into a particular style of communication: "Culture is, after all, a matter of members' achievement" (Houtkoop-Steenstra 1991, 248). Aspects of Deaf culture are evidenced in the talk and give the data a specific flavor.

Comparisons of the speakers' use of written English with their sign use may generate interesting information about personal styles of interaction as well as proficiency in both media. This would facilitate description based on increased knowledge of the parties to the talk.

One feature that emerged during analysis of openings to Minicom conversations is the frequent use of vocatives. This is wholly unlike the use of vocatives in BSL where it is very unusual for one person, within talk, to address another by their name or to latch a name onto the beginning or end of a comment. This is an English structure. Attention-getting procedures in BSL do not use vocatives but involve bodily movement, touch, and eye contact.

Overlap in Minicom conversations is also an interesting feature to consider. There is evidence that there is less overlap in telephone than face-to-face conversation and all indications are that there is even less in text telephone interactions.

The present study has shown both that detailed sequential analysis is possible for text conversations and that it is a useful tool for uncovering the delicate interactional accomplishments of Minicom users. It has also highlighted the increased communicative possibilities that this technology affords deaf people. Increased ease of communication strengthens the Deaf community, while simultaneously granting greater opportunities to interact with elements of the larger society.

**REFERENCES**

Atkinson, J. M., and J. Heritage, eds. 1984. *Structures of social action: Studies in conversation analysis.* Cambridge: Cambridge University Press.
Baker, C. 1977. Regulators and turn-taking in American Sign Language Discourse. In *On the other hand: New perspectives on American sign language,* ed. L. A. Friedman. New York: Academic Press.

Cagle, S. J., and K. M. Cagle. 1991. *GA and SK etiquette: Guidelines for telecommunications in the Deaf community.* Bowling Green, Ohio: Bowling Green Press.

Hopper, R. 1992. *Telephone conversation.* Bloomington: Indiana University Press.

Houtkoop-Steenstra, H. 1991. Opening sequences in Dutch telephone conversations. In *Talk and social structure: Studies in ethnomethodology and conversation analysis,* ed. D. Boden and D. H. Zimmerman. Cambridge: Polity Press.

Kyle, J. H., and B. Woll. 1985. *Sign language: The study of Deaf people and their language.* Cambridge: Cambridge University Press.

Lee, J. R. E. 1987. Prologue: Talking organization. In *Talk and social organization,* ed. G. Button and J. R. E. Lee. Clevedon, U.K.: Multilingual Matters.

McIlvenny, P. 1995. Seeing conversations: Analyzing sign language talk. In *Situated order: studies in the social organization of talk and embodied activities,* ed. P. Ten Have and G. Psathas. Washington, D.C.: International Institute for Ethnomethodology and Conversation Analysis and University Press of America.

Nash, J. E., and A. Nash. 1982. Typing on the phone: How the Deaf accomplish TTY conversations. *Sign Language Studies* 36:193–216.

Sacks, H. 1972. Lecture 1, spring. In *Harvey Sacks' lectures in conversation,* vols. 1 and 2, ed. G. Jefferson. Oxford: Blackwell.

———. 1972. Lecture 3, spring. In *Harvey Sacks' lectures in conversation,* vols. 1 and 2, ed. G. Jefferson. Oxford: Blackwell.

Sacks, H., E. A. Schegloff, and G. Jefferson. 1974. A simplest systematics for the organization of turn-taking for conversation. *Language* 50:696–735.

Schegloff, E. A. 1979. Identification and recognition in telephone conversation openings. In *Everyday language: Studies in ethnomethodology,* ed. G. Psathas. New York: Irvington Publishers.

———. 1986. The routine as achievement. *Human Studies* 6:111–52.

Schein, J. D., and R. N. Hamilton. 1980. *Impact 1980: Telecommunications and deafness.* New York: Deafness Research & Training Center, New York University School of Education.

# Part 2 **External Context**

# Sign Languages as a Natural Part of

# the Linguistic Mosaic: The Impact of

# Deaf People on Discourse Forms in

# North Bali, Indonesia

*Jan Branson, Don Miller, and I Gede Marsaja*

This paper examines the use of signed discourses in the villages and towns of north Bali in Indonesia. Over the last few years we have been studying the social, cultural, and linguistic practices of a community of deaf people living in a village in North Bali (see Branson, Miller, and Marsaja 1996). At the same time, we have been studying the linguistic practices of students at the school for the deaf, SLB Bagian B,[1] in the nearby town of Singaraja. Although the village sign language has developed over many generations as a village language, the sign language of the students in the school has developed in the school and is unrelated to the sign language of the village.

The village that has been the focus of our attention is here referred to as *Desa Kolok,* Deaf Village. The village contains a hereditary deaf population (the *kolok*) who have been part of the village for at least twelve generations. Their sign language, known as the *kata kolok,* deaf talking, makes full use of the kinds of syntactical and lexical devises that characterize so many sign languages. The language is known and used not only by the deaf, but by the majority of hearing villagers (the *inget*) as well. Children signing in the street will often turn out to be hearing. Although many of the hearing and the *kolok* themselves see the *kolok* as having a distinct identity as a kind of subcommunity within the village, the *kolok*

---

1. Sekolah Luar Biasa translates as "School Outside the Normal." Bagian B translates as "Section B," the section for the deaf.

are fully integrated into village life and achieve their prime identity from membership of kin and ritual communities, which make no distinction between *kolok* and *inget* as far as obligations are concerned.

While we were aware that villagers from some neighboring villages found the integration of the *kolok* into village life surprising (see Branson, Miller, and Marsaja 1996, 46–48), but the contours of attitudes toward deaf people in villages in the region and toward the use of signing needed to be documented. The research in Desa Kolok and in the school raised a number of questions:

- Was the language used by the villagers in Desa Kolok restricted to the village?
- If it had spread, where had it spread to and who now used it?
- Was there a Deaf community linking deaf people in surrounding villages?[2]
- If so, did the Deaf community use a common sign language?
- Were there other Deaf communities in the surrounding areas with their own languages?
- What about isolated deaf people, how did they communicate?

This paper sets out not only to answer these questions but also to examine the impact of social and cultural factors on the discursive practices of deaf people living in north Bali. In documenting and seeking to explain the discursive processes through signing in north Bali, we also examine attitudes to deafness throughout the region, attitudes that vary significantly. These attitudes are influenced by a wide range of social and cultural factors that can only be understood through an appreciation of the region's ethnography, in the context of a society undergoing significant social and cultural changes in response to national and international pressures. The next section outlines the social and cultural shape of north Bali.

## BALI AND THE REGION OF BULELENG

Bali is a luminous mosaic of Southeast Asian civilization. Though small by the standards of Java or continental Asian societies, it is both a product and a producer of a spate of ideas and imagery that draws on numerous

2. In the West much emphasis is placed on the notion of a Deaf community that transcends normal geographical boundaries, so that there is even talk of an international Deaf community.

great historical streams—Malayo-Polynesian, Megalithic, Indian, Chinese, Islamic, and Western, as well as its own local innovative genius—and it composes a complex and cosmopolitan society of highly diverse organization (Barth 1993, 9).

Bali lies east of Java in the Indonesian archipelago. It has long been a well-known tourist destination, attracting tourists with images of white sandy beaches, majestic active volcanoes, smiling people, elaborate colorful rituals, and a feast of art and artifacts: painting, dance, drama, shadow puppets, and stone and wooden sculpture. Most descriptions of Balinese society and culture have painted a picture of social and cultural homogeneity. Balinese society is characterized as a hierarchical society, a caste-based society ruled by the high-caste descendants of rulers from the Javanese Hindu kingdom of Majapahit, who fled to Bali in the fifteenth century. These migrants are also assumed to have brought Hinduism with them and established the lavish culture that dominates tourist images of Bali. While Hinduism, or rather Hindu-Buddhism, came to Bali long before the Majapahit migration (see Miller 1982, 1983), the picture painted in these conventional descriptions of the Balinese does apply in general terms to south Bali, where Majapahit elites settled and where modern tourists and expatriate "experts" are to be found. But as we cross the mountains and head north, the picture changes.

Throughout the higher reaches of the mountains and down through the foothills and the narrow coastal plain to the north, the picture is very different. The hierarchical society of the south, ruled by ritual and secular elite castes, gives way to more egalitarian social environments. Elite castes are conspicuous by their virtual absence, with priests and village leaders coming from what in the south are considered commoner castes. But through the hills and down onto the north coast there is no sense of commoners. Clan affiliations are important and there is ranking among clans, but there is no sense of hierarchy. The ritual environment is less ornate but still colorful and complex. Substantial differences in ritual traditions exist throughout the region, even between neighboring villages.

Socially, culturally, and linguistically, the central volcanoes therefore provide a clear division between the hierarchical and highly colorful south, well known as an exotic tourist destination, and the less well known and more egalitarian center and north. In the north, the mountains run virtually down to the sea, leaving little or no coastal plain. We decided to restrict our search for other Deaf communities to the north central region of Bali, the region of Buleleng. This was also the region from which most of the students came who attended the specialist school for the deaf in the northern capital Singaraja. The region includes only two urbanized centers: Singaraja, the old Dutch capital with a population of around 50,000; and Seririt, a much smaller market town 20 kilometers to the west. Most people live on the narrow coastal plain and in the numerous small villages in the foothills behind. Singaraja is now a large market and educational center and lies roughly in the middle of the northern coastline. Patterns of movement of people tend to radiate in and out of Singaraja as well as within markets in local areas. General movement from west to east across Singaraja is less common.

The region of Buleleng is rugged and socially, culturally, linguistically, and ecologically diverse. It has a population of 564,523 spread through 145 villages, stretches just over 100 kilometers along the north coast, and penetrates just 20 kilometers into the hills at its widest point along the central part of the region. The population is predominantly Hindu-Buddhist, but immigrant Bugis and Javanese communities are to be found along the coast, with Arab and Chinese populations in Singaraja. One old Muslim village, recently studied by Fredrik Barth (1993), is to be found in the foothills above Singaraja. Its people speak Balinese but lead a relatively autonomous religious life. High in the hills are populations described as Bali Aga and Bali Mula/Asli. These populations are seen as having social and cultural practices that are particularly ancient and less influenced by the Majapahit migration than those in the foothills and on the coast. But their faith still has a vital Hindu-Buddhist quality, and all Buleleng villages have a strong religious association with ancestors. Linguistically, the mountain villages have languages distinct from the Balinese of the foothills and plains, but operate readily in Balinese as well. There were few deaf people in the Bali Aga/Mula villages and one adult in the Muslim village. The vast majority of the deaf people living in Buleleng are Hindu-Buddhist.

Among the Balinese we have dealt with, there is a very strong sense of community, of links that bind people together not only as residential communities but as ritual communities. Shared ritual obligations define the relationships that are ultimately binding and exclude the ephemeral links established beyond the community through personal, individual association at work, school, university, and so on.

In the analysis that follows it is vital that we move beyond the ethnocentrism of Western notions of community and identity, and of obligations associated with ties of friendship and the like, orientations that are associated with the breakdown of community and the emergence of individualism as the dominant value in capitalist societies. Much of the analysis of the data will hinge on understanding the dispositions of these Balinese toward links with people inside and outside their ritual communities.

In most Western societies, social life is coordinated in the main through depersonalized institutions and associations to which people are tied as individuals. Personal subjectivity is individuated, and social honor ideologically assumed to be a reflection of individual achievement. The sense and experience of hereditary communities has been replaced by a rampant individualism, where face-to-face relationships have been replaced by secondary relationships, where the roles of kinship and religious association have been replaced by a wide range of depersonalized institutions—the school, the university, the voluntary association, the nightclub, the hospital, the business enterprise, the bank, the amusement park, and the nation.

In contrast, the nature and role of communities and their linguistic qualities and practices are very different in Bali. Social relationships are still to a large degree coordinated through multigenerational, communal obligations. Personal subjectivity derives in large part from a hereditary communal association with others. In rural Bali the focus is on the village-based community. In urban Bali, although the focus shifts in part to the school and the office, identity comes from shared ritual associations. People do form friendships with other individuals in the market, on laboring sites, in the office, and at school and university, but these links are beyond community. They are individual links. They do not involve ritual obligations and in no way challenge or compare with the links of community.

## COMMUNITY AND IDENTITY IN AND BEYOND DESA KOLOK

When we were first working among the *kolok* of Desa Kolok, hearing villagers were adamant that the *kolok* were a unique aspect of their village life and that there were no communal links between the *kolok* of Desa Kolok and *kolok* elsewhere. The only other deaf people mentioned at all, apart from the deaf children at the school, were a few *kolok* in a neighboring village, but the links were seen as ephemeral. The *kolok* themselves mentioned other *kolok* in the neighboring village but did not regard them as part of their community. They were, after all, from another village.

In searching for an understanding of linguistic developments beyond Desa Kolok, we especially wanted to determine if sign languages were used in multigenerational rather than individual contexts. We also wanted to determine how signing was integrated into the linguistic practices between generations. Although she does not consider signing as a medium for linguistic activity, McMahon makes a vital point about languages when she writes, "speakers must learn their native languages in such a way as to allow communications with the generations above and below them: since language is a vehicle of communication, it would be failing in its primary function if it did not allow parents to be understood by their children, or grandchildren by their grandparents" (1994, 5).

Apart from the linguistic and personal links established through the deaf school in Singaraja, we were therefore concerned with those links that were not bound to the modern occupations or education, links that involve the development of multigenerational discursive processes. Later in the paper, we will return to the impact of individually based relationships through work and education, as well as the impact of new ideological and political forces associated with the nation and the region on these "traditional" discursive processes.

All Balinese are involved with people outside the village through links of kinship. Clan links extend well beyond the village and marriages are increasingly formed with people outside. Village membership may also involve historical links with other villages, as the history of Desa Kolok will show. In addition, Balinese people have always traveled quite long distances to markets. Markets rotate on three, five, and seven day cycles, with sellers and buyers attending markets outside their local area.

And so networks spread out from the village. But it is the identity associated with the family temple and its location in a specific village that remain central to a person's identity. The sense of community is not of a finite population but of shifting communal obligations associated with kin- and territory-based associations. A person's identity and worth is associated with their place in a complex web of ritual duties, duties that establish the sense of belonging that is vital to a secure identity. To understand the way this sense of community operates both within and beyond the village, we must understand the importance to the villagers of Bali of the island's temples, large and small, that are to be found in the thousands. People have ritual obligations to a range of temples within and beyond the village. Household temples, family temples, and clan temples link people through kinship. A range of village temples link the community to the wider cosmos, to the forces of good, evil, creation, sustenance, and destruction; the temples bind humanity into the wider picture, providing a framework for individual human beings to engage in strategic ritual action to cope with the vagaries of a life lived in close association with nature.

In relation to ritual obligations, the *kolok* from Desa Kolok do not have their own special ceremonies. Their identity as *kolok* is irrelevant to their performance of family-based, clan-based, and village-based ceremonies. They do, however, tend to attend the family-based ceremonies of other *kolok*, even when no ritual obligations apply. Attendance by nonkin at these ceremonies (such as the "earthing" of a child at three months of age: the *telu bulanan*, when a child, having survived those dangerous first three months, joins earthly humanity by touching the ground for the first time) is not problematic and the *kolok* attend as fellow *kolok*. To be *kolok* in Desa Kolok is to share an identity integral to the identity of the village as a whole. To be *kolok* is not to be marginal, as the origin myths of the village show.

## THE BALINESE COSMOS

The Balinese Hindu-Buddhist cosmos is linked directly to the world of experience, to the mountains, the coastal plains, and the sea. The uranian, or heavenly sphere, is the world of the sun and the mountain—the source of the rivers that run down to fertilize the receptive, impure female world of fertile coastal plains, the crops that nurture and sustain life. The uranian sphere is identified with gods. The earthly sphere is identified with goddesses: Bhatari Uma, who cares for rice shoots, and the all important Dewi Sri, mother of the ripening harvest. In this earthly world, disaster or the threat of disaster is never far away and comes in one of the forms of the destructive demoness Bhatari Durga.

The world is fraught with danger, and the villagers' views of their place in it involve constant concern with the ordering of time and space and with strategically positioning themselves vis-à-vis the plethora of cosmic forces. Temporally they (women in particular) must observe a complex array of rituals. The day, the month, and the year are subdivided to generate times when rituals must be observed: times of danger demand ritual action, auspicious times must be celebrated. The life of each individual is itself a stream of rituals, of "life-crises," as humanity walks the knife-edge path through the cosmos. Even in the production of goods and services, rituals stress the need for awareness of cosmic forces.

Throughout the villages, fields, towns, houseyards, and along the coast, temples and shrines provide a focus for constant ritual as space and time are brought together in strategies for survival. Village temples provide a focus for the realization of the village community, irrigation society or *subak* temples provide a focus for the farming community, market temples a focus for the merchant community, clan temples a focus for the intervillage clan-based community, household temples a focus for the local kin group and so on. Through their rituals the Balinese express and experience the hegemony of essential Hindu ideals of honor and shame, purity and pollution, superiority and inferiority, male and female.

Good and evil, beautiful and ugly, the human and the nonhuman, and the domesticated and the wild are all vital aspects of a complex and dangerous world. Western cosmology favors a unitary logocentric world positively valuing the singular, a "straightforward" unitary order that devalues the fragmentary, which is seen as chaos. This is not the cosmos as understood by the Balinese. For them, the coexistence of what to us may seem contradictory images is not problematic; it is normal, expected, and valued. Rich, uncertain, unpredictable diversity is not chaos, but the flux of nature and humanity.

When children are born with or develop characteristics that interfere with their potential to participate effectively in the community's economic, political, and ritual life—an inability to walk, an inability to use limbs effectively or to coordinate one's body, an inability to speak effectively, blindness, extreme mental retardation, and in some cases deafness—parents seek the advice of a healer or spirit medium and possibly hope for a cure. The reason for the problem will usually be assumed to lie in the family's failure to perform essential rituals or to observe marriage prohibitions.

As we shall see in the examination of the interview data, throughout particular parts of Buleleng, the possibility of a child being deaf is expected. In some cases the fact that a child is deaf is seen as normal, especially among those families—almost all in Desa Kolok—identified as *kolok* families. In some other families deafness is a possibility that is simply taken on board. In others deafness is seen as a problem to be treated and possibly cured through the services of a *balian*. Whatever the reaction, a deaf child is part of the diversity of nature.

The data revealed that to some degree, proximity to Desa Kolok influenced the attitude expressed toward the presence of a *kolok* child. But while proximity appeared in part to collate with shared or similar attitudes, another factor emerged as exerting a particularly strong influence: the diversity of attitudes was closely linked to the local cosmology, specifically to whether or not *kolok* were sanctioned in myth and legend as an integral and expected aspect of the cosmos.

## THE HISTORY AND MYTHOLOGY OF DESA KOLOK AND ITS *KOLOK*

The history of Desa Kolok is described in the ancient written record of its origin, the *prasasti*. The *prasasti* is written in an ancient script on bronze plates and is kept in a shrine in the *pura puseh,* also called the *pura desa.* On special occasions it is washed in holy water and honored before being replaced in its shrine. No one in the village can read the *prasasti,* but oral versions are handed down from generation to generation. The oral version of the *prasasti* for Desa Kolok states that the village was established in *Crawana* of *Caka* 1103 (July of 1181 A.D.) during the reign of King Sri Maharaja Haji Jayapangus. Prior to this, the village, which was called Desa Keraman, was much larger than the present village and included the area of Pakwan to the southwest of the present village. Desa Keraman was, of course, a ritual community focusing on the village temples. Between 1079 and 1088 A.D., during the reign of King Walaprabhu, the area's population increased and the villagers petitioned the king to establish separate villages. Desa Kolok and Desa Pakisan became two distinct ritual communities but some linkages remained. Today, the two villages share one of the temples in Banjar Klandis of Desa Pakisan, where among other shrines—or seats to which gods descend on auspicious days—is a shrine to a god bearing the name of the village of Desa Kolok. In the temple is a shrine to Bhatara Kolok, a deaf god.

There is also a story that the people from Desa Kolok and another neighboring village, Suwug, came from the nearby village of Sinabun. The people of Desa Kolok and Suwug also share a temple, Pura Menasa, in Sinabun. In Sinabun there are two temples, the Pura Menasa and the Pura Sakti, that contain shrines to the Bhatara Kolok. In Suwug there is also a shrine to the Bhatara Kolok in Pura Lebah.

Within the cultural context of the villages of Desa Kolok, Desa Suwug, Desa Sinabun, and Desa Pakisan, deaf people are integral to the villagers' cosmology. Villagers saw the shrine to Bhatara Kolok as the reason why there are always *kolok* in these villages. When asked about the reason for the prevalence or origins of deafness within Desa Kolok, both deaf and hearing villagers from Desa Kolok and these surrounding villages told the following story. This *konon* or legend has been handed down over many generations from parents to children. All the villagers we asked provided almost identical versions of the same story. The story is as follows:

> A long time ago there was a couple who lived in the village and wanted to have children. After some time, when no child had arrived, they decided to seek help from the gods. A close member of the family went to the children's cemetery at midnight to find some *pelangkiran* to bring back to the family temple.[3] At the cemetery he met a deaf ghost. Later, when the couple had a baby, the baby was deaf.

The story of the deaf ghost is a graphic and enduring part of the current village beliefs. It was not difficult to find villagers who reported seeing the ghost. In fact it was assumed that the village cosmos contained *kolok* ghosts. The origins of the *kolok* and their ongoing presence was explained in a way that incorporated the *kolok* into all aspects of village discourse, sacred and secular.

The cosmological presence, and indeed legitimacy, of the *kolok* is reinforced above all by the fact that there is not only a deaf god (the Bhatara Kolok) among the pantheon of local gods, but that the cosmological presence of the Bhatara Kolok is not simply theoretical but is frequently experienced. The Balinese Hindu-Buddhist cosmos contains myriad spiritual forces, some identified as gods, others as lesser spirits, and others identified with the ancestors. Communicating with the gods is a normal part of everyday Balinese life. Offerings must be made daily. At certain auspicious times the community directly engages in discourse with the gods through spirit mediums in trance. The spirit medium, or *balian,* is a hearing woman who cannot sign. In these ceremonies the gods' views, thoughts, and particular messages are conveyed through the *balian.* Suwug, within the sphere of the myths and legends of Desa Kolok, traditionally specializes in providing trance mediums through whom people consult their ancestors and establish discursive links with the gods.

3. When a young baby dies, special offerings called *pelangkiran* are placed near the grave site in the cemetery. When a couple is unable to have children, a close member of the family goes to the children's cemetery at midnight to find some *pelangkiran* to be offered in the family temple.

The Bhatara Kolok is associated with the temples mentioned previously. The Bhatara Kolok descends with other gods to the temples on their temple festivals, their Odalan. So, for example, we recorded the descent of the Bhatara Kolok to its seat in the Pura Lebah in Desa Suwug. A *balian* became possessed by the god and signed its responses. The signing of the god was interpreted for the worshipers by a temple priest, *pemangku*, from Desa Kolok. The Bhatara Kolok descended again the next day in Pura Menasa in Sinabun, on its Odalan, held annually on Pumama Sarsih Keenam. Again, one of the participants was possessed, and again it was a hearing woman who could not sign. In trance she "became deaf" and signed, and one of the temple priests, *pemangku,* from Desa Kolok acted as an interpreter during the trance sequence so that the message from the *kolok* god could be understood by all.

Villagers associated through myth and legend with Desa Kolok saw the existence of a deaf ghost and a deaf god as a sign that there will always be deaf people in their villages, that they are a normal and even essential part of the makeup of the village. Deaf people and signing are, according to deaf and hearing alike, integral to the everyday life of the village. But what of the discursive processes and orientations of people in surrounding villages and beyond. Did their cosmos, their habitus, include deaf people and signing? How did people communicate? To ask these questions coherently we had to approach the discursive practices of north Bali through a particular kind of theoretical framework.

## THEORIZING DISCURSIVE PROCESSES IN NORTH BALI

The focus of the paper is on "ways of communicating." In interpreting the dynamics of signing in the linguistic ecology of the area, we follow Mühläusler (1996) in eschewing approaches that focus on the "given languages" of a region, due to the problem of separating languages from other forms of communication. Whether the "ways of communicating" described here qualify as "languages" will be put aside for the purposes of this paper for two main reasons: (1) because, as Mühläusler stresses, linguistic ecology is not just made up of "languages," and (2) because for the majority people of north Bali whom we are dealing with, the question of when a way of communicating is a language is not an issue.

The analysis of the dynamics of selected discursive practices in north Bali will also draw on what has been dubbed "critical discourse analysis."

For as we examine the dynamics of change we will see that we are faced with an ecology in danger. The danger arises from the impact of political forces exerting effective dominance through a drive for linguistic uniformity and control. These forces serve not only to transform a complex linguistic ecology but to isolate and disable a group of people who were formerly a part of the ecological diversity. We will also draw on the work of the French anthropologist Pierre Bourdieu (1977), specifically on his concept of "habitus." Unlike the concept of a "linguistic ecology," which focuses on the whole, the concept of a linguistic habitus takes us to the heart of linguistic practice as cultural practice as we examine the way individual Balinese are creative, strategic agents in the production and reproduction of the linguistic environment.

As we explore the dynamics of discursive practices through signing in north Bali we also engage in a critique of Western orientations toward signed discourse from two perspectives: an historical examination of the transformation of attitudes toward language in the West, and a comparative analysis of discursive processes in the West with those of north Bali. To understand what is happening in Buleleng in terms of discursive processes, the paper looks at these discursive processes as the dynamic aspect of the region's linguistic ecology. This perspective has been adopted, following Mühläusler (1996), because of its concern with the dynamics of the wider "environment" in which discourse occurs, the dynamics of the linguistic mosaic, and its focus on communicative action rather than on "languages" as distinct entities. Mühläusler objects to approaches that focus on a region's "given languages" on two grounds: the lack of linguistic criteria for deciding in all instances on a determinate number of languages in a postulated ecology, and the problem of separating languages from other forms of communication.

It is the second criterion that is particularly pertinent in the context of understanding the dynamics of linguistic processes in north Bali. We are concerned with the ways in which the people of north Bali communicate with each other. At the same time we are concerned with current pressures for change that threaten the region's complex discursive environments. These pressures are associated with economic and political processes often seen to be outside the field of linguistics. "The ecological metaphor in my view is action oriented. It shifts the attention from linguists being players of academic language games to becoming shop stewards for linguistic diversity, and to addressing moral economic and other 'nonlinguistic' issues" (Mühläusler 1996, 2).

We deal with these "nonlinguistic" issues by bringing the work of Pierre Bourdieu to bear on Mühläusler's concept of linguistic ecology. Following Bourdieu, we view the linguistic environments we deal with as cultural environments of a particular kind, through a view of culture that focuses on the dynamics and variability of cultural practice rather than on culture as singular and uniform. Such a view of culture recognizes that people are cultural strategists, using the symbol systems of their cultures—dress, language, the arts, work, leisure, and so on—to express themselves and to understand and communicate. Their strategic practice is structured by the sociocultural environment, by what Bourdieu (1977, 72) calls *habitus*: "systems of durable, transposable *dispositions*, structured structures predisposed to act as structuring structures, that is, as principles of the generation and structuring of practices and representations." These dispositions are not random but are interrelated with one another; they are structured to form a style or way of doing things. The practices and views generated by the habitus can be "objectively 'regulated' and 'regular' without in any way being the product of obedience to rules, objectively adapted to their goals without presupposing a conscious aiming at ends or an express mastery of the operations necessary to attain them, and, being all this, collectively orchestrated without being the product of the orchestrating action of a conductor" (Bourdieu 1977, 72).

Culture thus understood is a dynamic, overtly social, and shared process. It is the means through which people express and experience community membership, their sense of belonging, and their claim to belong. It is also the way through which they assert, embody, and express differences within, as well as between, societies and groups. Culture serves not only to unite but to divide.

In the linguistic environments of north Bali, people strategically manipulate their linguistic skills to satisfy their needs. They do so in terms of their linguistic habitus, which are dynamic and changing, influenced by shifting linguistic, cultural, economic, and political conditions. We are faced in the region with a complex linguistic ecology, a polylingualism that also involves different forms of communication. It is also an ecology under threat, an ecology experiencing an all-too-familiar decline in the face of national and international pressures for linguistic and cultural conformity and uniformity. Mühläusler recently warned of "the inability of most practicing linguists to understand what is happening around them, that their very object of study is disappearing at an alarming rate, that the transition from polylingualism to monolingualism is accelerating, and that the prospects of survival of traditional languages *and forms of communication* are very slim indeed" (Mühläusler 1996, 1, emphasis added). Not only are the trends toward monolingualism being felt in north Bali, but the legitimacy of different forms of communication, including the signing mode, is being questioned.

## SURVEYING THE DEAF PEOPLE OF NORTH BALI

How did we collect the data? The rugged mountainous terrain meant that if we wanted to be sure that we had found all sign languages we needed to visit every village and every household containing a deaf person, no matter how remote. Initial contact with each village was made through the village head, the Kepala Desa. The Kepala Desa identified deaf people in the village and gave permission for us to visit their families. Contact was then made with almost every deaf person and their family. The visits usually took several hours each with the family often joined by neighbors. After the necessary polite formalities were completed, an informal semistructured interview was conducted and usually videotaped. This pattern of two and sometimes three or more visits to each village has provided a reliable guide to the distribution of deaf people through the villages and to their discursive practices.

The survey covered every village in the region of Buleleng in central northern Bali, consisting of the districts of Tejakula, Kabutambahan, Sawan, Buleleng, Suksada, Banjar, Seririt, Busungbiu, and Gerokgak. The survey figures are based on interviews with the head of each village, where possible with the *kolok* of the village, and with other villagers. All the *kolok* in the region have been surveyed. Follow-up interviews were also conducted with many of the *kolok*, to allow for filming and to ensure detailed coverage of the various cultural and linguistic situations in which *kolok* were to be found.

This process was very slow, because many village houses could be accessed only on foot in very rugged terrain. Expeditions into the hills on foot ensured that all *kolok* were contacted. For example, we were walking with filming equipment to where we expected to find two deaf siblings. The terrain became more and more rugged and the vegetation harder to penetrate. We came upon a farmer in his field hut who said that we would not be able to access the house from this direction. We asked if there were any other *kolok* nearby, and were told that there were. We followed the farmer's instructions and were met by a mature fluent signer living in an environment in which signing was an accepted way of communicating among his family and his neighbors. The figures in table 1 are therefore a reliable guide to the distribution of deaf people through the districts of Buleleng.

Two things emerge from table 1. First, the level of deafness among the region's general population is higher than levels in the West and is closer to the rates reported in the nineteenth century in Europe and America. Second, there appear to be pockets of deafness, the most obvious being Kubutambahan, the region that includes Desa Kolok, where the rate of deafness is 1 in 550. In the survey area there were 145 villages. The *kolok* were to be found in 88 of the villages (60 percent). Of these, 69 villages had more than one *kolok,* and several villages (apart from Desa Kolok) had between 5 and 18 *kolok.* On the basis of current assumptions among academics involved in deaf studies and sign language research, the conditions and potential for the development of sign languages or small Deaf communities appears to be clearly present. There appears to be no lessening of the incidence of deafness over time, as 38 percent of these deaf were under twenty years of age, 59 percent between the ages of twenty-one and fifty-five, and 3 percent between fifty-six and eighty. This means that the need for sign language use is at present not declining.

Current Western academic approaches to the occurrence of sign languages assume that apart from the development of signing in deaf school environments, the incidence of deaf children being born to deaf parents is

TABLE 1. *Deaf and Hearing Population of Buleleng by District*

| Name of District (from east to west) | Population by Gender | | Total Population | Number of *Kolok* | Ratio of *Kolok* |
|---|---|---|---|---|---|
| | Male | Female | | | |
| Tejakula | 27,595 | 27,980 | 55,575 | 22 | 1 in 2500 |
| Kubutambahan | 23,921 | 24,201 | 48,122 | 88 | 1 in 550 |
| Sawan | 27,761 | 30,214 | 57,975 | 50 | 1 in 1160 |
| Buleleng | 54,688 | 56,396 | 111,084 | 75 | 1 in 1500 |
| Sukasada | 29,759 | 31,319 | 61,078 | 20 | 1 in 3050 |
| Banjar | 30,247 | 31,728 | 61,975 | 44 | 1 in 1400 |
| Seririt | 32,072 | 33,552 | 65,624 | 36 | 1 in 1800 |
| Busungbiu | 20,680 | 21,557 | 42,237 | 15 | 1 in 2800 |
| TOTAL | 277,138 | 287,385 | 564,523 | 370 | 1 in 1500 |

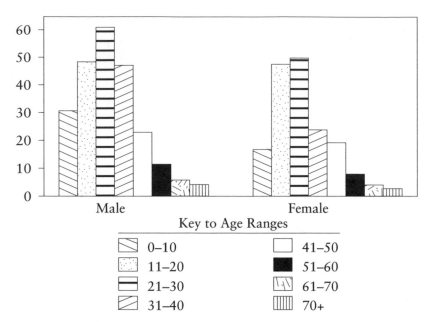

FIGURE I. *Distribution of Deaf Population of Buleleng by Age*

of vital importance to the development and survival of sign languages. It might therefore appear, on the basis of the statistics alone, that the vast majority of deaf in Buleleng would have no contact with signing in their immediate environment, especially given the rugged terrain and the isolation of many villagers. In Buleleng, only 9 percent of the *kolok* had one or more deaf parents with a further 5 percent having close deaf relatives.[4] Of the *kolok* with deaf parents, 22 (76 percent) lived in Desa Kolok, 1 in a neighboring village, 4 in Singaraja, and 1 far to the west. Eighty-five percent of the *kolok* had no family-based contact with deaf people. Multi-generational deafness was to be found in only 5 out of the 88 villages containing deaf people. Did this mean that the vast majority of *kolok* in

4. These figures are in line with current assumptions about the overall occurrence of deafness, that is, that ninety percent of deafness occurs randomly through the population. In the West, the impact of the distribution of deafness on the transmission of sign language has been well documented. Because ninety percent of deafness occurs randomly, the problem of the transmission of sign language is critical. Deaf children are unlikely to have deaf parents and deaf parents are most likely to have hearing children. Therefore the transmission of sign languages across generations is rare.

Buleleng had no contact with sign language? The interviews with deaf people proved otherwise.

But before we move beyond the overall statistics, it is important to outline the general occupational and educational contours of the deaf population. The occupational figures are interesting for two reasons: first, the figures establish the social status of deaf adults relative to the general population and thus help to determine how each deaf person's particular social position influenced their discursive practices; and second, the occupational figures help gauge how much contact deaf people were likely to have with the wider population inside and outside their village.

## Occupations

As the figures in table 2 show, the *kolok* of Buleleng were involved in a wide range of occupations. Where possible these figures are related to the general figures for Buleleng, but the categories are in some cases problematic. The official statistics tend to use Western categories such as "unemployed" and even "housewife," despite the fact that they are inappropriate. The vast majority of the deaf population, and indeed the overall population of Buleleng, are involved in village-based production. In such a productive environment, unemployment rarely, if ever, exists. Home-based activities are as much part of the productive system as those activities pursued outside the home.

The occupational and educational figures show that the deaf population of Buleleng had substantial contact with people outside the immediate household, therefore involving them in a wide range of social contexts. As Van Dijk (1997, 2) points out, discourse "focuses on the properties of what people say or write in order to accomplish social, political, or cultural acts in various local contexts as well as within the broader frameworks of societal structure and culture." When people engage in discourse they do so as members of specific social categories usually made up of "complex combinations of social and cultural roles and conversely, by accomplishing discourse in social situations, language users at the same time actively construct and display such roles and identities" (Van Dijk 1997, 3). The deaf population of Buleleng interacts with the wider society through a wide range of occupations. Leaving aside those who were at school and those under the age of thirteen years, only 15 percent had no ongoing employment outside the home. The range of jobs was quite widespread and not dissimilar to hearing members of the population with the

TABLE 2. *The Occupations of Deaf People in Buleleng.*

| Type of Employment | Number Employed (N = 174) | Percentage | Type of Employment | Number Employed (N = 174) | Percentage |
|---|---|---|---|---|---|
| Laborer | 78 | 44.8 | Spirit medium | 1 | 0.6 |
| Farmer/ | | | Stone polisher | 1 | 0.6 |
| cattle breeder | 34 | 19.5 | Palm sugar | | |
| Servant | 10 | 5.7 | maker | 1 | 0.6 |
| Merchant | 10 | 5.7 | Beauty salon | | |
| Tailor, sewer | 8 | 4.6 | worker | 1 | 0.6 |
| Stonemason | 6 | 3.4 | Maker of | | |
| Weaver | 4 | 2.3 | offerings | 1 | 0.6 |
| Mechanic | 3 | 1.7 | Tour guide | 1 | 0.6 |
| Fisherman | 3 | 1.7 | Baker | 1 | 0.6 |
| Painter | 3 | 1.7 | Hotel clerk | 1 | 0.6 |
| Housewife | 2 | 1.1 | Teacher of | | |
| Driver | 2 | 1.1 | the deaf | 1 | 0.6 |
| Shoe maker, | | | | | |
| repairer | 2 | 1.1 | | | |

exception of office workers, where deafness could be seen as a barrier to employment.

Although the deaf people of Buleleng participated in a wide range of occupations, the proportion of laborers to farmers was the reverse of the overall population. By far the largest occupational category for the *kolok* was laborer. The latest figures relating to the total population of Buleleng show 12 percent of the population over ten years of age who were in the workforce were laborers and 51 percent were farmers (Kantor Statistik Kabupaten Buleleng 1997, 77). The high proportion of laborers reflects the lack of access to clerical occupations and the generally poorer condition of the deaf population. In terms of contact between deaf people and the outside world, however, laboring brings deaf people into constant contact and communication with hearing people and sometimes with other deaf people. Twenty-nine percent of the *kolok* old enough to be in the workforce had received some type of skill training. This skill training consisted largely of on-the-job apprenticeship. In the case of traditional occupations such as weaving, the occupations were concentrated in villages that specialized in these occupations, indicative of the fact that for the vast proportion of the *kolok*, skill training was in the family.

## Education

In terms of educational background, 70 percent of the total deaf population over the age of six years had never been to school. This compares with 18 percent for the overall population of Buleleng. Of the current school age children, 36 percent of the *kolok* had never been to school. This compares with 2.5 percent for the overall school age population of Buleleng. Of those *kolok* who were attending school, 84 percent were attending an SLB, most in Singaraja. Of those aged between sixteen and forty, 64 percent had never been to school. Of those who went to school in this older age group, 67 percent had attended an SLB compared with 84 percent of the under-sixteen group. The rate of school attendance has almost doubled in the last twenty years, with an increasing proportion attending the special school, a direct contrast to schools in the West where mainstreaming has led to the closure of some schools for the deaf. This increase in school attendance is not only confined to the deaf, however. For example, between 1970 and 1996 the number of primary schools in Buleleng more than doubled, from 267 to 553 (Kantor Statistik Kabupaten Buleleng 1997, 84).

Not surprisingly, a very high proportion of those who had attended school lived in one of the two urbanized centers of Singaraja or Seririt. Generally, the more remote the village from Singaraja the less likely the children were to go to school, as schooling became less accessible and less relevant to their future occupations. The exception was a rich village that was engaged in coffee production and prided itself that all the children went to school. This did not necessarily mean school in Singaraja. Several deaf children from the village had been sent to Java for their education. Even so, only 4 percent of the *kolok* had proceeded beyond primary school.

## Marriage

Marriage is extremely important in Bali. It is through marriage that people become completely human, through the union of male and female aspects. Full membership rights of the village through the village council, and full family responsibilities including membership of the *sanggah,* the clan temple council, are bestowed only on marriage. Just under half (43 percent) of those *kolok* twenty and over had married, thus, theoretically at least, qualifying for full village membership. A few had been divorced or widowed and some had married two, three, or even four times. Over one-third of the married *kolok* (37 percent) had married other *kolok* and almost all marriages had produced one or more children. Sixteen of the marriages had produced one or more deaf children. With the exception of two families, they all lived in Desa Kolok. Language transmission in Desa Kolok is therefore direct among the immediate or extended family. It is customary for unmarried children to remain at the family home. Although most of the *kolok* either lived with their spouse, or parents if they were unmarried, a small number (23) lived either with brothers or sisters or a member of the extended family.

It is very difficult to reach statistically relevant conclusions in relation to specific villages from the marriage figures, because the number of *kolok* in most villages is so low. But it is worth noting that two areas had high percentages of marriages—the "urban" areas of Singaraja and Seririt, and Desa Kolok and the villages linked to it by myth and legend. Not only did Desa Kolok have 85 percent of its *kolok* over twenty years of age married, but in the surrounding villages, the percentages were also higher than average at 62 percent. If you remove Desa Kolok and its cosmological partners from the marriage statistics, the percentage of kolok over twenty who are married falls dramatically. When you also remove a neighboring village where *kolok* have close contact with the *kolok* of Desa Kolok, the figure falls even further. Marriage for a *kolok* therefore appeared to be more difficult beyond the sphere of influence of Desa Kolok and its cosmology. What then of the high rates in Singaraja and Seririt? Here the urban environment, ease of contact with outsiders, and high levels of employment outside the home appeared to facilitate marriage. The statistics from the regional office with regard to marriage give figures for those over the age of ten years (see table 3). Although there are a higher proportion of deaf in the ten to twenty age group among the *kolok* than in the wider population, the figures do show that it is only in and immediately around Desa Kolok and in Singaraja and Seririt that deaf people are as likely as hearing people to marry.

### Signing as a Widespread Discursive Activity

The general statistics collected through the survey show a high proportion of deaf people, particularly in the area around Desa Kolok. They also reveal several villages apart from Desa Kolok with between five and eighteen deaf residents. As already indicated, the conditions and potential

TABLE 3. *Marital Status of Buleleng Population Over Ten Years of Age*

| | Total Population (N = 451,888) | | Deaf Population (N = 336) | |
|---|---|---|---|---|
| | Number | Percent | Number | Percent |
| Not married | 160,756 | 35.6 | 237 | 70.5 |
| Married | 291,132 | 64.4 | 99 | 29.5 |

Source for overall Buleleng figures: *Kantor Statistik Kabupaten Buleleng* 1997, 60.

for the development among these groups of sign languages or small Deaf communities appeared to be present, but a very different picture emerged through the interviews with deaf people.

In the villages bordering Desa Kolok, the sign language in use among the deaf people interviewed was clearly closely related to the sign language of Desa Kolok. In one neighboring village, some of the deaf people knew and interacted with some of the *kolok* from Desa Kolok, but only on a casual basis. They communicated with hearing members of their family and neighborhood through signing. Yet in no sense did they or others in their community see the *kolok* as members of a "Deaf community." Their community membership was focused on their family and village.

As we moved away from the immediate neighborhood of Desa Kolok we came into contact mostly with individual deaf people living as integral members of wider hearing communities defined in terms of kinship and ritual association. The following incident outlines the dramatic nature of what we found. We were on our way to interview a mature male *kolok* in a village some distance from Desa Kolok. With us was a fluent hearing signer from Desa Kolok. The local *kolok* had learned that we were on our way and came out to meet us. He came toward us signing fluently, obviously very happy to meet us. His signing was completely unintelligible as far as our Desa Kolok friend was concerned. When we tried to sign to the local *kolok,* he laughed at our signing but began to mime in order to communicate. Members of his family and close neighbors soon joined us. All communicated readily with the local *kolok* through signing and acted as interpreters. "Where had he learned his sign language?" we asked. He saw this as a funny and unnecessary question. He had learned it in the family, of course. "Were there other *kolok* in the family either now or in previous generations?" "No," came the reply. "Did he have contact with any other *kolok* in the village?" Again a very funny question: "No. Why would he do that?" "Had he met any *kolok* from Desa Kolok?" Again much laughter: "Yes, but they talked in a very funny way. I couldn't understand them."

This fluent and complex signing was therefore a localized language developed by the local community as they developed effective communication with this deaf person. It was a natural and expected part of the linguistic environment, given the existence of, and therefore the need to communicate with, a person who could not hear. This experience was repeated over and over again. Signing was not a deaf activity at all but rather a way of communicating that occurred readily and naturally when there were deaf members of the community. The following case studies illustrate the main trends found through the interviews.

### Case Study 1: Adult Male in Desa Kolok

Gde[5] is a mature and influential member of the village. His parents are hearing but have deaf relatives and ancestors. Gde has both deaf and hearing siblings. He is currently married to a hearing woman and has been married twice before, both times to hearing women. He has a number of children, one of whom is deaf. Gde has some land that he farms and also breeds his cow. He also works drying coffee beans for a local coffee merchant. Gde has learned to read and write but has no formal education. He travels into Singaraja frequently and has a good knowledge of the area.

Gde is an active member of the village council and also interacts energetically within the *kolok* community, coordinating practices and performances of the *kolok* dance troupe. He lives in an environment where active communication with deaf and hearing people is fluent through the *kata kolok*. He is a highly valued and well-liked member of the village community.

### Case Study 2: Young Adult Siblings in Desa Suwug

Made and her brother Ketut are deaf siblings. Both their parents and other siblings are hearing. They live in Desa Suwug, a village with cosmological links to Desa Kolok. Made was married to a hearing man but is now divorced. She works as a laborer in the village market. Their mother claims that Ketut was deaf because he had been brought up by his

---

5. Gde, Ketut, etc., are birth order names and so are constantly repeated throughout the population.

sister. She did not elaborate on this theory but the explanation was regarded as quite reasonable by others present (see also case study 3).

Ketut feels discursively comfortable at home and in his immediate neighborhood with his deaf sister and hearing neighbors and friends. His signing is basically recognizable to the villager from Desa Kolok. His best friend is a young hearing man. After the interview he rushed down into the main area of the village to tell everyone about our visit and about the interview. He was signing rapidly in a hearing audience with no barriers to comprehension or participation.

At the time of the interview, Made was still in the market. We met her in the market where she communicated freely through signing with sellers and customers.

### Case Study 3: Young Adult Siblings in Banyuatis

Banyuatis is 50 kilometers northwest of Singaraja, in the hills. It is a wealthy village producing coffee and cloves as cash crops. There are eighteen deaf people in the village, some in very remote houses, and although there is a sense of there being a "local" signing system, there is no sense of a Deaf community.

Gde, Made, and Ketut are deaf siblings with hearing parents. Gde and Made are male and Ketut female. All have been to the deaf school in Singaraja, Gde and Made each for nine years, and Ketut for six years. Gde's mother said he became deaf due to illness. Made is assumed to be deaf because he grew up with his deaf brother. Gde had been taken to *balians* throughout Bali in an attempt to cure his deafness but the same had not been done for Made or Ketut. Gde lives at home with his parents, while Made is married to a fellow pupil from the deaf school, has a hearing daughter, and runs a small shop in the village. Ketut is fourteen, unmarried, and lives at home helping her parents. All sign fluently using some school signs as well as local community signs. Gde is friendly with an uneducated deaf boy, Komang, who sometimes visits Gde and uses local signing. Komang has a wide range of hearing friends with whom he signs freely. Gde, Made, and Ketut all sign freely with the local hearing community.

### Case Study 4: Young Adult Male in Sidetapa

Sidetapa is forty kilometers west of Singaraja. Wayan has been deaf from birth and lives with his grandparents, helping them in their farming activities. He has never been to school and has virtually no contact with other deaf people. He signs fluently both in the context of the family household and with a large number of hearing friends in Sidetapa and neighboring villages. He identifies very strongly with his village and the people of his village and sees no special connection with other deaf people. His signing is local and cannot be understood by the people of Desa Kolok.

## ETHNOGRAPHIC SUMMARY

In Buleleng, there are only two groups who congregate together by virtue of being deaf—the deaf people of Desa Kolok, and current and former pupils from the deaf school in Singaraja. Otherwise, deaf people focus on their village-based communities, seeing no particular reason to socialize with other deaf people. Signing is referred to in Desa Kolok as the *kata kolok,* and is therefore seen as a way of communicating used by and with the *kolok.* In many other situations, signing is simply seen as a way of communicating when *kolok* are present, it in no sense belongs to the *kolok.* The results of the survey of the deaf people of Buleleng can be summarized as follows. Regarding the use of sign languages, there are three distinct ways of communicating:

1. through the *kata kolok,* the sign language centering on Desa Kolok and used in the villages around Desa Kolok;
2. through the sign language of the deaf school in Singaraja, used primarily in urban Singaraja; and
3. through local community-based sign languages developed within the family and immediate neighborhood, the isolated, variable languages used among deaf people in the majority of villages.

In villages that have historical, legendary, and mythic links with Desa Kolok, deaf people are an expected and integral part of humanity and of the wider cosmos. The likelihood of deaf people to marry in this environment is the same as for the wider population, and there is no expectation that deaf people will develop speech. In families in villages beyond the sphere of influence of Desa Kolok, the birth of a deaf child is less expected and more problematic. Outside of Desa Kolok, Singaraja, and Seririt, deaf people had a significantly lower rate of marriage.

In families with deaf children, whether in the villages or towns, there are two distinct orientations toward deafness and the use of signing. First, where there has been no contact with the deaf school, local community sign languages develop readily and naturally as the expected mode of communication. There is no expectation that the deaf person will develop speech. Second, where there has been contact with the deaf school there is a tendency to regard the deaf child as not "normal" and to regard the development of speech as both possible and desirable.

Education does not increase chances of marriage or employment for a deaf person. This is probably due to the fact that education brings negative attitudes toward deafness and negative self concept and it only opens up a few additional employment varieties in the towns.

In the villages of north Bali we find widespread and fluent use of signing among both deaf and hearing people where deaf people are to be found. In some cases the signing is associated with a specific Deaf village community and is identified as the "talking" of that community. While the community is therefore the focus for this sign language, their hearing family members and neighbors all enter readily into discursive interaction through the sign language. Signing is an accepted mode of interaction in Desa Kolok between deaf and between deaf and hearing. In neighboring villages where deaf people have interaction with the deaf of Desa Kolok, the same sign language is used.

But there are many deaf people who do not have any interaction with the deaf of Desa Kolok and thus have no contact with their sign language. And yet throughout the narrow plains and rugged hills of north Bali, in villages, many extremely remote, we found deaf people interacting with family members and fellow villagers through complex signing systems. In many cases the signing is associated with one deaf person and has been initiated and developed by hearing members of the family. But it is not just miming, it is the fluent use of arbitrary signs with a coherent structure.

## INTERPRETING THE DATA

An examination of the social organization of signed discourse in north Bali reveals some marked contrasts to Western assumptions about the formation of Deaf communities and their links to signing processes. In Desa Kolok there is a clear Deaf community. Being *kolok* involves you in a range of social activities that take you beyond traditional village communal processes. The *kolok* cross conventional kinship boundaries to attend each others' weddings and other rites of passage and generally operate at the village level as a group. This interaction is in addition to their participation in conventional kin and community-based activities. Some of the *kolok* in neighboring villages are linked to Desa Kolok by marriage and have contact with the *kolok* there, using the same sign language but not engaging in the communal activities.

Beyond Desa Kolok and its immediate neighbors, the only way in which deaf people come together as a Deaf community is among the pupils and former pupils of the deaf school in Singaraja. These links are in the form of casual visits to each other's homes. Otherwise, deaf people do not come together or seek each other out. In fact, many found the following question very strange: "Do you have close contact or any contact at all with other deaf people in this village or neighboring village?" The response was generally, "Why?" Such links on the basis of deafness were seen as completely meaningless. Social relationships were governed to a large extent by kinship and clerkship and to a lesser degree by shared work environments. If other deaf people were beyond the bounds of kinship and clerkship, there was no more reason to contact them than there was to contact anyone else outside the bounds of normal face-to-face relationships. Communication within the clan-based neighborhood was signed and thus effective. The response to the question about contact with other *kolok* often included the comment, "I can't understand their signing; they sign in a funny way." Communication through signing was more meaningful with the hearing people of the immediate community than with *kolok* from other communities.

In north Bali, deafness does not define a person's identity and therefore does not link one deaf person to another. Even if they are in contact with people from other villages on a work site, they do not see their links with other deaf people on the work site as being qualitatively different from those with hearing people. Friendships develop among workers but for deaf workers these friendships are not at all influenced by whether a person is deaf or hearing.

This raises important questions about the social conditions required for the development of communal links based in deafness. The communal links that exist among the *kolok* in Desa Kolok are an extension of kin-based obligations. The long-term presence of an hereditary deaf population has resulted in *kolok* being a cultural category. Their difference is acknowledged and integrated in the social organization of the village. Their cultural identity is to a degree based on their deafness, but only partially so.

For the majority of the people of north Bali, communication is not limited by notions of what is or isn't language. Communication is interaction among people. To communicate with people who are hearing, you speak, and if they are deaf you sign. One does not expect deaf people to speak, nor to understand speech. It is a normal discursive process.

## THE LINGUISTIC ENVIRONMENT IN NORTH BALI

Traditionally, written language was the language of elites and priests, far removed from most people and their everyday lives. Textual literacy was very specialized. Few learned the languages involved, let alone the literary skills to read them. Although there were literary texts, particularly poetic forms, which were read or sung aloud in a secular context, access was restricted to the leisured elite. Other texts were even more restricted and much further removed from the spoken word:

> Unlike narrative texts, *there are no contexts in which speculative, "metaphysical" texts*—texts recounting offerings and mantras to cure illness, invoke a deity, or liberate the soul; those narrating mystical connections between divinities and categories of persons; or those concerning the structure and origins of the cosmos—*are voiced;* some say they cannot even be discussed (Weiner 1995, 83, emphasis added).

Even further removed were the priestly texts, which were regarded as sacred, dangerous, and having magical powers, and which could only be studied by those trained and consecrated. Even today in Desa Kolok, the bronze plates (*prasasti*) recording the origins of the village and its population are sacred, stored in the village temple and the subject of important village ritual. No villagers can read them, nor do they expect to be able to do so. That is the business of elites and far removed from the everyday life of the village.

Although the narrative, "metaphysical," and sacred texts remain the province of cultured and sacred elites, most secular written language is in the national language, Indonesian, which is quite distinct from local spoken languages. The parents of the deaf children are, therefore, working from an oral base in developing communication through sign. And they are working in an environment that is not dominated by ideas of "language." In their linguistic mosaic, the spoken languages find no formalization in a written form. The linguistic skills that parents bring to bear on the development of signed communication are unreflexive oral skills.[6]

In north Bali we find deaf individuals naturally using the signing mode from birth. They sign extremely well. The source of their language is parents, relatives, and neighbors who in most cases have not signed before. They have developed signs to communicate with the deaf child and have developed fluent communication with the deaf person through sign. But it could be hypothesized that while the parents might or might not develop sign language, their deaf children do develop the signing into a language—a language developed fully possibly in only one individual but used at a different level by surrounding hearing people.[7]

## LANGUAGE, SOUND, AND THE WESTERN INTELLECTUAL TRADITION

The language situation in the West is very different from that in Bali. The definition of language tends to be identified with sound. Linguistic discourse must therefore be through speech or through its representation as writing. Someone who cannot speak, has until very recently, usually been assumed to be deprived of language.

Hearing people who interact with deaf people assume that the deaf must learn to speechread and speak if they are to participate in the discursive processes of the hearing society. This approach to discursive processes is tied to the long-term development of a particular view of lan-

6. In theorizing the relationship between the spoken language of the parents and the language that develops in sign, it must be pointed out that the relationship is qualitatively very different from the relationship between a dominant literate language and the signed forms developed for educational purposes, for example signed English or signed Indonesian. In the case of manual codes such as signed English, the signed code is designed and developed by teachers for classroom use. It is based not on the vagaries of spoken, natural language, but on formalized written language. Signed English, in structure and delivery, is therefore very formal and far removed from much everyday spoken English.

7. It is important to relate this material to recent work on Nicaraguan school children (Kegl 1994; Senghas 1994; Senghas, Kegl, and Kegl 1994). That research shows that when school pupils learn signing late, they do not develop sign lan-

guage itself, a view of language that emerged in the Renaissance and became particularly reinforced during the Enlightenment. This view of language was particularly given legitimacy by the rebirth of the ancient philosophy of Aristotle. It was Aristotle (1910, 536b, lines 3–4) who in the fourth century B.C. said, "Men that are born deaf are in all cases also dumb; that is, they can make vocal sounds, but they cannot speak." With regard to the nature of language, Aristotle observed that

> voice and sound are different from one another; and language differs from voice and sound. . . . Language is the articulation of vocal sounds by the instrumentality of the tongue. Thus, the voice and larynx can emit vocal or vowel sounds; nonvocal or consonantal sounds are made by the tongue and the lips; and out of these vocal and nonvocal sounds language is composed (1910, 535a, line 27, and 535b, line 4).

From the Renaissance, the impact of Aristotle on the evaluation of the deaf and their signing was profound. Not only did this view devalue the language of the deaf (their signing seen simply as gestures and mimicry, not as language), but their path to language was seen to lie in training them to articulate "vocal and nonvocal sounds" to produce language.

To come much closer to the present, Walter Ong, philosopher of language, went so far as to claim that, "until the pedagogical techniques for introducing deaf-mutes more thoroughly, if always indirectly, into the oral-aural world were perfected in the past few generations, deaf-mutes always grew up intellectually sub-normal. Left unattended, the congenitally deaf are more intellectually retarded than the congenitally blind" (1967, 142).

Ong looked to the work of B. Siertsema for support. Siertsema, in her critical survey of glossematics, claimed that sound was an essential element of language per se, and that "all other possible substances of expression besides sound are only secondary and only try to represent in a more or less successful way spoken language" (1965, 10). Even as late as

---

guage but remain at a less complex structural level (cf. Chomsky 1986, 1996). They gesture but do not develop a fully fledged language. Children of former pupils and those who live with older siblings and relatives who were pupils do develop fully fledged language, unlike their parents, siblings, or relatives. They live and communicate together, but only the child who has learned to sign from birth develops the language.

1982, Ong (1982, 7) wrote that "the basic orality of language is permanent." He continued that

> Wherever human beings exist they have a language, and in every instance a language that exists basically as spoken and heard, in the world of sound. . . . Despite the richness of gesture, elaborated sign languages are substitutes for speech and dependent on oral speech systems, even when used by the congenitally deaf (1982, 7).

According to influential Western linguists and philosophers of language, then, language as a concept and as a discursive process is linked directly to the ability to articulate a range of physical capabilities associated with the reception and reproduction of sound (see also Eco 1995, 174). This sound-based view of language emerged slowly from the sixteenth to the nineteenth century, often through encounters with the deaf and sign language. These encounters at times gave signing linguistic status and at others denied it (see Mirzoeff 1995).

Prior to the Renaissance, however, there is evidence of an approach to discursive processes much more akin to what we find in north Bali. Effective discursive processes do not appear to have been tied to speech. People lived in what has been called a "linguistic mosaic."[8] People switched from language to language, and possibly from mode to mode, depending on the discursive processes involved. Spoken language was not dominated by written language.[9] Each had its place and qualities. The written word often had magical qualities and was far removed from everyday discourse, which was about communicating, not about "language." In monasteries, for example, where silent orders were to be found, interaction was through signing. Illuminated manuscripts and signed conversations dominated many a monk's life. And in the monasteries, deaf children found a home and were educated through sign language. In the medieval world at large, signing appears to have been simply one possible discursive mode.

8. A concept introduced by a discussant, Professor Yamuna Kachru of the Department of Linguistics at the University of Illinois, at a session of AILA 96 in Finland, who pointed out that in many non-Western situations literate and nonliterate languages coexist perfectly naturally and effectively in a "linguistic mosaic," as people switch from language to language depending on the discursive processes involved. The Western model remains an essentially monolingual model

But the world of learning was to change dramatically. As rebellious clerics sought to question the authority of the church and its remoteness from the people, they turned away from the use of Latin and provided access to the word of God through the languages of everyday life. Soon intellectuals turned away from simply interpreting the word of God and sought knowledge and progress in human knowledge by questioning all that had previously been taken for granted as God-given. And again they did so not in the old language of scholarship, Latin, but in their own essentially parochial languages. They made demands on their local languages that had never been made before. And as they turned to question all around them, they began to theorize all that had previously simply been accepted aspects of life, including their language. And so the signing of, and with, the deaf that had been part of an untheorized discursive field for generations, became enmeshed in the search for the understanding and control of language.

These changes were associated with new demands on language. Language was no longer an aspect of discursive processes that was taken for granted, but the clue to the development of humanity in its own terms through its own efforts. Language had to satisfy the demands of philosophy and science, not just the demands of day-to-day interaction. The question asked of any language and any mode was "is it an effective vehicle for creative intellectual activity?" The change was marked in many countries by the development of academies to coordinate the use and development of the national language as a language of philosophy and science. Language academies were established in Italy in 1582, in France in 1635, and in Spain in 1713. Moves to do the same in Britain were frequent during the seventeenth and early eighteenth century (made by such writers as John Dryden, Daniel Defoe, and Jonathan Swift), but were never successful (see Crystal 1987, 4). But the linguistic self-consciousness of the English was no less intense, with dictionaries and grammars making their presence firmly felt. Roy Harris sums up this new consciousness of language as Europe entered the eighteenth century:

---

in so far as people are assumed to have a "first language," even in a multilingual situation. One language is assumed to be primary.

9. Here it should be noted that the concept of a "linguistic mosaic" supports the argument that writing systems did not necessarily develop to represent speech. "[I]t may be argued . . . that writing systems were created not to represent speech, but to communicate information. The relation to speech is at best indirect" (Olson 1996, 65ff, quote at 68).

Enlightenment thinkers treated language as an important topic for at least three interrelated reasons. First, arguments advanced by Descartes had refocused attention on language as holding the key to the basic difference between animal nature and human nature. Second, the origin and evolution of language were seen as bound up with the origin and evolution of society. Third, the explanation of the origin and diversification of language was an area in which the authority of the Bible was most conspicuously open to challenge (1995, 272).

North Bali is not medieval Europe, but it seems likely that medieval Europeans would have understood the Balinese linguistic environment more easily than most contemporary linguists. The fruits of the Enlightenment have generated a linguistic consciousness in the West, and increasingly in non-Western countries, which blinds Western intellectuals to a wide range of linguistic possibilities. They think in terms of "languages" and in terms of "first" and "second" languages, as though monolingualism is normal.

## DEAFNESS AND IDENTITY

### Deafness and Identity in the West

It was in the eighteenth century, during the so-called Enlightenment, that Western philosophical writings began to define individuals as having a shared identity through deafness. Deaf people were suddenly assumed to be of a kind and their signing was said to be a universal language, understood by all deaf people throughout the world. It was also assumed to be a primitive language, maybe even the original language of humanity, and a language shared not only by deaf people but by those people defined as "primitive," such as the American Indians and Australian Aborigines. These ideas were evident, for example, in the eighteenth-century writings of Lord Monboddo in his discussion, "Of the several methods of communication in use among men before the invention of language" (1773, chapter 2). Such a view of the universality and primitiveness of sign language was even more marked by the intensely imperialistic nineteenth century, as exemplified in the writing of Arthur Hartmann. He wrote that sign language is universal, and that deaf-mutes throughout the world should be able to communicate with each other immediately. He claims characteristically that "deaf-mutes can easily communicate with savages, who also employ signs, in consequence of the defective development of their articulate speech. The gestures of savages and deaf-mutes are like the dialects of a primitive language" (1974, 111). At the same time, the identity of deaf people was being defined in medical terms as a pathological condition: "deafness." To be deaf was to be a particular kind of human being who engaged in equally different and marginal discursive practices.

From the late eighteenth century on, the West defined deaf people as "disabled." The deaf and their disability–deafness–were coupled with linguistic isolation because of the prevalent oralist views of language. In multiple ways deaf people were marginalized in society. Deafness became the prime mark of identity. Given the individualistic nature of their societies and the consequent need to find an identity linked to one's individual qualities, being deaf became an essential aspect of subjectivity and the basis upon which to associate with others of "that kind." The complete marginalization of signing as a linguistic activity also restricted the ways of communicating within Western societies and resulted in the emergence of signing communities that were also Deaf communities.

## Deafness and Identity in Bali

In Bali, similar processes, imported from the West and interpreted in an Indonesian way, are transforming the cultural and linguistic environment. Deaf education has been essentially oralist in its orientation and has been carried out within the context of special schools labeled "abnormal." For example, Sekolah Luar Biasa (SLB) means "school outside the normal." Indeed the word "normal" is often used instead of "*biasa*" and is increasingly applied to deaf people, even in Desa Kolok.

In addition to the disabling processes associated with education, the "masks of benevolence" (Lane 1992) are also emerging in other guises. Deaf people are seen as the responsibility of the Department of Social Services (Departemen Sosial), and as disabled people in need of special assistance. For example, on the economic front, among projects such as providing the *kolok* with goats to rear and breed for sale, the government has provided the *kolok* with funds to set up a business manufacturing a soybean-based food called *tempeh*. The *kolok* have been extremely successful in the enterprise, and they value the extra money the business brings in. But it marks them as different from the rest of the community and in need of special treatment because they are deaf. In the ritual sphere, at the suggestion of the village head, a musician has established a *kolok* dance troupe that performs both in and outside the village. Even if the people of Desa Kolok simply see it as a special activity performed by their *kolok,* as far as outsiders are concerned, the *kolok* perform as deaf people, not simply as members of the village community. As people *"luar biasa,"* their performance is interpreted as evidence of progressive policies on the part of the village administration.

The luminous mosaic, the flux of nature in all its diversity, is being challenged by ideas of what is normal versus what is pathological. The habitus of villagers and officials alike are being transformed as orientations toward humanity focus on the new concept of "normality." Deaf people become the object of charitable works. Difference is less valued and less tolerated. And so, too, is the case in relation to the linguistic environment, Bali's linguistic mosaic.

## THE CHANGING LINGUISTIC ECOLOGY OF BULELENG

Just as the oral linguistic diversity of Bali is being challenged by the uniform adoption of the national language—Bahasa Indonesia—as the language of education and of all official activity, there are strong pressures for signing to become formalized, nationalized, and subordinated to the national spoken language (Branson and Miller 1998, 20). People throughout Bali and Indonesia in general are aware of a signing interpreter on the television during news broadcasts. The signing on the television is incomprehensible for all the deaf in Buleleng, even among the school children and staff at the school for the deaf. The new national sign language is embodied in the recently published *Signed Indonesian Dictionary,* or *Kamus Sistem Isyarat Bahasa Indonesia* (Departemen Pendidikan dan Kebudayaan 1994).[10] The school for the deaf has a copy of the dictionary and the government recently gave a copy of the dictionary to the Kepala Desa's office in Desa Kolok. The village has not made any move to use the signed version of Indonesian, but it now has sitting on the shelf a formal, print-based product with an official seal of approval. As we wrote recently,

10. See Branson and Miller (1997) for a detailed discussion of the origins and content of the dictionary.

the potential impact on the linguistic status of the *kata kolok* can be gauged by the following incident. When talking about the *kata kolok* with some shop keepers in Singaraja who came from neighboring villages, we were told that the signing used by the *kolok* of Desa Kolok was not correct sign language but that the correct signing was the one used on the national news. The impact of linguistic nationalism cannot be underestimated (Branson and Miller 1998, 20).

The pressures toward uniformity rather than diversity and regional idiosyncrasy are strong, both with regard to the evaluation of deafness and of ways of communicating. These pressures are evident in emerging values among some parents and neighbors of deaf people. Parents of deaf children educated at a deaf school expected that their children should speak rather than sign. These same parents also stressed the problems with regard to their children finding employment and generally interacting with the wider society.

The linguistic habitus is changing. Although Bahasa Indonesia might be seen to be simply an additional element in the linguistic mosaic of the region, used in official and educational contexts but giving way to more local discursive modes in other situations, the relative authority of different ways of communicating is by no means equal. Bahasa Indonesia is the language of authority and power, the medium through which people gain access to educational, political, legal, and economic resources. It is the language not only of the nation, but of nationalism, the language that binds people to the origin myths of Indonesia, to its fight for independence, and its emergence as a world power. The motto of the nation is *Binneka Tunggal Eka,* Unity in Diversity, but the unity lies in Bahasa Indonesia and its cultural associations. And it is the unity rather than the diversity that is increasingly valued.

And so people's dispositions toward ways of communicating are being transformed as their linguistic conditions of existence change. The government brings in a national language and a national education system, as well as a national administrative system. And the television beams forth images that place in doubt the linguistic mosaic so readily accepted before. Deaf people become a uniform category to be accessed through a uniform sign language, and so they become marginalized from cultural and linguistic communities of which they were formerly an integral part. The ecology has thus been transformed, diversity and flux potentially giving way to monoculture.

In Buleleng we find deaf individuals naturally using the signing mode from birth. The source of their language is parents, relatives, and neighbors who in most cases have not signed before. They have naturally turned to signing to communicate with the deaf child and have developed fluent communication with the deaf person through sign. As we have already hypothesized, while the parents might or might not develop sign language, their deaf children do appear to develop the signing into a language—a language that in some instances is developed fully in only one individual but used at a different level by surrounding hearing people. As parents and neighbors are pressured ideologically or otherwise, through changes in conditions of existence and subsequent changes in the linguistic habitus, to regard signing as an inappropriate communicative response to deafness or to regard the appropriate signing to be that available through official channels, language death will occur, not just the death of ways of communicating.

## CONCLUSIONS

The linguistic ecology of much of Buleleng is diverse. It is a linguistic mosaic that concentrates on "ways of communicating" and that accommodates and promotes a linguistic diversity to match the region's human and cultural diversity. Signing is used readily and effectively, integrating deaf people into the discursive processes of village-based communities even where they are not an expected or unproblematic aspect of human diversity. Over virtually the whole of Buleleng, deafness in a child is seen as problematic, but its occurrence is accepted and does not result in the deaf child's exclusion from the community's discursive processes, as is so often the case in the West. Discursive practices are expanded to include all.

Although multigenerational sign languages only develop where hereditary communities are found, signing as a way of communicating is part of the linguistic habitus throughout the region. Why this is so is a matter for speculation, but it is clear that people focus on ways of communicating. In Bourdieu's terms, signing is a doxic—that is, a natural and untheorized—aspect of the linguistic environment. It is Westerners and Western influences that focus on "language." As Van Dijk (1997, 1) indicates, when we examine discourse as social interaction, we focus "on the properties of what people say or write in order to accomplish social, political, or cultural acts in various local contexts as well as within the broader frameworks of societal structure and culture." In Buleleng, when deaf people are part of the community, all people use signing as a way of communicating in order to accomplish the social, political, and cultural acts of the community.

Much of the academic literature has assumed that a Deaf community of some kind must exist for sign languages to emerge. Isolated deaf people have been assumed to be linguistically isolated and deprived. This is not the case for the vast majority of deaf people in Buleleng in north Bali. Not only do these isolated deaf people communicate freely through signing with family and fellow villagers, but they appear to develop the local signing into full-fledged language. And so we have hypothesized that while hearing parents might or might not develop a sign language, their deaf children do appear to develop the signing into a language. Their innate linguistic orientations take the raw material provided by parents and neighbors and mold them into a language, a language that may live for only one generation or may be handed down to the children of these deaf individuals.

But this flexible, diverse linguistic environment is clearly under threat. As Mühläusler (1996, 2) points out, the ecological metaphor brings to the fore the vital importance of linguistic diversity, drawing attention to moral, economic, and other nonlinguistic issues. As deafness and signing are problematized through the transformation of conditions of existence via education, television, and the forces of national conformity, signing is no longer doxic, no longer an unquestioned natural way of communicating with deaf people, but a matter for speculation. Although these influences have by no means impacted all the people of Buleleng, particularly in the rural areas, current trends threaten the delicate linguistic ecology of the region and in the process threaten to marginalize and disable its deaf people.

The detailed analysis of the signing of the deaf people of Buleleng is currently under way, but the interviews have clearly shown that we are dealing with discursive practices that do not conform with premises on which much sign language research has rested to date. The linguistic analysis of a selection of these sign languages will include comparisons with the spoken Balinese of the region, but it is already clear that in the vast majority of cases in Buleleng, sign languages develop from an oral language base. They are also constantly used by bilingual hearing people who shift constantly between spoken Balinese and the local sign languages. This in no way supports conclusions that sign languages are derived from, or dependent upon, spoken languages (cf. Ong 1982, 7), but the relationship is historically, culturally, and linguistically complex. Balinese has very flexible word order and a syntactical structure like many documented sign languages. The move between modes might be relatively unproblematic in this case and therefore the syntactical relationship between the signed and spoken languages might remain closer than is the case, for example, between Auslan and English or ASL and English.

Our studies illustrate the dangers inherent in approaches to sign language analysis that attempt to generalize for a unitary category of "sign language." In the same way, there is no sense in which generalizations should be based in deafness. Deaf people are not a unitary category; their lives and discursive practices are culturally defined. As we approach the study of sign languages internationally, we must not take our ethnocentric assumptions about sign language, language, the culturally Deaf, or the physically deaf, with us. We must expect the unexpected and realize that the sign languages of Western countries are but a small proportion of the sign languages to be found throughout the world. Sign language studies must be informed by a sociolinguistics that is anthropologically sophisticated and capable of dealing analytically with the cultural diversity of humanity and its ways of communicating.

## REFERENCES

Aristotle. 1910. The works of Aristotle, transl. D'Arcy Wentworth Thompson. In *Historia animalium,* vol. 4, ed. J. A. Smith and W. D. Ross. Oxford: Clarendon Press.

Barth, Fredrik. 1993. *Balinese worlds.* Chicago: University of Chicago Press.

Bourdieu, P. 1977. *Outline of a theory of practice.* London: Cambridge University Press.

Branson, Jan, and Don Miller. 1998. Nationalism and the linguistic rights of Deaf communities: Linguistic imperialism and the recognition and development of sign languages. *Journal of Sociolinguistics* 2(1):3–34.

Branson, Jan, Don Miller, and I Gede Marsaja. 1996. Everyone here speaks sign language too: A deaf village in Bali, Indonesia. In *Multicultural aspects of sociolinguistics in deaf communities,* ed. Ceil Lucas, 39–57. Washington, D.C.: Gallaudet University Press

Chomsky, Noam. 1986. *Knowledge of language: Its nature, origin, and use.* New York: Praeger.

———. 1996. *Power and prospects: Reflections on human nature and the social order.* Boston: South End Press.

Crystal, David. 1987. *The Cambridge encyclopedia of language.* Cambridge: Cambridge University Press.

Departemen Pendidikan dan Kebudayaan. 1994. *Katnus sistem isyarat Bahasa Indonesia.* Edisi Pertama, Jakarta: Departemen Pendidikan dan Kebudayaan.

Eco, Umberto. 1995. *The search for the perfect language.* Oxford: Blackwell.

Harris, Roy. 1995. Language. In *The Blackwell companion to the Enlightenment,* ed. John W. Yolton, Roy Porter, Pat Rogers, and Barbara Maria Stafford, 272–74. Oxford: Blackwell.

Hartmann, Arthur. 1974. *Deafmutism and the education of Deaf-mutes by lip-reading and articulation.* New York: Gordon Press.

Kantor Statistik Kabupaten Buleleng. 1997. *Buleleng Dalam Angka 1996.* Kantor Statistik Kabupaten Buleleng, Singaraja, July.

Kegl, Judy. 1994. The Nicaraguan sign language project: An overview. *Signpost* 7(1): 24–31.

Lane, Harlan. 1992. *The mask of benevolence: Disabling the Deaf community.* New York: Knopf.

McMahon, April M.S. 1994. *Understanding language change.* Cambridge: Cambridge University Press.

Miller, D. B. 1982. The Brahmin/Kshatriya relationship in India and Bali. *South Asia* 5(1): 54–60.

Miller, D. B. 1983. Hinduism in perspective: India and Bali compared. *RIMA,* December: 36–63.

Miller, D., and J. Branson. 1989. Pollution in paradise: Hinduism and the subordination of women in Bali. In *Creating Indonesian culture,* ed. P. Alexander. Oceania Ethnographies 3. Sydney, Australia: University of Sydney.

Mirzoeff, Nicholas. 1995. *Silent poetry: Deafness, sign, and visual culture in modern France.* Princeton, N.J.: Princeton University Press.

Monboddo, Lord (James Bumett). 1773. *Of the origin and progress of language,* vol. 1. London: Cadell.

Mühläusler, Peter. 1996. *Linguistic ecology: Language change and linguistic imperialism in the Pacific region.* London: Routledge.

Olson, David R. 1996. *The world on paper: The conceptual and cognitive implications of writing and reading.* Cambridge: Cambridge University Press.

Ong, Walter. 1967. *The presence of the word: Some proglemena for cultural and religious history.* London: Yale University Press.

———. 1982. *Orality and literacy.* London: Methuen.

Senghas, Ann. 1994. Nicaragua's lessons for language acquisition. *Signpost,* vol. 7, no. 1, Spring: 32–39.

Senghas, Richard, J. Kegl, and Judy Kegl. 1994. Social considerations in the emergence of Idioma de Signos Nicaragiiense (Nicaraguan Sign Language). *Signpost,* vol. 7, no. 1, Spring: 40–46.

Siertsema, B. 1965. *A study of glossematics: Critical survey of its fundamental concepts.* The Hague: Martinus Nijhoff.

Van Dijk, Teun A., ed. 1997. Discourse as social interaction. *Discourse Studies* 2. London: Sage Publications.

Weiner, Margaret J. 1995. *Visible and invisible realms: Power, magic, and colonial conquest in Bali.* Chicago: University of Chicago Press.

# Italian Sign Language and Spoken Italian

# in Contact: An Analysis of Interactions

# between Deaf Parents and Hearing Children

*Sabina Fontana*

In Italy, there has been no research yet into the linguistic outcome of interactions between deaf parents and their hearing children. Whereas some deaf parents expose their children to sign language, others tend to mix signs and Italian words or simply to voice their sign language. Very rarely do deaf parents use only spoken Italian with their hearing children. The code chosen by deaf parents is mirrored in the language of their hearing children. The linguistic outcome of this contact is unique and linguistically relevant.

Situations of language contact have been investigated by Lucas and Valli (1989) and by Lucas (1991) as far as American Sign Language (ASL) is concerned. The outcome of the linguistic contact between ASL and English has been defined *contact signing* because "it exhibits features of both languages" (Lucas and Valli 1989, 11). The hypothesis of a Pidgin Sign English (Woodward 1973) has been excluded because the sociolinguistic situation in the American Deaf community does not represent a typical pidgin situation. In fact, Lucas and Valli argue that "pidginization . . . is clearly the result of a unique kind of language contact and the key elements in understanding the pidginization process appear to be the relative access to the target model, the lack of a mutual intelligible language among interlocutors, the immediate need for communication and the interruption of access to one's native language" (1989, 38). None of these sociolinguistic requisites can be found in the American Deaf community nor in the Italian Deaf community.

The outcome of the language contact situation depends very much on the context in which data have been collected. It is crucial that the data are collected in an interactional and informal context because the outcome is affected by the nature of the situation and by the interlocutor. Lucas and Valli point out that "the first step toward understanding language contact in the deaf community involves recognizing the complexity of the contact situation with respect to not only the characteristics of participants but also the varieties of language available to those participants" (1989, 12).

In particular, apart from the formality or informality of the situation, the outcome of the linguistic contact is determined by the addressee's bilingualism or monolingualism and by the interlocutor's language acquisition background.[1] Observational evidence has shown that when the addressee is hearing, the deaf person will mouth words or shift to spoken language. As Lucas and Valli maintain, "Deaf individuals not only can sign quite differently with other deaf individuals than with hearing individuals but also can initiate an interaction in one language and radically switch when the interlocutor's ability to hear is revealed" (1989, 14).

This study analyzes the outcome of the language contact between deaf parents and hearing children in familiar and informal settings. In order to observe the importance of these settings, the interaction between the deaf informants and a monolingual Italian speaker in a semiformal situation was also taken into consideration. This paper will use the term *family variety* to characterize the language used in these interactions, in order to emphasize the fact that the variety belonged to this particular family and that its existence in other similar cases has not yet been proven. Before analyzing the morphological and syntactic characteristics of contact signing, it is essential to discuss the linguistic situation in the Italian Deaf community.

## THE LINGUISTIC SITUATION OF THE ITALIAN DEAF COMMUNITY

Several authors (Stokoe 1969; Lee 1982; Tessarolo 1990) have arrived at different conclusions after analyzing the linguistic interaction between Deaf and hearing communities. The issue of bilingualism in such cases appears to be quite complex, not only because spoken language and sign lan-

---

1. For the purposes of this paper, bilingualism will refer to a person who has either a passive or active competence in both spoken language and sign language. Monolingual will refer to a person fluent in only one language.

guage do not have the same status, but because they exploit different modality of communications, one of which (the vocal-aural modality) is not naturally accessible to deaf people.

Stokoe (1969) analyzed the linguistic situation of the Deaf community in terms of *diglossia,* applying the concept Ferguson (1974) used in the context of spoken languages. Diglossia refers to a situation in which two forms of speech are used by a community in different contexts. He posited the concept of a sign language continuum representing a scale of all the varieties of ASL and manual English produced by Deaf and hearing signers. Manual English is "not spoken but uttered in 'words' which are fingerspelled or signed" (Stokoe 1969, 28). In Stokoe's analysis, the American Deaf community was not using two varieties of the same language but two different languages, Manual English and ASL. Lee verified all the characteristics described by Ferguson for spoken language diglossia, finding that none were directly applicable to today's American Deaf community. She found that "code-switching and style shifting rather than diglossia appear to be the norm" (Lee 1982, 127). In her opinion the shifting is determined by the topic, the signer's attitude toward ASL or English, and by the addressee. She mentions an example of a fluent signer who started using a form of Pidgin Sign English (PSE) with a bilingual hearing person, but then switched to ASL because the topic required more spatial details.

Tessarolo suggested that Deaf people were in a situation of pseudo-bilingualism, which is a kind of false bilingualism. "False bilingualism arises . . . when one of the two languages has progressed up to the level of a code and is endowed with certain cultural and institutional functions, whereas the other system has stopped at the level of usage" (Tessarolo 1990, 90).

Whereas deaf people typically learn spoken language through formal teaching, sign language tends to be acquired naturally either from other deaf children or from deaf parents. Because spoken language input is reduced with respect to sign language input, the competence in spoken language will depend not only on the educational background but also on the life experiences of people who are deaf. This suggests a continuum of spoken Italian varieties used by deaf people that range from a variety strongly influenced by sign language to a variety closer to the one used by native Italian speakers. The less deaf people know the spoken Italian grammatical system, the more they will use sign language grammar when they interact with hearing monolingual Italian speakers. These varieties can be considered in terms of interlanguages or elementary learning varieties (Klein 1984) that are systematically based on hypotheses. Such hypotheses can be confirmed or not by the native speakers. If they are not confirmed, the speaker gradually eliminates them from the system. By doing so, the system is gradually modified in the direction of the variety used by natives. Typically, interlanguages are varieties of a second language that are strongly dynamic and unstable.

Generally, the learning varieties of deaf people are not as dynamic because spoken Italian exploits a modality that is not accessible for deaf people. Often, such varieties appear to be fossilized or shifted very slowly on the continuum of learning varieties. In fact, such hypotheses regarding deaf people are idiosyncratically confirmed by native Italian speakers. Observational evidence shows that monolingual Italian speakers shift to a sort of *foreigner talk* supported by gestures that are either conventional or invented on the spot. Foreigner talk is the simplified register that native speakers consider to be appropriate to communicate with foreigners, and it is also used with Deaf people.

Therefore, three varieties can be potentially involved during an interaction between hearing and Deaf people: Italian Sign Language (LIS), the learning variety of spoken Italian used by deaf people, and the simplified register of spoken Italian used by hearing people. If the interaction occurs between Deaf people and hearing people with sign language competence, the phenomena of codeswitching and/or code mixing can be predicted. If the addressee is a monolingual Italian, the Deaf person will use his learning variety of Italian with gestures mixed with signs whereas the hearing person will use a simplified register supported by gestures.

## THE PRESENT STUDY

Two different kind of interactions have been taken into consideration: Deaf bilinguals with hearing bilinguals and a hearing monolingual. There were five informants, four of whom belong to the same family (see table 1 on p. 153). The parents are deaf and the two children are hearing. One of the children was the study's investigator. The fifth was a hearing friend of the children who was often invited to the house. Most of the interactions between the parents and children occurred in an informal familiar setting, whereas the interaction between the Deaf informants and the monolingual Italian speaker occurred in a semiformal situation. The formality of the situation is determined by the following variables: setting in which the interaction occurs; degree of intimacy between the speaker and the interlocutor. The interactions between the monolingual Italian speaker and the Deaf informants have been examined according to Joos' (1968) framework. The register (or "style" in Joos' terms) chosen appears to be consultative because it implies the constant adjustment of the speaker's speech according to the feedback given by the listener.

None of them, apart from the investigator, knew that the videocamera was taping their conversation. The fact that the investigator was also an informant has enabled a deeper analysis of the sociolinguistic variables that determined shifts in register or modification of the linguistic code.

TABLE 1. *Characteristics of the Informants*

| Informants | Age | Languages | Other Information |
|---|---|---|---|
| Deaf Informant 1: the mother | 52 | LIS Good knowledge of spoken Italian and interested in improving it | Born deaf from hearing parents Attended residential school |
| Deaf Informant 2: the father | 54 | LIS Poor knowledge of spoken Italian and no interest in improving it | Born deaf from hearing parents Attended residential school |
| Hearing Informant 3: the son | 22 | Spoken Italian Passive LIS competence | Frequent contacts with deaf people (his parents' friends) Student at the local university |
| Hearing Informant 4: the investigator | 25 | Spoken Italian Passive LIS competence | Frequent contacts with deaf people (her parents' friends) Student at the local university |
| Monolingual Informant 5: a male friend of the son and daughter | 28 | Spoken Italian | No contacts with deaf people Attended high school |

Gumperz maintains that "the investigator's skill in managing interaction is an important factor in sociolinguistic elicitation. . . . The most successful investigators are those who can utilize their own background knowledge of the culture in elicitation" (1972, 25).

The informants could be videotaped only during lunch or dinner time in order for the interaction to be clearly visible. In particular, the Deaf informants were also videotaped in the absence of their hearing children in order to verify that the language chosen when interacting between each other was sign language. The data consist of two hours of interactions and nine different communicative situations.

The Deaf informants are sign language users and members of the Deaf community. They were born deaf and learned sign language from their peers at a residential school, although the school supported the oralist method. Both work with hearing people. Although they share a similar educational background and similar life experiences, their competence in spoken Italian is different. In fact, the first Deaf informant is much more interested in improving her spoken Italian and continuously asks questions about the acceptability of some of her constructions. Deaf informant 2 has a minimal command of Italian and does not show any interest in improving it. He simply voices his sign language rather than using a learning variety.

The Deaf informants speak when they interact with their children. They have used sign language only with other Deaf people. Consequently, their hearing children have been exposed to sign language but were never encouraged to use it either with their parents or with other Deaf people. Rather, both of them remember having been asked by some hearing members of their family to always use their voices when communicating with their parents. They can be said to have a passive competence, which means that they can understand sign language, but they cannot sign properly. Only recently (after this study) has one of them (the investigator) attended formal courses in sign language. The other hearing informant is a monolingual Italian speaker and does not meet Deaf people on a regular basis.

## INTERACTIONS BETWEEN DEAF BILINGUALS AND HEARING BILINGUALS

The linguistic outcome of the interaction between Deaf bilinguals and hearing bilinguals in this study can be defined as *spoken sign language*. In fact, the hearing and Deaf bilinguals use a code totally based on the structure of LIS. Most of the lexical items are expressed by signs and the corresponding words. A few elements are expressed just vocally whereas others are only manual. The shift to one modality or another is determined by different reasons in hearing and Deaf bilinguals' utterances. The hearing informants codeswitch to spoken language because they are unsure about the signs to use and therefore rely on speechreading rather than using fingerspelling. The hearing informants codeswitch to sign language if a sign is idiomatic or has particular oral components.

The Deaf informants do not codeswitch in the same way. The informant with a minimal command of Italian codeswitches frequently. Apparently, some cases can be justified with the lack of a particular Italian lexical item that can co-occur with the sign. Deaf informant 1 codeswitches less than the other three and always from sign language to spoken language even when she interacts with the other Deaf informant. These shifts of modality do not appear immediately justifiable, but the co-occurrence of the two codes is the norm.

### Hearing Informant Data

It has been already pointed out that the utterances are prevalently based on LIS grammar. Both the Deaf and the hearing informants use facial expression to convey interrogatives, negatives, and to roleshift. For example:

| Hearing Informant 4: | |
|---|---|
| *spoken* | eat what, meat and what. . . . |
| *nonmanual* | interrogative facial expression |
| *signed* | EAT WHAT, MEAT |

The utterances of the hearing informants cannot be considered in terms of spoken Italian grammar because they would appear absolutely destructured and idiosyncratic. In fact, the visuo-gestural component and the knowledge of the particular family code are both required for the correct understanding. For example, the following utterance, based on roleshift, could not be understood by people who do not know this particular code.

| | | | | | |
|---|---|---|---|---|---|
| *spoken* | Giorgio said nooo, because | Corallo [a computer shop] sale, | sale | nothing, phone | |
| *signed* | GIORGIO SAY NO BECAUSE INDEX | SALE, SALE NOTHING, PHONE | | | |
| *spoken* | Corallo, phone done, | I said sale | how much, sale done, | £. 3.500.000 SALE DONE | |
| *signed* | INDEX, PHONE DONE SAY SALE | SALE DONE 3.500.000 SALE DONE | | | |
| *spoken* | Giorgio | chosen, | Giorgio | pffff | |
| *signed* | UNRELIABLE | CHOSEN GIORGIO LOST | | | |

*Giorgio said no because Corallo hasn't reduced yet (the computer), he told me to call Corallo and I did it. I asked Corallo, 'how much has to be reduced?,' and he answered at me that he had already reduced it. The price of the computer (3.500.000 million lira) has been already reduced (and it was still so expensive). Giorgio is not reliable, so he lost his battle (to buy the computer in that shop).*

This example shows clearly how the utterance functions according to LIS grammar rather than spoken Italian grammar. The hearing informant roleshifts to Giorgio first, then he tells what he did: "phone Corallo." Then he shifts to himself, "I said sale how much," and then roleshifts to Corallo, the shop owner, who says, "sale done £.3.500.000 sale done." Finally, he becomes the narrator and comments on the episode by codeswitching twice. In the first example, UNRELIABLE, codeswitching to sign language occurs for discourse cohesion. In fact in the family variety system, the meaning "unreliable" is conveyed only by a sign. If hearing informant 4 decided to maintain the spoken language, then he had to use a sentence rather than a single word, which might have caused the collapse of the interaction either because it was unintelligible for the Deaf addressee or because it shaded the topic of the utterance (Giorgio).

The other phenomenon of codeswitching seems to be determined by the specific oral component of the sign LOST. In fact, it is characterized by mouthing "pfff," which is an obligatory morpheme of the sign. Without that specific mouth pattern, the same sign would mean "dead."

In the utterance above, the morpheme "done" (*fatto*) follows the same LIS functions: it expresses completion and can be compared to the Italian tense form of *"passato prossimo."* Other interesting morphological phenomena can be found in this utterance:

| | | | |
|---|---|---|---|
| *spoken* | ( . . . ) fed up | still study study | |
| *signed* | ( . . . )FED-UP | STUDY | |

The verb "study" is expressed in both ways and interestingly it is modified to express aspect not only in signs but also in the spoken component, in which the verb is repeated twice.

Apparently, the hearing informants choose lexical forms which belong to LIS with the same meaning. Some items are used only in the familiar context. For example, "fed up" (*stufa*) seems to be used by all the family as an interjection and sometimes as an adverb. In Italian it is only used as an adverb. Furthermore, the suffix "*a*" should be modified for the number and the gender whereas in the data we found the form *stufa* was used to refer to either a woman or a man.

### Deaf Informant Data

The Deaf bilinguals use a similar code to interact with the hearing bilinguals. The utterances are characterized by sign language morphological and syntactic sign language processes even if they are mostly voiced.

---

**Deaf Informant 1**

| | |
|---|---|
| *spoken* | you not understood, expenses many,  light, house. . . . future, |
| *signed* | INDEX NO UNDERSTAND EXPENSES MANY   LIGHT, HOUSE. . . FUTURE |
| *spoken* | when you   grown up, married,   family, job, children,  problems, |
| *signed* | INDEX GROW-UP, MARRIED, FAMILY, JOB, CHILDREN, PROBLEM, |
| *spoken* | light, telephone, money   finished   quickly |
| *signed* | LIGHT, TELEPHONE, MONEY FINISH QUICKLY |

*You don't understand, (I have) to spend a lot of money for the light and the house. In the future when you grow up and you get married and you have to think about your family, your job, your children, you'll have many problems, electricity bill, telephone bill, your money will finish quickly.*

---

In the utterance, the Deaf informant uses the time adverb to refer to the past as in LIS and locates all the possible expenses, for example, LIGHT, HOUSE in the neutral space. The Deaf informant uses facial expression to disambiguate the utterance and ultimately with the same function of intonation in spoken language.

Another example shows how the superlative of the adjective "big" is realized through the facial expression instead of the morpheme "*issimo*" in Italian.

*spoken*   Aunt   said shop   biiiig

*signed*   AUNT SAY SHOP [very]-big

In this example, the spoken component "big" appears to accompany the movement of the hands from the neutral space outward by prolonging the vowel "i."

In conclusion, the Deaf and the hearing bilinguals appear to use a similar code even if the incidence of signs is higher in the Deaf bilinguals' utterances. In both cases, the utterances are based on LIS morphological and syntactic rules. The hearing and Deaf bilinguals make frequent use of nonmanual features in sign language that appear to play not only a grammatical role but also contribute to the decodification of the sentence. In addition, the Deaf informants sign slightly more than the hearing informants. The 33 utterances of the Deaf informants are characterized by 121 signs, whereas in the 22 utterances of the hearing informants, we count 79 signs. Whether these utterances can be considered entirely sign language even if voiced has still to be verified.

## INTERACTION BETWEEN THE DEAF BILINGUALS AND THE HEARING MONOLINGUAL

The interaction between the Deaf informants and the hearing monolingual has thrown light on the roles played by independent social variables such as the interlocutor and the situation. The communicative situation is formal: the hearing monolingual is a friend of the children who often is invited to the house. He does not know sign language nor has any contact with Deaf people. His utterances are marked in that particular context. In fact, the concept of markedness depends on the perspective which has been chosen (Renzi 1988, 116). In this case, the morphological and syntactic structure as well as the choice of words is different from the one pointed out in the hearing and Deaf bilinguals' utterances. The hearing monolingual speaks Italian and uses gestures and facial expression in a nonconventional way to communicate with the Deaf informants:

### Hearing Monolingual

*spoken*   In May. They catch the plane in Rome. . . . They join a group they don't know . . .

*manual*   [nonconventional gestures which accompany every item]

The conversation collapses because the Deaf informants show that they have not understood the message. The hearing monolingual informant looks for the support of the hearing bilinguals. Interestingly, hearing informant 3 interfaces between the two interlocutors by simply translating the message in their conventional code and adding a piece of information that she got before:

---

### Hearing Informant 1

| | | | | | |
|---|---|---|---|---|---|
| *spoken* | they Rome | together | group not know | | Italy |
| *signed* | ROME TOGETHER GROUP NO KNOW COMING-FROM-ALL-OVER ITALY | | | | |

---

When conversing with the hearing monolingual, the deaf informant with some command of Italian modifies her register and builds sentences that are perfectly acceptable in Italian:

---

### Deaf Informant 1

| | | | | |
|---|---|---|---|---|
| *spoken* | do you want bread with mushrooms | | | |
| *signed* | WANT | | | |
| *spoken* | I always bought bread with olives, today I have seen bread with mushrooms, that's new, | | | |
| *signed* | BUY | OLIVE | SEEN | THAT'S-NEW |
| *spoken* | bought I am curious | | | |
| *signed* | BUY | CURIOUS | | |

---

The number of signs used has decreased. The Deaf informant is clearly speaking Italian and also trying not to make mistakes. She inflects the nouns to express number (olives or mushrooms) and although her use of past verbs is not perfect (e.g., in "I bought," have is missing, but "I have seen" is correct), she successfully inflects verbs in the present tense (e.g., "do you want"). This example illustrates Giles' (1977) theory of accommodation. According to this model, three different linguistic phenomena can occur during the interaction between two people belonging to different social or linguistic communities: speech divergence, convergence, or nonconvergence. In this particular case we have convergence on one side and nonconvergence on the other. In fact, whereas the Deaf informant converges to a language variety that is similar to the one used by the addressee, the monolingual speaker simply does not know how to adapt to the register of the Deaf person. In particular, he does not know that he should speak more slowly and that he should choose different words.

The other Deaf informant does not shift register. His variety is not different from the one used with the hearing bilinguals apart from the disappearance of codeswitching.

| | Deaf Informant 2 | |
|---|---|---|
| *spoken* | eat difficult. | We try |
| *signed* | EAT DIFFICULT | WE TRY |

The shift from an informal and familiar variety to a semiformal register of another language implies some competence in that language. The Deaf informant is competent in sign language and has very little knowledge of Italian, so the shifting of register cannot occur.

## CONCLUSION

The analysis of these data has pointed out that the outcome of the linguistic contact is affected by social variables such as the interlocutor and the situation. The effect of such variables depends on the ability of the speaker or signer to shift from one language to another, and ultimately on his or her competence in the two languages. If the speaker or signer does not have competence in the language of the addressee, he or she will not shift register and therefore will not converge.

When the two languages are continuously in contact, as in the case of deaf parents and their hearing children, the outcome of the linguistic contact appears to be a stable form of *spoken sign language*. It does not seem appropriate to apply the label of code mixing because the morphological and syntactic features of this code belong to LIS. None of the sentences are characterized by morphological or syntactic phenomena from spoken Italian. Even the lexical choice appears to refer to LIS.

It might be possible that the Deaf informants have started to voice their sign language simply because their children were able to hear. We have seen that if an interlocutor is hearing, Deaf people modify their linguistic code even if the hearing interlocutor is bilingual. It is also important to add that although the investigator is now able to sign quite fluently with other Deaf people, the language chosen to interact with her parents has not changed. Likewise, her parents still do not sign to her.

Spoken sign language is only one of the possible outcomes of linguistic contact. Deaf parents with hearing children provide a unique linguistic situation in which two languages are in constant contact in a natural setting. It is reasonable to hope that researchers will start to investigate the language used in mixed families.

## REFERENCES

Ferguson, C. A. 1974. La Diglossia. In *Linguaggio e Societa,* ed. P. P. Giglioli, 281–300. Bologna, Italy: Mulino.

Giles, H. 1977. *Language, ethnicity and intergroup relations.* London: Academic Press.

Gumperz, J. J., and D. Hymes. 1972. *Directions in sociolinguistics: The ethnography of communication.* New York: Academic Press.

Joos M. 1968. The isolation of styles. In *Readings in the sociology of language,* ed. J. Fishman. The Hague: Mouton.

Klein W. 1984. *Zweitspracherwerb. Eine Einfuehrung.* Koenigstein/Ts.: Athenaeum.

Lee, D. M. 1982. Are there really signs of diglossia? Reexamining the situation. *Sign Language Studies* 35:127–52.

Lucas, C. 1994. Language contact phenomena in Deaf communities. In *Perspectives on sign language structure,* ed. I. Ahlgren, M. Bergman, and M. Brennan. Durham: ISLA.

Lucas, C., and C. Valli. 1989. Language contact in the American Deaf community. In *The sociolinguistics of the Deaf community,* ed. C. Lucas. New York: Academic Press.

Renzi, L., ed. 1988. *Grande grammatica Italiana di consultazione.* Firenze: Il Mulino.

Stokoe, W. 1969. Sign language diglossia. *Studies in Linguistics* 21:27–41.

Tessarolo, M. 1990. Deaf people bilingualism as pseudo-bilingualism. In *Current trends in European sign language research,* ed. S. Prillwitz and T. Vollhaber. Hamburg: Signum Press.

Volterra, V., ed. 1987. *La lingua Italiana dei segni. La comunicazione visivogestuale dei sordi.* Bologna: Il Mulino.

Woodward, J. 1973. Some characteristics of Pidgin Sign English. *Sign Language Studies* 3:39–46.

# GET-TO-THE-POINT: Academic Bilingualism and

# Discourse in American Sign Language and

# Written English

*Karen Christie, Dorothy M. Wilkins,*

*Betsy Hicks McDonald, and Cindy Neuroth-Gimbrone*

In recent years, a number of educational programs for Deaf students in the United States have begun to adopt a bilingual philosophy in order to encourage the formal development of language skills in both American Sign Language (ASL) and some form of English (see Strong 1995). The impetus of this change has come from social movements calling for the recognition of the United States as a multicultural society, and research in bilingualism concerning how minority language students can best be educated in the language and culture of the majority without giving up their own (Cummins 1979; Jankowski 1997). At the same time, there has been increasing research in ASL linguistics as well as anthropological research describing Deaf culture (see Lane, Hoffmeister, and Bahan 1996 for a review of these studies).

Information from these areas of research and philosophies related to social change have led educators to the realization that Deaf people, like those from other minority language groups in the United States, have a right to instruction in their language—ASL, a fully accessible, natural language (Newport 1990; Cummins and Danesi 1990; Johnson, Liddell, and Erting 1989). Support for the minority language and direct instruction leads to a "common underlying proficiency" that will contribute to greater achievement in majority or second language development (Cummins 1979; Cummins 1995; Philip 1995). Thus, the development of Deaf students' conceptual proficiency in ASL provides a strong foundation for the acquisition of English academic skills. Although the traditional educational goal of teaching English to Deaf students is expected to be more successfully accomplished in a bilingual program, such a program also incorporates direct instruction in ASL and the use of ASL as an academic language. A bilingual educational experience provides Deaf students with a positive cultural identity and the opportunity to develop positive values regarding both languages and cultures (Kuntze and Bosso 1994; Mason and Ewoldt 1996, among others). The goals of such programs are for Deaf students to become bilingual in ASL and written English; students are expected to use both languages in the academic setting.

## DISCOURSE STRUCTURES IN BILINGUALISM

### Bilingualism

Although the situation of Deaf students learning printed English may be viewed as a unique language learning situation, literature in second language learning has provided information concerning how one's understanding of a first language can be utilized in the development of academic writing. Kaplan (1966) analyzed approximately 600 compositions written by students of English as a second language. He noted that the students' application of "rhetorical logic" in their English compositions and use of subsequent structures in their paragraph development (such as the types of parallel construction, degree of subordination and coordination, use of digression, and degree of directness in tackling the subject of the composition) occurred in ways consistent with other students from their first-language groups. For example, French writers digressed to a greater degree than that usually allowed for in written English. Chinese and Korean writers developed their compositions in a way that would be considered too indirect for native English readers. Finally, Kaplan noted that the conventions for how to open and close written academic compositions differed across the language groups.

Kaplan concludes that non-native users of English need to analyze the rhetoric or discourse structures of their first language and learn how this contrasts with the written discourse structures, expectations, and standards of judgments in the educational systems of the second language. This supports Cummins' (1979) contention that students' second language acquisition builds on concepts developed first in their primary language.

Kaplan (1966) also noted comments instructors of English as a second language made regarding their students' compositions, which were strikingly similar to comments we have made and also heard from post-secondary instructors of Deaf students. The "lack of cohesion," differential use of subordination and digression, and "weak organization" have been comments made by both groups of instructors. Such information lends support for the approach of teaching contrastive discourse analysis to Deaf students in English courses.

Additionally, support for teaching contrastive discourse analysis is evident from comments we have noticed from Deaf students regarding interpreted lectures or signed lectures by hearing (or nonfluent ASL-using) instructors. Deaf students note that such lecturers tend to "beat around the bush" in terms of getting to the point of the lecture. When the point of the lecture is finally directly stated, most grumble that had the lecturer made the point earlier the examples and ideas in the lecture would have been more easily understood. Such experiences lead Deaf people to silently encourage lecturers to "GET-TO-THE-POINT."

Thus, when a non-native lectures in ASL and when a non-native writes in academic English, information about audience expectations and culture conventions across two languages are at play and seem best to be addressed at a discourse level (see also Kaplan 1972). This article first focuses on instruction in discourse features in ASL. It then explores discourse features in written English to enable Deaf students to more effectively give lectures on academic topics in ASL and write compositions in English.

## ASL

Research describing discourse features in ASL (Baker 1977; Prinz and Prinz 1985; Wilbur and Petitto 1983; McIntire and Groode 1982; Roy 1989) is still a relatively new area. Most of these studies focus on dyadic conversation; however, Roy describes the microfeatures of an expository ASL lecture. She identified focal episodes (the introduction), developmental episodes (the body of the talk), and closing episodes. Our understanding of ASL discourse in contrast to the discourse of spoken English borrows heavily from the teaching and analysis done by M. J. Bienvenu (1993) and Betty Colonomos (1989).

### Definitions of Discourse

Generally, discourse refers to any sequence of two or more utterances produced by a single speaker or by two or more speakers interacting with one another (Wilbur and Petitto 1983). In this paper, the sequence of utterances can refer to both face-to-face presentations and written communication. Discourse features are sociocultural conventions that establish expectations and provide a structure concerning how language is both used and understood. Discourse structures vary depending upon the type of interaction, such as how to have a dialogue, carry on teaching events, perform poetry for an audience, tell a story, and so on. All of these situations have basic rules of discourse. The type of interaction is one feature that determines the sign choices: the pace of signing; how to open a conversation, handle turn-taking, and close a conversation; and the variety of nonmanual signals.

### Definitions of Register

Joos (1968) described particular linguistic features that dynamically correlated with the social context. He identified five groups of registers: frozen, formal, casual/informal, and intimate (however, see Zimmer 1989). More recently, ASL research has included descriptions of features of ASL registers and analysis of indicators of registers (Bienvenu and Colonomos 1989; Shaw 1987; Zimmer 1989).

Use of a particular register is usually determined by situations and participants. For example, a frozen register is generally used in ceremonious situations such as religious ceremonies and club or organization events. The uses of a frozen register include the Pledge of Allegiance, the "Star Spangled Banner," the Lord's Prayer, and "The Buff and Blue Song" from Gallaudet University. Many of the frozen features of an ASL register are borrowed from English print. Formal registers are used when speakers are on stage making formal presentations to an audience. In these situations, the speaker signs much more slowly and uses a larger signing space, scanning eye contact, frequent rhetorical questions, and extensive use of metaphors. The consultative register can be utilized in the classroom and at workshops or meetings. Linguistic features of consultative ASL include fingerspelling more frequently and mixing sentence structures. Casual or informal ASL registers occur at informal gatherings. Each of these types of registers influences the features of the language appropriate to the situation.

### Discourse Overview

For our purpose, students created ASL personal narratives for academic settings. This means a student needed to use the features found in either a formal or consultative type of register. Students making a classroom presentation related to a personal experience needed to include features of both formal and consultative registers. The students studied models of personal narratives in ASL and the discourse features of ASL. Six different presentations performed by Bienvenu were shown (see appendix A on p. 178 for an example). The presentations all incorporated features of ASL discourse. Students watched the presentations and identified aspects of ASL discourse from the presentations. In this manner, students' metacognitive skills were developed through opportunities to recognize and analyze ASL presentations on the discourse level.

Our focus for teaching academic bilingualism includes ASL discourse and written English discourse. We use figure 1 to help students to visualize the contrasts between the discourse features that they have experienced across two languages and two cultures. Figure 1 illustrates three different structures—ASL discourse, spoken English discourse, and written English discourse—that are used in academic and other formal-consultative situations. These structures are visual representations of the framework or schemata people use for communicating particular information. They also represent the expectations of the audience to whom the information is being communicated. Such "expectations" are culturally and linguistically determined.

The first configuration in figure 1 shows that a person giving a presentation in ASL directly states the point or topic of the lecture at the beginning. In contrast, a presenter using spoken English (the middle configuration) tends to make the point of the presentation much later. This contrast allowed our students to understand why they seemed to feel impatient when some of their instructors don't "GET-TO-THE POINT." Written English for the production of an academic essay is different from both an ASL presentation and a spoken English presentation. This third configuration shows that the point of the essay (or the thesis statement) occurs at the end of an introductory paragraph. The point is often summarized at the beginning of the concluding paragraph and support for the point is elaborated on in the middle, or body, paragraphs.

### Features of ASL Discourse

Features of ASL discourse that guided the students' creation of an ASL formal narrative are features that occur in most ASL registers. In particular, the students created a narrative presentation for an audience of ASL

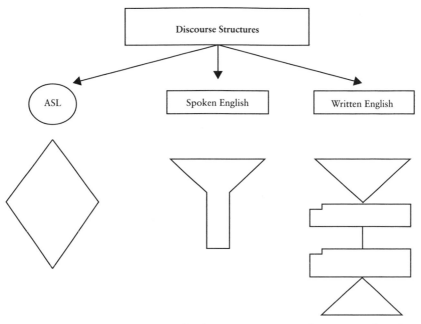

FIGURE 1. *Discourse Structures. The discourse structures first appeared in three different sources. The ASL structure first appeared in Bienvenu and Colonomos (1989), the spoken English structure in Neuroth-Gimbrone (1995), and the written English structure in Reid (1998).*

users. Bienvenu (1993) and Roy (1989) describe the features of ASL discourse in terms of the opening, middle, and closing features. The opening feature of ASL discourse includes the main point, or the obligatory focus, which makes up introductory statements. This opening feature includes the topic of the presentation and can include the speaker's reason for choosing that topic. Another discourse feature is digression, in which the speaker may add information such as historical background or an opinion. During a presentation, a number of developmental episodes or explanations of significant points make up the main body of the presentation. If a speaker makes a mistake during the presentation, he or she needs to know the appropriate strategy in ASL for repairing mistakes. Repairs in ASL can be needed for "slips of the hand," incorrect information, or failure of memory. Finally, a presentation in ASL needs to be ended. The obligatory closing episode of a presentation reminds the audience or listener of the topic and the significance of the topic in the speaker's presentation.

## METHOD

### Subjects

The subjects of this pilot research project were fourteen preparatory Deaf students at the National Technical Institute for the Deaf (NTID). All subjects were highly skilled in ASL, as measured by the sign instruction placement interview (SIPI). The students were deemed "preparatory," based on the scores they received on the California Reading Test (scores ranged from 6.0–7.4) and Michigan Test of English Language Proficiency (scores ranged from 44–57) that were used for initial placement. The effect of these scores was that most of the students would not receive program acceptance for technical majors without intensive English course work. The intensive English course at NTID meets for five hours, twice a week; students enrolled in the pilot program divided their time between both programs.

### Instructors

This twenty-week pilot course (two quarters, four hours a week) involved team teaching with two Deaf instructors from NTID. One instructor was from the American Sign Language and Interpreting Education Department and the other instructor was from the English Department. Although the former was responsible for primary instruction concerning ASL discourse and the latter was responsible for primary instruction concerning written English discourse, both instructors were bilingual in ASL and written English. Class instruction and discussion occurred in ASL.

### Course Goals

The course was designed to facilitate Deaf students' development of academic bilingualism. Deaf students need to be able to use both languages for academic purposes (such as formal presentations in ASL in addition to written documentation in English) in order to have a successful and relevant college career. Although students' acceptance in their major depended primarily on their improvement in written English, the research suggests that by adopting a bilingual philosophy that includes instruction and progress in both languages, Deaf students improve in their academic use of both ASL and written English. Further, in order to foster the development of written English, research has shown there needs to be a strong foundation of those skills in the students' dominant language. Finally, it has been documented that when the students' dominant culture and language is valued by their educational institutions, there is greater academic achievement (Cummins 1979).

With these ideas in mind, we identified three primary goals:

1. metacognitive skill development, to facilitate Deaf students' awareness of the similarities and differences in the presentation of information in two languages and discourse structures and across two cultures;

2. transference abilities, to facilitate Deaf students' abilities to utilize this knowledge of linguistic concepts in ASL to English print in their development of ASL and written English; and

3. cross-cultural analysis, to facilitate Deaf students' abilities to analyze information in both languages and judge their appropriateness related to the cultural conventions of the languages using appropriate linguistic and cultural experience, knowledge, traditions, and expectations.

The level of language instruction began with discussion about discourse. We viewed discourse as the structure or framework into which information or experience is fit. This approach followed a holistic, top-down approach in language instruction and focused on deductive processes in analyzing personal narrative schema across both languages and cultures. This process contextualized further instruction and practice in other levels of language instruction such as syntax and word or sign choice.

## INSTRUCTION IN ASL

The goal of instruction and practice in ASL was to create a personal narrative that would be judged as an academic presentation and could be analyzed as possessing critical features to both the narrative form and ASL discourse. We began with instruction in ASL because we supported Cummins' (1979) contention that valuing and developing students' metacognitive skills development in their primary language would transfer to greater achievement in their second language (see also Neuroth-Gimbrone and Logiodice 1992).

### Narrative Models

Students initially were shown examples of personal narratives in ASL. The creators of these narratives ranged from other NTID students to Deaf people valued for their knowledge and use of ASL. This exposure led to a discussion and the development of an ASL discourse evaluation form based on discourse features of ASL (see appendix B on p. 181).

### Creating the ASL Narrative

Students were asked to choose from a list of topics and prepare a personal narrative in ASL. Topics included "my most embarrassing moment," "my first car," and "my earliest memory." Although most information students are asked to present and write about in academic settings is less personal, we thought that it would be best to begin with topics requiring students' personal experience or knowledge and later gradually decontexualize the information being communicated and move to more expository forms.

Students were then videotaped signing their prepared personal narratives (see transcription of an example, appendix D on p. 184). Students paired up and watched each others' narratives. The signer and the partner worked together to evaluate the videotaped narrative using the evaluation form. Most students had little trouble creating and signing an interesting and complete narrative, although the most frequently missing discourse element was their closing. Most simply ended the narrative by signing ME-FINISHED.

Following the feedback sessions with their partners, the students created a second draft of their videotaped story (see appendix E on p. 185). The students' second draft was evaluated in a number of possible ways: with their partner, in a conference with a teacher, or with full class discussion. Although discourse structure as outlined on the evaluation form remained the targeted elements for evaluation, at this stage students often discussed changes in sign choice and syntax structure.

By the final draft, students had created a personal narrative in ASL with openings and closings highlighting the point of the story. They effectively used digressions, repair behavior, and repetition. Thus, in the process of creating a personal narrative in ASL, Deaf students learned how to analyze their language on the discourse level.

### INSTRUCTION IN WRITTEN ENGLISH

Following the creation of ASL personal narratives, students were asked to retell the personal narrative in written English. In particular, the retelling needed to follow conventions of academic English essays (as opposed to, for example, literary or creative writing). It was to be written not only to communicate the story, but also to show mastery of the essay form following "institutional-based discourse."

## Narrative Models

Because the content and structure of the narrative had already been clearly developed by the students in ASL, the focus in this portion of the course was to facilitate the students' presentation of the same story in written English. We followed basically the same process described above. The students read and analyzed written English essays developed from ASL narratives and were given other examples of written English narrative essays. Following this, an evaluation form was developed along with a discourse structure chart (see appendix F on p. 187).

## Creating a Written English Essay

The process from ASL to written English began with students watching their own videotaped narrative and making "conceptual notations" on a piece of paper. The purpose of using conceptual notations was primarily as a memory aid and a technique used to aid transference from ASL to written English. Students' conceptual notations were highly individualized, consisting of English words, English glosses of signs, drawings, and sometimes English phrases or sentences (see table 1). Table 1 also shows the opening and closing points appropriate for a narrative ("most embarrass—swim team").

After students had made their conceptual notations of the ASL narrative, the videotape was put aside, and we discussed the expectations of

TABLE 1. *Conceptual Notation Sample.*

| | |
|---|---|
| MOST embarrass—swim team | shot |
| Goal beat him, nervous | swim |
| think positive | faster and beat him like boat |
| Other team think I am nothing | "+"close to face . . . |
| I must beat to show them | finally, touch wall for finish |
| alone, think | "GO, GO and more" |
| Get ready and set up on block | happen Dream |
| start heart beating | Most embarrass—swim team |
| look at each other | |

academic English essays. Although students showed a surface awareness of the discourse structure of English essays (an introduction, body paragraphs, and a conclusion), they admitted to having problems of squeezing out enough words to create an introduction and conclusion, being puzzled about the structure of body paragraphs, and uncertain about how to keep the story from being judged as going "off the point."

With their first draft developed from the conceptual notations and memory, students worked with their partners using the evaluation form for elements in written English discourse. A typical example of one rough draft (see appendix G on p. 188) shows the student's struggle with introductions and conclusions. In terms of introductions and conclusions, this example indicates that the student wrote following a framework more similar to ASL discourse structure than that of an academic essay structure in written English. At the end of the rough draft evaluation, most students became more aware of the "discourse structure" of their own writing and the necessity to not merely "transcribe" their ASL narrative, but truly recreate it.

### INTRODUCTIONS AND CONCLUSIONS

Because most of our students were native or near-native users of ASL, they seemed to already have an unconscious discourse structure or story schema for ASL narratives. Many had exposure to skilled adult models of ASL. Analyzing the discourse features of ASL proved to be a task to which they brought a lot of background experience.

Analyzing the discourse features of written English and creating written English essays initially seemed overwhelming. But as the students had gained knowledge and vocabulary related to discourse analysis in ASL, they began to follow analogous steps in analyzing and creating English narratives. Eventually, the students would ask us why no one had ever "told" them all this before.

Like Kaplan (1966), we felt a necessity to focus on the practice of introductions and conclusions in the students' second language, written English. During our class discussions with the students, they also showed an awareness that a one-sentence introduction and conclusion was not enough, but they felt at a loss for how to elaborate and make the introduction and conclusion longer. In this section, we focus on instruction concerning the academic conventions and expectations in writing introductions in English essays.

In trying to develop how to teach assumptions implied in the rhetoric of academic English, we discussed how to describe appropriate approaches to particular writing topics. For example, there are numerous ways to begin an essay with the topic of "my most embarrassing moment." We began by teaching about some of the more typical ways to introduce such a topic, moving from a general introduction to the topic and leading to its direct statement. Although we wanted to avoid stereotypical writing with a focus only on form at the expense of meaning, our goal in this part of the course was to teach the cultural conventions—the audience expectations and the expectations of institutional-based discourse—that must be demonstrated in order to pass the writing requirements for their undergraduate degree. One way we felt we could do this was by example.

When introducing the topic of "my most embarrassing moment," one could describe the embarrassing moments of a number of people (e.g., Gerald Ford) before leading to the point of the essay. Another way to introduce the topic would be to provide the reader with a scrapbook of moments describing one's scariest moment, one's proudest moment, finally focusing on ones' most embarrassing moment. A third way would be for the introduction to inform the reader about necessary background information. Appendix H on p. 189 shows one student's development of an introduction to include more background information. It also included another introductory technique—a shift in expectations. These were some of the examples students were given in regard to creating an introduction that "leads to the point" and "introduces the topic."

These examples of typical introduction techniques struck our students as beginnings that were way off the point, but their awareness of differences in the types of discourse structure required for introductions across ASL and written English increased. One student explained that hearing teachers reading English compositions did not like picking up a composition and being "smacked in the face" with the point in the first sentence. The introduction was viewed by this student as a gentle guiding of the reader to the topic while giving the reader an opportunity to "get their mind into focus."

In regard to conclusions, it was emphasized that the students needed to elaborate beyond the events described in their ASL narrative. Students noticed, for example, that model written English conclusions often ended by stating the lesson that was learned or the understanding achieved by an event. One of our students then described the ending of an English essay as a slow moving away from the topic; a slow motion placing of the paper from a hand-held reading position to a position on a table. If the teacher is confident that the student has learned from this experience, he teased, then he or she will be able to get a good night's sleep.

The writing process continued in a manner analogous to that of the process in developing a personal narrative in ASL. Students were expected to write a second rough draft that was evaluated either in a conference with teachers, with their partners, or during a class discussion. Again, as the drafts continued to improve in discourse structure, students' focus began to shift to language at the vocabulary or sentence level. At this level, students appeared to make linguistic choices based on knowledge of academic register. Often during the final draft stage, the students wanted to look back at their videotape in search of ways that the "richness" of their ASL narratives could be transferred to their English narrative by using more descriptive English words, phrases, or sentences.

## TEACHING CONTRASTIVE DISCOURSE: AN OVERVIEW

The process of creating narratives in ASL and written English for academic purposes was recognized as a process in the creation of cross-cultural "bridges" (Ball 1992). Students worked not only from one language and cultural traditions to another but also from a language that is used face-to-face to a language that is written.

The students taught us about their own process of moving from one language to another. At the first stage, ASL narratives were produced on videotape following the appropriate cultural conventions, discourse structures, and level of formality. As with most face-to-face languages, this language was contextualized. While it was recorded on videotape, all students gave their narratives in front of an audience of other Deaf students. Prior to writing their story in English, students used unique conceptual notations created for their own use. Although it has not been widely documented, many Deaf people appear to use particular forms of conceptual notations when remembering or preparing for presentations. This conceptual notation, although it occurred in a written form, was still highly contextualized. As the students began to develop their story in written English, they added many textual features such as sentences and paragraphs. On the discourse level, however, students appeared to maintain some cultural conventions that appeared in their ASL narratives. The final stage occurred when the discourse conventions of academic English were followed in a final draft (refer to appendix H, p. 189 for one example). Thus, the process of creating ASL narratives and subsequently written English narratives was one that included transfer of information across languages and cultures.

## SUMMARY

Discourse analysis between ASL presentations and written English essays has been described as a process that enables students to effectively organize their information depending on their purpose, their audience, and their language choice. As Ball has stated,

> discourse preferences, which are influenced by both social and cultural experiences, can have positive or adverse affects on students' academic experiences. An important task, therefore, for practitioners and researchers alike, is to investigate the relationships between students' informal language (face-to-face language) and the demands of academic discourse in schools and to explore ways of helping students use patterns associated with academic discourse successfully. (1992, 254–55)

This pilot course, shaped in great part by student feedback, allowed teachers from separate disciplines to work together and enabled students to bridge their knowledge between two languages. We approached the teaching of the course knowing that students had been required by the educational system to do many of these analysis tasks on their own. The development of materials and evaluation forms were created through teacher-student collaboration. All the students in this course were eventually accepted into their majors.

## REFERENCES

Baker, C. 1977. Regulators and turn-taking in American Sign Language discourse. In *On the other hand: New perspectives on American Sign Language*, ed. L. A. Friedman, 215–36. New York: Academic Press.

Ball, A. F. 1992. Cultural preference and the expository writing of African-American adolescents. *Written Communication* 9(4):501–32.

Bienvenu, M. J. 1989. ASL discourse samples: Elections, disability, interpreting, whales, loyalty, and caraway seeds. Unpublished videotape of a presentation at The Bicultural Center, Riverdale, Md.

———. 1993, Feb. ASL Discourse. Paper presented at the Lilac Chapter of American Sign Language Teachers Association Workshop, Rochester, N.Y.

Bienvenu, M. J., and B. Colonomos. 1989. Discourse structures (handout). Riverdale, Md.: The Bicultural Center.

Cummins, J. 1979. Linguistic interdependence and the educational development of bilingual children. *Review of Educational Research* 49:222–51.

———. 1986. Empowering minority students: A framework for intervention. *Harvard Educational Review* 56:18–36.

———. 1995, May 5. A framework for the education of bilingual students: To what extent does it apply to the education of deaf students? Paper presented at the ASL & English Literacy Series, Rochester, N.Y.

Cummins, J., and M. Danesi. 1990. *Heritage languages: The development and denial of Canada's linguistic resources.* Toronto: Garamond.

Jankowski, K. A. 1997. *Deaf empowerment: Emergence, struggle, and rhetoric.* Washington, D.C.: Gallaudet University Press.

Johnson, R. E., S. K. Liddell, and C. J. Erting. 1989. *Unlocking the curriculum: Principles for achieving access in deaf education.* Washington, D.C.: Gallaudet University Research Institute.

Joos, M. 1968. The isolation of styles. In *Readings in the sociology of language,* ed. J. Fishman, 185–91. The Hague: Mouton.

Kaplan, R. B. 1966. Cultural thought patterns in inter-cultural education. *Language Learning* 16:1–20.

———. 1972. *The anatomy of rhetoric: Prolegomena to a functional theory of rhetoric.* Philadelphia: Center for Curriculum Development.

Kuntze, M., and E. Bosso. 1994, Oct. 14. Developing ASL and English literacy. Paper presented at the ASL & English Literacy, Rochester, N.Y.

Lane, H., R. Hoffmeister, and B. Bahan. 1996. *Journey to the DEAF-WORLD.* San Diego: Dawn Sign Press.

Mason, D., and C. Ewoldt. 1996. Whole language and deaf bilingual-bicultural education—naturally! *American Annals of the Deaf* 141(4): 293–98.

McIntire, M., and J. Groode. 1982. Hello, goodbye, and what happens in between. In *Social aspects of deafness,* vol. 1, ed. C. Erting and R. Meisegeier, 299–347, Washington, D.C.: Gallaudet University.

Neuroth-Gimbrone, C. 1995. BLANK-FACES: Decontextualization and lexicalization in American Sign Language and English. Unpublished manuscript.

Neuroth-Gimbrone, C., and C. M. Logiodice. 1992. A bilingual language program for deaf adolescents, *Sign Language Studies* 74:79–91.

Newport, E. 1990, May 16. Critical periods and creolization: The effects of input and age on the acquisition of ASL. Paper presented at the NTID ASL Lecture Series, Rochester, N.Y.

Philip, M. 1995, Feb. 10. Classroom strategies for developing literacy in ASL and English. Paper presented at the NTID ASL and English Literacy Series, Rochester, N.Y.

Prinz, P., and E. Prinz. 1985. If only you could hear what I see: Discourse development in sign language. *Discourse Processes* 8:1–19.

Reid, J. M. 1988. The process of composition. Englewood Cliffs, N.J.: Prentice-Hall.

Roy, C. B. 1989. Features of discourse in an American Sign Language lecture. In *The sociolinguistics of the Deaf community*, ed. C. Lucas, 231–51. San Diego: Academic Press.

Smith, C., E. M. Lentz, and K. Mikos. 1988. *Vista: Signing naturally, teacher's curriculum guide, level 1*. Berkeley: Dawn Sign Press.

Strong, M. 1995. A review of bilingual/bicultural programs for Deaf children in North America. *American Annals of the Deaf* 140(2):84–94.

Wilbur, R. B., and L. Pettito. 1983. Discourse structure in American Sign Language conversations (or, how to know a conversation when you see one). *Discourse Processes* 6(3):225–41.

Zimmer, J. 1989. Toward a description of register variation in American Sign Language. In *The sociolinguistics of the Deaf community*, ed. C. Lucas, 253–72. San Diego: Academic Press.

## A Description of an ASL Presentation

For an example of discourse structures and register use in ASL, we showed the class an unpublished videotape of M. J. Bienvenu's (1989) discussion of interpreting. This presentation will be described in detail to provide readers with some background information concerning the structure of an ASL presentation.

Bienvenu first informs the audience that she will be discussing a current issue related to the field of interpreting. (This information is communicated in a space to the left of the audience. She then shifts her body somewhat to the space to the right in order to describe her view of the interpreting field and her description of the qualities an interpreter should have.) This description includes factors such as knowledge, skill, and fluency in two languages and two cultures. Although interpreters should know one language and culture thoroughly and natively, they should also have an in-depth knowledge of the second language and culture. Interpreters equally respect, value, and have a passion for both languages and both cultures. Interpreters should be culturally and socially competent interacting with members of both cultures. In this way, interpreters should continually upgrade their skills and knowledge.

Bienvenu then shifts her body to the center and signs NOW, an equivalent move to beginning a new paragraph in written English. With this move, she rhetorically asks if the interpreting field today matches these definitions. This question occurs with the sign SAME moving from the audience's left (the interpreting field space) to its right (the definition space). The importance of the question is emphasized with the sign QM and the connotation "think about it." Her body shifts back to the left and she asks a series of questions concerning the interpreting field today. ("How many times have you seen interpreters say, 'Deaf people need interpreters' or 'I need to train deaf people about how to use an interpreter,' or 'Deaf people need help?' How many times have you seen those comments made by interpreters?" she asks.) With these questions, Bienvenu appeals to audience members' shared experience in order to strengthen her argument. Her brief nod at the end of the series of questions communicates that of course the audience members are familiar with these comments and know what she is talking about.

She follows these questions by a digression about the national Registry of Interpreters for the Deaf (RID) and interpreting training programs. She describes RID (signed in the upper left area) as focusing primarily on the evaluation of interpreters, which she mentions as valuable and should continue. Bienvenu then asks, "If ninety-nine percent of the focus of RID is on evaluation, where is the attention to the teaching of respect related to languages and cultures?" (She emphasizes this question with extended signing of WHERE, head moved forward with eye gaze direct at the audience, and another Q question marker. She then throws up her hands and clasps them in a WELL gesture, signifying another shift.)

Bienvenu then turns her attention to the topic of interpreter training programs. Interpreter training programs tend to focus first on expressive interpreting from spoken English to ASL and then ASL to spoken English interpreting (voice). (This information is again signed to the left.) The justification for this process is that voice interpreting, in the minds of the interpreter trainers, is considered to be very difficult to master. They believe that it must be practiced only after expressive ASL skills have been taught. After training for only twelve weeks in an interpreter training program, an interpreter often returns from their first job saying, "Guess what? I interpreted for a Deaf person," as if it were a rite of passage that needs to be celebrated. "Right?" she asks. "How many people feel the same about that? How many people have experienced that? So, this means that after a short time any interpreter who gets a job voice interpreting really feels that they are successful and feels skilled. How many of you have experienced that?" Bienvenu admits that these are "tough questions," yet clearly tough questions which should not be avoided.

With the sign ANYWAY, Bienvenu moves back to the main point of her presentation. The point, she believes, is that the interpreter training programs need to have interpreters analyze why they became interpreters. Were they motivated by the "missionary" desire to help Deaf people, because they were fascinated with different languages, or because they feel like they are "a small fish in a big pond" in terms of the hearing community and want to join the Deaf community? Or are they trying to achieve the goals outlined above? (Bienvenu signs SAME from the space in which she established her definition earlier.) If an interpreter does have the same vision of an interpreter than Bienvenu described, then this means they will continue to develop their skills. This means that they will need to consistently interact with both Deaf people and hearing people. They will need to keep up knowledge and skill in ASL (after repair in signing English first) and also English. Bienvenu goes on to say that an interpreter needs to maintain their skills in English and will need to ask other hearing people for guidance related to the use of English in the hearing community. "Do interpreters continue to ask other hearing people for help related to English?" she asks. "Do they also take courses related to English? Do they take courses related to voice?" Interpreters who want to be like those described (in the right signing space) will need to take those types of courses.

Up until now, most of the people in interpreter training programs have believed that most interpreters should have these goals: to become skilled in voice interpreting, to become skilled signers, to be praised, and to get certified. These goals need to be set aside. The real goal is to be like the interpreters Bienvenu described (in the right signing space). Thus, with this point to the right, she clearly means that the real goal is to become the type of interpreter described above: one who focuses on the development of a person who is skilled in, knowledgeable of, and respectful of both languages and cultures.

## ASL Discourse Evaluation Form

Name: _____

Date: _____

Partner: _____


ASL Discourse: Personal Narrative


Topic: My most embarrasing moment

*Overall Evaluation*

|                        | Good | Satisfactory | Needs to Improve |
| ---------------------- | ---- | ------------ | ---------------- |
| Opening                | ✔    |              |                  |
| Digression             |      |              | ✔                |
| Repairs (when needed)  | ✔    |              |                  |
| Repetition             |      | ✔            |                  |
| Closing                |      |              | ✔                |


Suggestions:

## Transcription Conventions Used for Appendices D and E

| Symbol | Example | Explanation |
|---|---|---|
| Glosses | | |
| # | OK | Indicates a fingerspelled loan sign |
| - | THAT-ONE | When words are separated by a hyphen, they represent a single sign. |
| + | FEEL+GOOD | A plus symbol between words is used for compound signs and contractions. |
| ++ | ALONE++ | A second plus symbol indicates a repetition of the sign. |
| " " | "What" | Quotation marks around lower-case words indicate a gesture-like sign. |
| (2h) | (2h)(heads bow) | (2h) stands for "two-handed" and is used when a sign commonly one-handed is made with both hands. |
| ( ) | (think about) | Words in parentheses indicate an action or movement, or variable signs that change in different contexts. |
| *Italics* | *You*-SHOW-TO-*her* | Italicized words before or after inflecting verbs indicate the subject and object of the verb. |
| Adverbial Nonmanual Behaviors | | |
| mm | | Normal or with regularity |
| tight lips | | Lips tightly pursed |
| oo | | Abnormally so |
| Nonmanual Behaviors | | |
| rhq | | Rhetorical question |
| th | | Tongue slightly sticking out to indicate carelessness and/or disorganization |
| neg | | Negation |
| whq | | Wh-word question |
| open th | | Open mouth with tongue slightly sticking out to indicate boredom in addition to carelessness |
| pl | | Pursed lips |

## Symbols for Classifiers

| | |
|---|---|
| SC:__ "_____" | Semantic classifier sign representing a category of noun such as vehicle or person. Handshape is given, followed by information about specific movement italicized and in quotation marks. |
| ECL:__ "_____" | Element classifier indicating elements such as fire, water, and earth. |
| PCL:__ "_____" | Person classifier. |

System adapted from Vista curriculum (Smith, Lentz, and Mikos 1988).

## Gloss of a First ASL Personal Narrative

$$\overline{\text{rhq}}$$

MOST EMBARRASSED MOMENT "what" SWIMMING TEAM COMPETE

$$\overline{\text{mm}}$$

HAPPEN READY CONFIDENT   BIG EVENT   SCREWED-UP   NEVER BEAT-

"us" SINCE   ME   WANT   GOAL   BEAT      NOW ME READY

$$\overline{\hspace{3cm}\text{th}\hspace{3cm}}$$

SCL:2 *"dived into the water and swim"*   SCL:1 *"swim across the pool"*

$$\overline{\text{tight lips}}$$

FEEL CLOSE   ME THINK FINISH CATCH-UP-"another swimmer"

$$\overline{\text{tight lips}}\qquad\overline{\text{mm}}$$

catch-up-"another swimmer" ME SPOT-BY-THE-CORNER-OF-MY-EYE

$$\overline{\text{oo}}$$

AHEAD-"from another swimmer"   ME READY CONFIDENT SWIM TOUCH-

TO-END-OF-THE-EDGE TOUCH   FINALLY   ME JUMP-"with-joy" JUMP

$$\overline{\text{neg}}$$

another-person-"wave-no" MORE MORE   ONE-MORE ME GULP

"another-swimmer" SCL:V *"hit the wall of the pool and swim"*   ME

GULP   CONFESS   WALK-AWAY-"with-shame" "out" WALK-AWAY

PCL:5 *"audience looked at me"* NOTHING-TO-IT   UNDERSTAND NEXT

TIME   FROM-NOW-ON ME SWALLOW-WITH-PRIDE

## Gloss of a Final ASL Personal Narrative

$\overline{\text{whq}}$
MOST EMBARRASSED MOMENT "what" TO-THE-POINT SWIMMING

TEAM SCL:V"*butterfly*" #OK (sequence#1-indexfinger) LARGE PICTURE

$\overline{\text{open th}}$
FAR-OUT ME THINK+POSITIVE  WEAK   WILL BEAT-"us"

                                       $\overline{\text{pl}}$
ME(2h)ECL:V"*sweat*"ME THINK NOTHING   ME PATIENCE  NOTHING-TO-IT

                               $\overline{\text{rhq}}$
MANY YEARS  ME LOOK-AT  PONDER  OHH-ME-SEE  DO-DO  ME

THIRST WANT BEAT-"them" ME(2h)ECL:V"*sweat*" TIME  COMPETE TWO-

                                   $\overline{\text{rhq}}$
TEAMS CHALLENGE  CLOTHES READY FOR WARM #UP  DO-DO  THINK

WANT  HOW BEAT-"them" THINK+POSITIVE VERY-THIRST  ME THINK

NOTHING  TELL-STORY  NOTHING  LOOK-AT-"us-nothing"  LAUGH

GROUP-"team" BOY ME LONELY ME SCL:V"*walk alone*"  MY COACH

LEAVE-ME-ALONE++ ME scl:5"*walk alone*" (think about) OHH-I-SEE

READY  SCL:V"*get up on the stand*"  HEART-BEAT  (another swim-

mer) HEART-BEAT ME THINK  NOTHING (2h)SCL:V "*get up on the stand*"

LOOK-AT-"each-other"  READY (2h)(heads bow) GUN-SHOT  BOOOM

(2h)SCL:V*"jump into the pool and swim"*     SCL:1 *"swim across the*

*pool"* UNTIL ME THOUGHT OVER SEE POSITIVE-"sign-at-the-end-of-the-

line" ME SPOT-"by-the-corner-of-my-eye" AHEAD-"from-another-swim-

            <u>oo</u>
mer"     ME     READY CONFIDENT     BOW BOW     FEEL+good

swim-"like-boat"     WAVE-"ripple-effect" SCL:1*"swim across the pool"*

SWIM SCL:1*"swim across the pool"* POSITIVE CAME+CLOSE TOUCH-TO-

END-OF-THE-EDGE     "another-swimmer" SCL:V*"hit the wall of the pool*

                       <u>neg</u>
*and swim"* another-person-"wave-no"     NOT FINISH     MORE     MORE

                              <u>-rhq</u>
ME GULP SCL:1*"walk away with shame"*     MORE     WHY     HAPPEN

TO-THE-POINT     DREAM NOT PAY-ATTENTION COUNT SINCE     THOUGHT

                       <u>th</u>
ME COUNT (ALRIGHT)     PERFECT WRONG     CONFLICT HAPPEN     THAT-

ONE MY MOST EMBARRASSED MOMENT TO-THE-POINT SWIMMING TEAM

## English Discourse Evaluation Form

Name: _____

Date: _____

Partner: _____

### English Discourse: Written Personal Narrative

Title/topic: My most embarrassing moment

*Overall Evaluation*

|  | Good | Satisfactory | Needs to Improve |
|---|:---:|:---:|:---:|
| Introduction | | | |
|    leads to the topic | ✔ | | |
|    background info (if needed) | | | ✔ |
|    topic stated | | ✔ | |
| Body paragraphs | | | |
|    chronology of events | ✔ | | |
|    paragraph breaks | ✔ | | |
| Conclusion | | | |
|    re-states the topic | ✔ | | |
|    leads to closing | | | ✔ |
|    accept/lesson | | ✔ | |

Suggestions:

**Written English Discourse: First Draft Sample**

My Most Embarrass Moment

My most embarrass moment was swimming team. That happen when I was junior in high school and summer time. Another swimmer and I were very good competition.

The other swim team was very good team. I swam against the other swimmer. He was a strong and skill swimmer. My goal was to beat him. I become nervous. Often, he beat me in every event. I thought positive myself. Time got ready for swimming, thought about him, and really wanted to beat him. He thought that I was nothing person and I was alone to think about swimming. My coach left me alone. We got ready for getting up on the block. My heart started beating and looked each other. The official shot gun for starting. We dove into water. We swam for few laps. I looked at him and he was behind me. I felt confident and felt like boat wave. I looked at the cross paint on the wall. Finally I touched the wall, jump, and felt so happy for beating him.

I looked at him and he still swam for the other more laps. Then I looked at crowd who yelled, "GO GO GO!" and "Two more laps." I wore out. What happen? I was dream and not pay attention for counting laps. In the past time, I was good count and remember how many laps all the time.

That was my most embarrass moment about swimming team.

# Written English Discourse: Final Draft Sample

## My Most Embarrassing Moment

Before I was born, I think I was a swimmer. I grew up swimming in pools, rivers, lakes, and oceans. I loved to swim anywhere. When I was 11 years old, I joined a swimming team. My goal was to participate in the Olympics. Since I was 11 years old to junior year in high school, I improved as a swimmer and never made mistakes. I happened to make a big mistake that was my most embarrassing moment with the swimming team.

One time, we competed against another good swimming team. I swam against the other swimmer. He was a strong and skilled swimmer. My goal was to beat him. I become nervous. Often, he beat me in every event. I thought positively. Just before we swam, I thought about him and really wanted to beat him. He looked like he thought that I was nothing, and I was alone thinking about swimming. My coach left me alone.

We got ready to get up on the blocks. My heart started beating faster and we looked each other. The official shot the gun to start. We dove into water. We swam a few laps. I looked at him and he was behind me. I felt confident and felt like a boat making huge waves. I looked at the cross painted on the wall at the end of my lane. Finally I touched the wall, jumped up and down, and felt so happy to beat him.

I looked at him and was puzzled that he still swam for more laps. Then I looked at crowd who yelled, "GO GO GO!" and "Two more laps!" I felt like a complete idiot. I went back to swim for two more laps. I wore out. I had been dreaming and not paying attention to counting laps. I was embarrassed!

That was my most embarrassing moment on my swimming team. I learned my lesson. I asked my team for help counting for me. When I swam, I looked to my coach and he counted on his fingers for how many laps to go or put a flipboard with the lap number on it in the pool near the wall. Then, it never happened again.

# Footing Shifts in an Interpreted

## Mock Interview

*Melanie Metzger*

Interpreting has long been viewed as if an interpreter is merely a tool to interaction. For example, the traditional view assumes that doctor-patient discourse facilitated by an interpreter is a dyad rather than a triad. In conjunction with this view, the field of interpreting has perpetuated the expectation that interpreters not be involved in interpreted interactions. Evidence for this exists in the American Sign Language (ASL) interpreters' professional code of ethics. The third tenet of the code states that an interpreter "shall not become personally involved because in so doing he/she accepts some responsibility for the outcomes, which does not rightly belong to the interpreter" (Frishberg 1990, 197).

Research indicates, however, that people present in a situation do influence the interaction. In his description of the observer's paradox, Labov (1972) describes the problem that a researcher cannot observe what happens when he or she is not present in a situation. In addition, Gumperz (1982) discusses how people come to understand one another on the basis of cultural and other background knowledge, information that might not be accessible to an interpreter. Given these issues, a practical question emerges: Can interpreters remain personally uninvolved and avoid influencing outcomes?

Recent research (Roy 1989, 1993; Zimmer 1989) indicates that the presence of ASL-English interpreters does influence interactional discourse. Roy discusses the interpreter's impact on turn-taking, indicating that interpreters might select which speaker receives a turn, might omit information when turns overlap, and so forth. In analyzing the English portion of an interpreted encounter, Zimmer discusses ways in which interpretation, via features such as lengthy pauses, influences the interactants' behavior and possibly even their perception of one another. If it is true that interpreters influence an interaction by virtue of their presence and task, then interpreters are faced with a paradox. Like researchers who face an observer's paradox, interpreters seem to face an interpreter's paradox, in which an interpreter tries to provide access to an interaction as if she or he were not present.

This paper examines the negotiation and interplay of the interpreter's paradox within an interpreted encounter. In order to begin an examination of this issue, it is helpful to focus on the relative participant structures that occur within an interpreted interaction. Goffman (1981) discusses participant structures—footing—as one of the ways in which humans frame their encounters. To understand the footing shifts within interpreted interaction, then, it is first necessary to clarify what is meant by the terms frame and footing.

## LITERATURE REVIEW

This section addresses definitions of the terms *frame* and *footing*. The discussion includes examples of the ways in which these terms have been applied in the field of linguistics with an emphasis on examples of types of footing shifts in English and in ASL. Although few studies have addressed the issue, analyses of footing in interpreted interaction will also be discussed.

### Frames

The term frame is generally attributed to the work of Bateson (1972) and subsequently to Goffman (1974). Among various applications of the term in a variety of disciplines, linguists such as Fillmore (1976), Chafe (1977), Tannen (1979), and others have examined the evidence that language can provide for the ways in which people frame events. Bateson (1972) used the term frame to account for the ways in which interaction is understood. For example, animals engaged in fighting behaviors appear to be able to discern the difference between serious fighting and play fighting. According to Bateson, these are two different ways of framing activity.

Goffman (1974) uses Bateson's notion of frame and applies it to many aspects of human interaction. He defines frames as "definitions of a situation which are built up in accordance with principles of organization which govern events—or at least social ones—and our subjective involvement in them" (11). He discusses activities, such as fighting, and the ways in which these activities can be transformed into something entirely distinct, as in play-fighting. He also discusses numerous examples of frames and the ways in which they can be transformed.

Goffman (1974, 496–559) specifically addresses the application of frames to language. One way in which speakers are capable of framing or transforming their talk is by saying things as if they were more or less attributable to the speaker. For example, using a direct quote is one way of framing talk as if it were not the speaker's words.[1] Goffman provides an example in which an astronaut says, "My wife said I'd never get here." The wife undoubtedly did not actually use the first person pronoun; a direct quotation would provide a different frame, "My wife said, 'You'll never get there.'" This example demonstrates the difference between who is being animated (it is the wife's word supposedly being animated in the second sentence). Goffman emphasizes the possible roles of the speaker (as in animator, principal, and so forth). He addresses this in greater detail in later work (1981), which is discussed in the next section. The application of frames to linguistic forms is also addressed by Fillmore (1976).

Fillmore describes linguistic frames as linguistic knowledge and its organization. He discusses ways in which linguistic forms provide differing perspectives of an activity. He uses the example of a commercial transaction involving the sale of a parrot. Depending on which information is foregrounded, the event represents a given perspective:

> He sold her the parrot for $300.
> She bought the parrot for $300 (20).

Thus, the same event can be framed from the perspective of the customer or the merchant. An explanation regarding ways in which linguistic choices can frame events also appears in Chafe (1977). Chafe, like Fillmore, views a frame as a way in which an individual "chooses an appropriate selection of individuals whose involvement in the event he decides to express" (47). For Chafe, choices made regarding the agent, patient, and beneficiary are directly related to the way in which a sentence is framed. He discusses the following two sentences:

> The older boy handed/gave/passed the younger boy a banana.
> Two boys passed a banana (47).

In the first sentence, the frame remains the same regardless of the verb selected. But the frame for the event is different in the second sentence, in

---

1. When reporting another's speech, it is, of course, the speaker who is speaking the quotation. In fact, Tannen (1989, 101) addresses the notion of reported speech as a construction on the part of the speaker (constructed dialogue), frequently not reflecting anything actually uttered by characters within the story or anecdote being told.

which the agents' roles are not clearly distinguished from one another. Chafe carefully defines frame in a manner similar to Fillmore, and consistent with Goffman (1974), although Chafe's definition is somewhat more narrow than Goffman's. Not all linguistic definitions of the term are so narrowly defined, as can be seen in Tannen (1979).

As mentioned earlier, the term frame has been defined and applied within a variety of disciplines. Tannen (1979) provides a detailed description of this term, as well as other terms including schema, based on work in such fields as anthropology, psychology, and artificial intelligence. Tannen addresses the need to identify the ways in which structures of expectations manifest themselves in discourse. She identifies sixteen general types of evidence, including the use of discourse markers such as *anyway* and *but. Anyway* appears to mark defeat in an attempt to follow temporal order in the retelling of a short movie. The marker *but* is used to contrast with preceding statements, and can identify expectations about an event as being contrary to what actually occurred. Tannen also discusses the occurrence of false starts and negative statements as evidence of insecurity at a task, which reveals expectations about the definition of the task itself Tannen refers to frames and schema as structures of expectations, and thus, identification of expectations is used to identify such frames as the film-telling and interview-for-experiment frames.

It can be seen that there has been some variation in the definition of the term frame as addressed by various linguists. It is useful to recognize that there appear to be two basic constructs underlying the discussion of frames as addressed in the literature. Some scholars, such as Fillmore (1976) and Tannen (1979), allude to frames regarding activities, as in commercial transactions and the film-viewing frame. Frames have also been referred to in terms of participants, as in Fillmore (1976) and Chafe (1977) mentioned previously. These two constructs are consistent with Goffman's (1974) discussion of the framing of events as multilayered and complex. An event, such as a fight, can be framed as a transformed activity (*i.e.,* play) on the basis of its participants (*i.e.,* player vs. onlooker). The next section will focus on participation frameworks, which Goffman refers to as footing.

## Footing

Goffman discusses the production format, which includes an expanded definition of speaker and hearer roles. Hearer roles include ratified or unratified status, and whether or not someone is an addressed recipient.

Speaker roles refer to who is responsible as principal, author, and animator of utterances. Understanding these relationships within interactions can help clarify what linguistic evidence of footing might look like, and when shifts in footing occur.

Goffman (1981, 128) defines footing as "the alignment we take up to ourselves and the others present as expressed in the way we manage the production or reception of an utterance." To clarify this definition, Goffman points out that traditional views of interaction, based on speaker-hearer dyads, are too simple to describe real interactive discourse. For example, although a ratified addressee might be identifiable, there might also be unratified addressees (bystanders) who access a conversation. Similarly, a speaker can be discussed in terms of more than one simple role.

According to Goffman (1981), ratified hearers are those who have an official place within a social encounter. Once ratified, an individual can choose whether or not to attend to the discourse. In addition, participants can choose to address certain individuals, leaving other ratified participants as unaddressed recipients. Thus, it appears that Goffman makes two relevant hearer distinctions: ratified-unratified addressee, based on access to official status within an encounter; and addressed-unaddressed recipient, which is reserved for ratified participants. The remaining possible hearer status, then, is the unratified participant who has access to the encounter. Goffman refers to such an individual as a bystander. Although Goffman discusses additional complexities for hearer status by considering a variety of social situations, the divisions discussed here are sufficient for the present study.

Goffman describes three roles that a speaker can fulfill: animator, author, and principal. These three roles are not necessarily satisfied by the same person at the same time. A speaker generally functions as an animator, the "talking machine" (Goffman 1981, 144) that actually produces an utterance. A speaker can also function as an author of an utterance, the originator of the content and form of the utterance. Although a speaker can function as both animator and author, it is possible for a speaker to function only as animator. For instance, when an actress speaks the lines of Shakespeare, she functions as the animator, but not the author of her utterances. Finally, Goffman describes the role of principal as the one who is responsible for, or committed to, what is being said. Thus, when someone reads a statement for a political figure, it is presumably the politician whose views are being expressed. By distinguishing these three roles, what Goffman calls the production format, it can be seen that a speaker's relationship to utterances and addressees can be quite complex.

Understanding the production format within an encounter provides an avenue from which to analyze a speaker's alignment regarding interlocutors. Each potential alignment represents a unique way of framing the encounter. For example, by quoting someone else's words a speaker can imply a lack of responsibility for the content, denying principal status, even though the speaker is responsible for deciding the comment was worth reporting.[2] Evidence of various alignments should be available through linguistic analysis. In fact, Goffman (1981) suggests that changes in footing might even be evident through paralinguistic features of discourse.

### APPLICATION OF FOOTING TO DISCOURSE

Examination of footing, or the ways in which speakers frame their utterances in relation to participants, can be seen in the work of Gumperz (1982) and Tannen and Wallat (1987). In addition, Clayman (1992), Hoyle (1993), Locker McKee (1992), Schiffrin (1993), and Smith (1993) have devoted attention to this issue, applying the notion of footing to various genres of discourse.

Gumperz discusses a variety of features that provide information regarding the footing between a speaker and addressees. For example, Gumperz (1982, 34) describes a situation in which the "singsong" prosody of an utterance is understood by addressees to signal that the speaker is marking an animated utterance as representative of a stereotyped image; the speaker is not the principal of the utterance. Gumperz also discusses codeswitching as used in quotations, qualifying asides, and other circumstances. Gumperz addresses the relevance of contextualization cues in conversational discourse, and thus, some of his work is related to the notion of footing and footing shifts in interaction.

---

2. Tannen (1986) provides a clear example of this. When a person tells another about a comment or criticism made by a third person, it is generally the third person who receives blame for the comment, rather than the one who has repeated it in the new context. Thus, it is the principal who is held accountable, rather than the animator.

Another example of footing shifts is described in Tannen and Wallat (1987). Tannen and Wallat describe footing shifts as changes in frame.[3] In examining a pediatric medical interview, they identify footing shifts through changes in register. The pediatrician uses "motherese" with the child patient, a conversational register with the mother, and a reporting register to the video camera (which is taping the encounter for use by doctors-in-training). Goffman (1981) refers to this work as evidence of the complexities of footing shifts in interactive discourse.

An examination of footing in news interview discourse is conducted by Clayman (1992). His interest is in interviewers' achievement of neutrality, for example, by attributing strong opinions to others through the use of constructed dialogue of unnamed parties. Examples of this include indefinite or inexplicit noun phrases, as in "it is said," and "critics on the conservative side have said" (Clayman 1992, 170, 171). Evidence that interviewers are striving to remain neutral is based on the occurrence of self-repair to constructions such as these.

In examination of footing within sermons, Smith (1993, 160) discusses the use of a variety of forms, including pronouns, rhetorical question-answer sequences, and discourse markers. An example of the influence of pronoun reference occurs when preachers say, "I think" or, "it's interesting to me," instead of "we can see." Smith suggests that the use of first person singular identifies the preacher as author of the utterance, while use of first person plural implies that the preacher speaks on behalf of the audience as well. The various strategies addressed by Smith appear to demonstrate ways in which preachers represent role in the preaching task (for example, whether or not they present themselves as an authority or mediator).

Hoyle (1993) also discusses the role of pronoun reference in footing shifts. In her examination of footing in "sportscasting play," Hoyle describes shifts between first and third person pronouns as evidence that her study's subjects are shifting footing. As they play ping-pong, two boys comment on the game as if it were a tennis match on television, and so refer to themselves in the third person during "sportscaster talk" segments in the data, as in the utterance, "they're hitting it back and forth," which

3. This is consistent with the definition of frame as used in this paper, in which footing represents alignment between two or more people (*e.g.*, to whom am I addressing a remark? Who is the eavesdropper?). Frames of activities would describe an event (Are we arguing or teasing?).

refs to the boys themselves (Hoyle 1993, 117). The occurrence of questions, response cries, asides, and explicit frame-bracketing with terms such as "time out" all provide evidence of shifting footing between the boys animating their own utterances, and animating utterances of an imaginary sportscaster.

The concept of speaking for another is explicitly addressed by Schiffrin (1993), in an analysis of sociolinguistic interviews. Schiffrin discusses shifts in footing as interactional moves. That is, in two examples in which one person speaks for another, one can be seen as helpful and supportive and an extension of help provided in daily activities. Another example can be seen as putting words in someone's mouth, sharing information that might have been private, and seemingly doing so for some benefit of the speaker rather than the spoken for (Schiffrin 1993, 238–39). Schiffrin demonstrates that just as linguistic markers might identify shifts in footing, footing shifts themselves can assist in the understanding of discourse.

In this section, the examination of footing has focused on English discourse. Although little research has examined footing in ASL, Locker McKee (1992) examines footing in ASL lectures. On the basis of Goffman's (1981) discussion of lectures, Locker McKee addresses two types of footing in ASL lectures: quotations and asides. She discusses many linguistic and paralinguistic cues that mark shifts in footing, including body leans and stepping to the side as spatial markers of a different footing, and eye gaze to specify a particular addressee for asides. The use of performatives (for constructed dialogue), the lexical marker QUOTE, code switching, and prosodic changes are indicators of quotations; a shift in which the signer is animating an utterance attributed to another author. Locker McKee also discusses the use of STOP and INDEX-HOLD as discourse markers used to identify changes in footing.[4]

It is useful to see that footing within English and ASL can be identified on the basis of prosodic, lexical, and other features, and it can be marked in both languages. Although parallel features exist, the linguistic and paralinguistic markers within English and ASL are different. These differences make ASL-English interpreted discourse an interesting type of interaction in which to examine footing.

4. The gloss STOP refers to the one- or two-handed sign in which the signer's palm is forward facing the addressee.

Goffman (1981) discusses the various roles that a speaker can fulfill in his description of production format. The production format takes on unique dimensions when applied to the task of interpreting, in which an interpreter is hired to relay the utterances of others. Few have attempted to analyze footing in interpreted interaction, but Keith (1984), Edmondson (1986), and Wadensjö (1992) address the notion of production format in interpreted encounters, although they bring different perspectives to the task.

The notion of footing, as applied to interpreting by Keith (1984), is very focused on the task of interpreting itself. Keith suggests that an interpreter has two distinct footings: translation of utterances and comprehension of utterances. The latter might result in requests for clarification or repetition, whereas the former refers specifically to interpretations of utterances. In this way, Keith seems to separate footings on the basis of authorship. That is, when translating, the utterance originates within someone else. When requesting clarification, the interpreter is the original author of the utterance.

Edmondson (1986) attempts to apply Goffman's conception of the three speakers' roles (animator, author, and principal) to the process of interpretation. Further, he discusses Goffman's identification of hearer roles as addressee, hearer, and overhearer. Edmondson suggests that although interpreters are responsible for the formulation and production of utterances, they are not responsible for utterance meaning. Edmondson concludes that interpreters are not involved in interactions and that they are neither speakers nor hearers; rather, they depend on a completely unique cognitive process that requires both speaking and hearing be accomplished simultaneously.

Wadensjö draws a different conclusion. In her data-based research, she discusses the interpreted encounters as, "conditioned by the co-presence of at least . . . three persons, and one of these (the dialogue interpreter) characteristically relays between the others" (1992, 65). The interpreter's talk is analyzed as two types: relaying and coordinating talk. Through examination of the relaying done by interpreters, Wadensjö finds that interpreters' renditions sometimes closely parallel an original participant's utterance, sometimes contain somewhat more or less information than the original, sometimes summarize prior talk, and sometimes the interpreter's utterance is not based on a prior utterance. Based on the various types of renditions, Wadensjö (1992, 72) concludes that interpreters do

not function simply as "translation machines." In examining an interpreter's coordinating function, Wadensjö again identifies a taxonomy. For example, an interpreter might ask for clarification, prompt a response or turn from a primary party, explain what one party or another means, or explain that one party does not appear to understand another. In addition, Wadensjö points out that an interpreter influences the coordination of talk simply by relaying utterances; the course of a conversation is influenced, in part, by the content and form of the interpretation.

## Summary

In this section, footing has been discussed as applied to interpreted interaction. Edmondson's work, which is not data-based, seems to reflect the more traditional notion of interpreter as an uninvolved relayer of messages. Keith and Wadensjö seem to view interpreters in a more interactive light, acknowledging that interpreters shift footings as they attempt to comprehend and relay conversation. The ways in which interpreters negotiate footing shifts is still a relatively unexplored area.

The notion of footing is a way in which participation status can be framed within utterances. Research regarding footing in English and ASL discourse provides some examples of the types of linguistic evidence of footing that can be found in conversational interaction. Although some researchers have begun to explore the negotiation of footing in interpreted encounters, no one has examined footing in ASL-English interpreted interaction. Moreover, in signed-spoken language interpreting there is often an added complexity of potential bimodal utterances.[5]

## METHODOLOGY

The purpose of this study is to analyze ASL-English interpreted interaction in order to identify and categorize evidence of footing within the interpreted encounter. Examination of footing shifts in multiparty

---

5. Whereas spoken language interpreters are not expected to speak two languages simultaneously, ASL-English interpreters might attempt, or be expected to attempt, to communicate in both languages simultaneously. Unique features of language contact between signed and spoken languages is addressed by Lucas and Valli (1992).

discourse is complicated at best. Examination of the same in an encounter in which one party is an interpreter can become even more complicated. This section describes the methodology applied to this task, including a description of the data, informants, and procedures. (See appendix A on p. 217 for transcription conventions.)

## The Data

The data used in this study were obtained as a result of contacting interpreter education programs with a request for copies of videotapes of interpreted discourse to be used for analytic purposes. From several hours' worth of videotape, the data selected include two interpreted mock medical interviews that occurred in an interpreter education program. These data were especially interesting for the examination of footing shifts for an unusual reason. Role-playing during a mock medical interview was videotaped, then discussed by participants and teacher. After the discussion, the role-playing was reenacted with some alterations that appear to be related to issues of footing. The role-playing consists of a hearing woman playing the part of a medical doctor; a Deaf man playing the role of a patient; and an interpreting student who is not only playing the role of interpreter, but is actually interpreting between the hearing and Deaf interlocutors.[6]

## Informant and Situational Characteristics

Information regarding the background of informants, the location of the study, and the physical orientation between interlocutors is important in any study. This information might be pertinent to some aspect of the data and analysis, and helps to contextualize the event under examination.

Although it is difficult, if not impossible, to describe all the relevant background characteristics of informants, it is obviously important to understand something about the informants in order to understand the context within which the event occurred. Because of the relatively small size

---

6. The woman has never actually been a doctor, but the Deaf man has had experience being a patient. The topic of this medical interview does not really have personal relevance for him, however, so it differs from an actual medical interview, at least in an emotional sense.

of both the Deaf community and the interpreting community, some information has been excluded in order to protect the informants' anonymity.

The data set includes three informants: two hearing women and one Deaf man. One of the hearing women is an interpreting student in a class that includes role-playing as a means of preparing students for work as interpreters in real-life settings. The other hearing woman is also interested in interpreting, and although she is not a student in the class she has been invited to participate in the mock interview. She plays the part of the doctor. For both hearing women, English is a first language and ASL is a second language that is still being studied. The Deaf man is a native signer who attended residential schools as a child and often teaches ASL as an adult.

The role-playing takes place in the interpreting classroom, in which access to video cameras and related equipment are available and used on a daily basis. The three participants are essentially facing one another, although the interpreter is seated next to the "doctor" who is across from the Deaf "patient." The teacher and other students are present and observing the interaction as a part of class. Similar training activities, including role-playing that might represent other types of real-world encounters such as sales events or phone conversations, occur throughout the semester. Because this tape and the permission to use it for research purposes were obtained after the fact, the data minimize the effect of the observer's paradox. Moreover, because the students are accustomed to being videotaped on a regular basis, the camera is likely to have less of an impact than it might in a real medical setting.

One of the difficulties in collecting data from real-life interpreted medical interviews involves technological challenges. The necessary use of video technology in recording ASL data has long been faced by signed language linguists. Use of recording devices in interpreted interactions can be especially problematic. For example, in order to interpret between sign language and English, interpreters must be positioned so that they can both see and be seen by any Deaf consumers. Yet analysis requires that both the Deaf participants' and the interpreter's signing be visibly accessible in the camera view. Bringing additional cameras into the interview setting is not only intrusive, but challenging to coordinate for later viewing. Thus, one benefit of the data used here is the availability of advanced technology to make all parties visible on the screen. Because of these technological issues, these data offer access and insights potentially unavailable in actual interpreted medical encounters. Nevertheless, it cannot be denied that while simulating a medical interview, this event will clearly differ from medical encounters that occur in the real-world context of hospitals and clinics. Hopefully, this analysis can serve as a pilot study for future research regarding actual interpreted medical interviews.

## Procedure

Once the data were selected, each role-playing episode was transcribed in its entirety, including utterances from both interlocutors and from the interpreter. In an attempt to incorporate the interactive and overlapping nature of the interpreted encounters, a musical score format was used in the transcript.[7] The transcript consists of both the English and ASL utterances, the latter transcribed with the use of English glosses. In addition, information regarding nonverbal and nonmanual information, such as eye gaze, is included in the transcript.

Analysis of the data included identification of a variety of factors, including the originator of each utterance and whether or not that utterance was reanimated or omitted, the intended addressee on the basis of linguistic or paralinguistic cues, turn-sequences, false starts, repairs, occurrences of constructed dialogue, use of question forms, reference, and so forth. Each utterance generated by the interpreter as original author was identified and categorized on the basis of production format.

## ANALYSIS

The interpreter's paradox exists because interpreters are faced with the goal of providing access to interaction of which they are not a part, while they are, in fact, physically and interactionally present. In order to examine the interpreter's involvement in the interpreted encounter, the data were coded for all interpreter-generated utterances. These utterances represent a footing in which the interpreter is the primary author and animator. Each utterance was then identified as directed to either one or both of the interlocutors in terms of their hearer status, as ratified or unratified,

---

7. Eckert (1993) uses this format. Each line of transcript includes a space for every interlocutor. Like the staff of a musical score, each person's utterances appear on the transcript in relation to one another, clearly identifying overlaps, pauses, and silences. In this paper, there is one line for the doctor, one for the patient, and two lines for the interpreter. One interpreter line represents spoken utterances and the other signed utterances.

addressed or unaddressed. The utterances represent ten different functions that fall under two major categories: relayings and interactional management.

### Overall Results

Examination of interpreter-generated utterances indicates that interpreters do contribute to interactional discourse. Moreover, in these data, the interpreter frequently treats the Deaf interlocutor as a ratified addressee, leaving the hearing interlocutor excluded. Conversely, there is only one utterance for which the interpreter treats the doctor as a ratified addressee while excluding the Deaf interlocutor. Most utterances directed to the hearing interlocutor are both spoken and signed, allowing the Deaf interlocutor to access the utterance as an unaddressed recipient. Thus, the interpreter establishes different footings between herself and each of the other participants.

The interpreter generated thirty-one utterances (see table 1). Of these, twenty-six were directed to the Deaf patient and were signed only, thus denying the hearing interlocutor access as a ratified unaddressed recipient. One utterance was directed to the doctor only; it was spoken but not signed. Interestingly, this utterance was actually a repetition of an utterance generated by the Deaf interlocutor. Because the Deaf patient only signed the comment once, but the interpreter decided to repeat it, the repetition is considered here to be an interpreter-generated utterance. This occurrence will be discussed in more depth later. Of the total interpreter-generated utterances, there were four utterances for which the interpreter attempted to sign and speak simultaneously. For each of these utterances, the ratified addressed recipient was the hearing interlocutor, and the combination of speaking and signing created a footing in which the Deaf interlocutor was a ratified, but unaddressed, recipient.

TABLE I. *Interpreter-Generated Utterances During a Mock Medical Interview* (N = 31)

|  | First Mock Interview | Second Mock Interview | Total |
|---|---|---|---|
| Signed and Spoken | 3 | 1 | 4 |
| Spoken Only | 1 | 0 | 1 |
| Signed Only | 11 | 15 | 26 |

Preliminary examination of the results indicates that the interpreter created different footings with each interlocutor. She almost never allows the Deaf interlocutor to become an unratified addressee. However, the hearing interlocutor frequently received unratified status on the basis of the interpreter's footings. In order to get a better sense of the footings the interpreter created, and how they were situated within the interaction, it is useful to categorize the interpreter's footing types and their functions.

## Taxonomy of Interpreter Footings

One of the ways in which Goffman distinguishes footing is on the basis of speaker roles. As described earlier, it is possible for a speaker to employ any or all of the three roles: animator, author, and principal. The interpreter's utterances, for which the interpreter is primary author, seem to vary in terms of the principal role. Certain interpreter-generated utterances seem to function as a part of the interpretation process. That is, some information is available within the interaction and originates among the interlocutors, but for some reason the interpreter must generate an utterance in order to fulfill the goal of relaying that information. For at least some relayings the interpreter functions as animator and author, but not as principal. For other interpreter-generated utterances, the interpreter appears to be managing some aspect of the interaction. For these utterances the interpreter appears to fulfill all three speaker roles.

RELAYINGS

When an interpreter relays what other people say, generally the original speaker can be thought of as a primary author and the interpreter as the secondary author and animator. Thus, relayings for which the interpreter is primary author are somewhat unique. Examples of these include source attribution, requests for clarification, explanations, and repetitions.

In interactional discourse people generally are able to identify speakers on the basis of voice recognition and location. When discourse is funneled through a single individual, the interpreter, information regarding the location and identity of the source (the original animator) is potentially lost. Moreover, if the interpreter engages in self-generated utterances, there is potential confusion over whether a particular utterance has originated from the interpreter or an outside source. Thus, it is not surprising to find that some of the interpreter-generated utterances are devoted to source attribution. Of the thirty-one utterances in this study, seven specifically identify the original animator of the upcoming utterance (see table 2). The interpreter appears to fulfill all three speaker roles for this utterance, because no one but the interpreter has contributed this information to the discourse. If the interpreter provided incorrect information about the source, it is the interpreter who is responsible for the incorrect content. Thus, the interpreter is not only animator and primary author, but also principal for such utterances.

The most frequent form of source attribution is a single indexical point in the direction of the speaker. In example 1 that follows, the interpreter has just finished introducing herself to the doctor and patient, and the doctor begins the medical interview:

---

### EXAMPLE I

Dr.:  And how are you feeling this morning?

Int.:  (point right)                              HOW FEEL? ALRIGHT MORNING?
        *She said,*            *"How are you feeling? Are you alright this morning?"*

---

The point to the right is directed toward the doctor. Just prior to this example the interpreter has been functioning as author of her own introduction, and this point indicates a shift in footing such that the doctor is the primary author of the upcoming utterance. It seems the index pointing is comparable to the use of pronouns as markers of footing (cf. Hoyle 1993; Smith 1993).

It is interesting to note that six of the seven source attributions coincide with a shift in footing either between speakers, as in example 1, or within a single interlocutor's utterance. However, one source attribution does not seem to coincide with any footing shift. Nevertheless, there is a considerably long pause between utterances in that case, and the interpreter might be indicating that the footing has not shifted, despite the time lapse.

TABLE 2. *Relayings During a Mock Medical Interview* (N = 17)

|  | First Mock Interview | Second Mock Interview | Total |
|---|---|---|---|
| Source Attribution | 4 | 3 | 7 |
| Requests for Clarification | 0 | 1 | 1 |
| Explanations | 4 | 4 | 8 |
| Repetitions | 1 | 0 | 1 |

A second interesting aspect of source attribution is that all seven occurrences are directed to the Deaf interlocutor. The interpreter never authors any utterance designed to clarify for the hearing interlocutor whether an utterance originated from the patient or the interpreter. In addition, although the interpreter provides this information to the patient, she does not do so consistently. There are many cases in which a shift in footing occurs and there is no mention of source. One area for future research would be to identify whether professionally certified interpreters provide source attribution, whether they do so consistently, and if not, what circumstances seem to elicit such utterances.

Another type of utterance for which the interpreter fulfills all three roles is requests for clarification. This is an interesting type of footing because the interpreter might be clarifying the content for which someone else is principal. There is only one occurrence of a request for clarification, which occurs in the second mock interview. At this point in the interview, the doctor has told the patient that he should not eat spicy foods. The patient is concerned about giving up Mexican food and is asking the doctor if he can eat the food if he removes the spicy jalapeno peppers:

---

EXAMPLE 2

Pat.: THAT REMOVE++? J-A-L-A P-E-P-P-E-R-S REMOVE (point forward) EAT CAN?
*What if I remove those? If I remove the peppers, then can I eat it?*

Int.: The . . . jalapeno peppers . . .

(leans forward)    CAN EAT J-A-L-A-P-E-N-O? O-R WHAT SAY?
*You can eat the jalapeno peppers? Or . . . what did you say?*

---

In this example, the interpreter is trying to clarify what the patient said. Consistent with Locker McKee (1992), the interpreter's shift in footing is evident due to a forward body lean and direct eye gaze. In addition, consistent with Gumperz (1982), she codeswitches, which is a clear indication of a change from addressing the hearing interlocutor (in English) to the Deaf interlocutor (in ASL).

The interpreter also provides explanations. Explanations are the most common type of utterance: eight of thirty-one utterances are explanations. There are two types of explanations in the data. The interpreter explains event-related information, and the interpreter explains why the doctor has spoken to the interpreter as a ratified addressee. There are three examples of the former in the data. In example 3, the interpreter informs the patient that a third person, a nurse, has just come in. After the interpreter explains that the nurse has just come in, she goes on to relay what the nurse has said to the doctor.

---

### EXAMPLE 3

Dr.:     Uh, I do have a list of uh, food that I'd like you to: . . . try to stick to-

Nurse:                                    excuse me, doctor

Int.:                    HAVE LIST FOOD RIGHT- NURSE CL:1

*I have a list of food right—a nurse just came in.*

---

The second type of explanation occurs when the doctor directs an utterance to the interpreter as addressee. An example of this occurs when the doctor asks the interpreter how to sign a word:

---

### EXAMPLE 4

Dr.:     What is- is there a sign for ulcer?

Int.:     PRO:3 PRO:1 SIGN FOR U-L-C-E-R PRO:2? ASK-PRO:1 QUESTION
*She asked me, "What's your sign for ulcer?" She asked me a question.*

---

The interpreter signs the question, including the doctor's footing shift from treating the interpreter as an unratified addressee, or bystander, to a ratified addressee. The interpreter points to the patient, eyebrows raised, indicating a question to him. She then explains to him that the doctor has asked her a question.

Another example of an explanation occurs when the interpreter accidentally touches doctor's arm while signing WELL. The doctor pauses, and asks the interpreter if there is problem:

---

### EXAMPLE 5

Dr.:   = the:n there . . . is there a problem? oh. -then it can become infected and =

Int.:                 s'cuse me

Int.:   WELL . . .    EXCUSE PRO:1 TOUCH (to doctor) DOCTOR-LOOK-AT-me
       *then . . .*    *Excuse me. I touched the doctor and she looked at me.*

---

The interpreter apologizes to the doctor, to indicate the touch was accidental, and then explains what just happened to the patient. Although the apology is both spoken and signed, the explanation is only in ASL.

The doctor, unaware of this subordinated communication, has continued with the medical interview. Some of the medical information is not present in the interpretation as a result of the overlap.

The two types of explanations in these data include explanations about the event and explanations regarding why the hearing interlocutor has spoken to the interpreter. Given a larger corpus of data, it would be interesting to examine whether or not interpreters ever provide explanations to hearing interlocutors, and if so, in what circumstances.

The last type of relaying to be discussed are repetitions. Obviously, some repetitions originate from speakers other than the interpreter. There is, however, one example in the data in which the interpreter, as secondary animator, decides to reanimate the utterance due to an overlap in the talk:

---

### EXAMPLE 6

Dr.:   = have milk, but have it with a meal, and try to limit how much milk you have, so that you're not just . . . uh,=

Int.:             CAN HAVE . . .       WITH FOOD . . .
            *You can have milk with food . . .*

Dr.:   y'know, maybe drinking a gallon of milk on an empty stomach.

Int.:              What do you mean, limit? What do you mean limit?

Int.:   TRY LIMIT++
      *but try to limit*

Pat.:              LIMIT? MEAN LIMIT? NOT-UNDERSTAND LIMIT?
      *Limit? What do you mean by that? I don't understand what you mean.*

---

The repetition occurs in the interpreter's second utterance. It is interesting to note that the Deaf interlocutor responds at an appropriate moment in the interpreter's discourse, after she signs LIMIT. The interpreter necessarily lags behind the doctor's speech; in her second utterance the interpreter is animating what the doctor said in his first utterance. Due to this lag, the Deaf interlocutor, who does not interrupt the conversation from his perspective, is reanimated by the interpreter during the doctor's utterance, causing an overlap in the English dialogue.

When the doctor completes her turn, the interpreter then reanimates her interpretation of the patient's question a second time so that it can be heard by the doctor. In this manner, the interpreter has taken responsibility for resolving the overlap by alleviating it. If she did not, it is conceivable that one or the other interlocutors would have taken on responsibility for the repetition. For example, the doctor might have asked the patient what he just said, which the interpreter could have interpreted. Conversely, if the doctor did not respond to his question the patient could have authored a repetition himself. Roy (1989) discusses the role of the interpreter in turn-taking. An examination of the affects of footing shifts on turn-taking in interpreted interaction is another area for future research.

This section has described the interpreter's footing while relaying tasks, including source attribution, requests for clarification, explanations, and repetition. The most common of these tasks are source attribution and explanations. In considering the interpreter's paradox, it is interesting to note that at least two of these categories, source attribution and requests for clarification, appear to be required components of interpreted interaction. That is, an interpreter cannot interpret if she or he does not understand, and the interlocutors cannot make sense of an interaction if they do not know who is responsible for the utterances. Clearly, some interpreter-generated utterances are essential to the task of interpreting interactive discourse.

INTERACTIONAL MANAGEMENT

Interpreter's utterances can also be seen in relation to the structure of the interpreted encounter. The footing types that occur within this category are introductions, responses to questions, explicit frame bracketing, procedural instructions, prompts, and interference.

In the first mock interview, the interpreter introduces herself by signing and speaking simultaneously. This is a footing in which the interpreter is addressing both interlocutors. The code choice is somewhat awkward, and evidence of this appears in the form of errors or self-repairs in both languages:

---

EXAMPLE 7

Dr.:                                                        Oh, you're the interpreter =

Int.:   and I'm gonna be the sign lang-language interpreter for today.

Int.:   POSS:1 SIGN LANGUAGE INTERPRETER LANGUAGE NOW PRO:1 PRO:3 PRO:1 OH =
        *I'll be the sign language interpreter- language today. I-She said I- "Oh =*

Dr.:                                        = for today. It's nice to meet you.

Int.:                                           Thank you, it's nice to meet you too.

Int.:   = INTERPRETER NOW PRO:1 #OH #OK PRO:1-NICE MEET PRO:1 THANKS NICE MEET-
        YOU SAME
        *= I'm the interpreter for today, oh, okay. "I- "It's nice to meet me." Thanks, it's
        nice to meet you too.*

---

In her first utterance, the interpreter treats both interlocutors as ratified addressees. In her next utterance, the interpreter responds to the doctor as they exchange greetings, resulting in an unaddressed recipient status for the patient. It is interesting to note that this footing is apparently noticed by the Deaf interlocutor, and in the re-enactment of the interview, the introductions are initiated by the patient, not by the interpreter:

---

EXAMPLE 8

Pat.:  HELLO PRO:1 INTRODUCE PRO:3 POSS:1 INTERPRETER (name) PRO:3 (nods)
       *Hello. I'd like to introduce you to the interpreter. Her name is —.*
Int.:  Hi. I'd like to introduce you to the interpreter. Her name is  —.

---

When the Deaf patient handles the introduction of the interpreter, the interpreter does not generate utterances and does not have to make code choices that start the interview on any particular "footing." Introductions can be handled in other ways as well. For instance, the interpreter could choose to introduce herself in one language at a time. Each of these options seems to result in a different footing, whether interpreter-initiated or not. Future research regarding the impact of the various footings on different genres of interaction could clarify whether any particular footing is most likely to minimize the interpreter's paradox.[8]

Another type of structural footing shift occurs when questions are directed to the interpreter. These questions can come from either the hearing or the Deaf interlocutor, and examples of both occur in the data though they are somewhat different in character. For example, the doctor may direct questions to the interpreter during the course of the interview. This was seen in example 4, on p. 207. In this example, the interpreter does not respond to the doctor's question. She interprets what the doctor said and adds her explanation, but all this is done in ASL and is not accessible to the doctor. Thus, the interpreter shifts footing, but not in harmony with the doctor's shift to interpreter as an addressed recipient. This example differs somewhat from those occurrences in which the patient asks a question of the interpreter.

There are two differences between example 4 and example 9, which follows. First, the patient never asks a question of the interpreter during

---

8. The underlying assumption here is that although interpreters cannot help but influence interaction, they can attempt to minimize their influence. To what extent this is possible and whether this is even an appropriate goal are important areas for future examination. Nevertheless, it seems to be consistent with the ways in which many researchers attempt to cope with the observer's paradox.

the course of the interview. The only time the patient treats the interpreter as an addressed recipient is when the doctor is temporarily called out of the room. The second difference between these two examples is that the interpreter responds to the patient with a much different footing. While the interpreter does not comply with the patient's request, she does provide an answer to his question, filling the empty slot in the patient-initiated adjacency pair (Schegloff and Sacks 1973):

---

### EXAMPLE 9

Pat.: UH U-L-C-E R TRUE MEAN RIGHT PRO:3?
*Hmm, is an ulcer really what she said it is?*


Int.: PRO:1 TRUE EXACT KNOW U-L-C-E-R? No. PRO:1 ASK-ASK-TO DR. POSS:3
*I just don't know much about ulcers. Better ask the doctor.*

---

In example 9 the interpreter accepts the footing established by the patient and responds to his question. In these data, there are seven occurrences in which the patient asks the interpreter a question and she generates a response, albeit without complying with the request for information or assistance. In addition, there are two occurrences (one in each mock interview) in which the doctor asks the interpreter a question. In the first of these two occurrences, the interpreter does not respond to the doctor, but tries to elicit a response from the patient by explaining the situation (see discussion on relayings). In the second, the interpreter first explains the situation, and then shifts the interpreting frame and provides procedural instructions to the doctor. Despite the fact that these footing types occur in response to questions, they are included in the taxonomy on the basis of their function, such as explaining or providing procedural instructions (see table 3).

TABLE 3. *Interactional Management During a Mock Medical Interview* (N = 14)

|  | First Mock Interview | Second Mock Interview | Total |
|---|---|---|---|
| Introductions | 2 | 0 | 2 |
| Responses to Questions | 3 | 4 | 7 |
| Explicit Frame Bracketing | 0 | 1 | 1 |
| Procedural Instructions | 0 | 1 | 1 |
| Prompts | 0 | 2 | 2 |
| Interference | 1 | 0 | 1 |

When the interpreter shifts the interpreting frame, she does so explicitly and with a specific lexical item, SUSPEND. Consistent with her other utterances, however, this frame-shift utterance is only accessible to the Deaf interlocutor. It occurs in the second mock interview just prior to a footing shift in which the interpreter speaks directly to the doctor, providing procedural instructions in response to the question, "Is there a sign for ulcer?":

---

EXAMPLE 10

Int.:        Um . . . you might wanna . . . ask him . . . if there's a sign . . . for ulcer

Int.:    SUSPEND DON'T-MIND PRO:1 ASK-TO (patient) SUPPOSE SIGN U-L-C-E-R
*Hold on a minute . . . you might want to ask him if there's a sign for ulcer.*

---

There are two footing shifts in example 10. The first is the explicit frame-break (cf. Hoyle 1993) directed to the patient in the form of a lexical item. The second occurs in the simultaneously produced instructions addressed to the doctor, in which the doctor is essentially being told to redirect her question to the patient. As in the earlier example of simultaneous production, there are some awkward pauses and errors in both the signed and spoken message. Nevertheless, both the doctor and the patient appear to understand the content. Example 10 includes the only occurrences of either an explicit frame-break or procedural instructions.

Another type of footing that occurs in the data is prompting. There are two examples of prompts. The following example occurs just prior to the segment included in example 10. In the second mock interview, when the doctor asks the interpreter how to sign ulcer, the interpreter engages in four types of footing shifts: the first just prior to the interpreted utterance, an explanation (i.e., "she asked me a question"); the second right after the interpreted utterance, a prompt (example 11); the third, a frame-break; and the fourth a procedural explanation (example 10). The prompt is an encouragement from the interpreter for the patient to respond to the doctor's question (cf. Wadensjö 1992).

---

EXAMPLE 11

Int.:    ASK-TO (interp)       SIGN U-L-C-E-R WELL?
*She asked me a question . . . about the sign for ulcer. What do you think?*

---

The sign glossed as WELL is articulated with an open hand, palm up in front of the interpreter, and directed toward the patient. It co-occurs with raised eyebrows, indicating that it is a question. The patient does not answer the question, and when the doctor directs a follow-up comment to the interpreter, "I'm just curious," the interpreter then shifts footing again beginning with the explicit frame-break seen in example 10.

The order in which these four footing types occur is interesting. Because the interpreter appears to be reticent to actually address utterances to the doctor, it appears that the interpreter might actually be attempting to shift footing between herself and the doctor as little as possible, increasing the nature or degree of the shift as necessary. Thus, the interpreter's footing shifts might represent a set of strategies that represent the interpreter's attempt to cope with her paradoxical situation.

The last type of footing shift occurs as a result of the physical environment. During the first mock interview, the interpreter accidentally touches the doctor's arm while signing. This situation was discussed in reference to example 5 on p. 207. This example was discussed earlier as an example of an explanation. Prior to the explanation, however, the interpreter shifts footing by code switching and simultaneously signing and speaking a comment directed to the doctor as an addressed recipient, with the patient as unaddressed recipient. The interpreter shifts footing by excusing herself for accidentally touching the doctor. As mentioned earlier, it is interesting to note that after excusing herself, the interpreter does not explain to the doctor why the doctor was seemingly tapped on the arm. This type of interference, based on the physical environment (e.g., being seated next to someone while signing) is similar to Hoyle's (1993, 128) discussion of footing shifts resulting from interference, as when a dog gets in the way of the ping-pong game and interrupts the sportscaster talk.

Six different types of footing have been discussed in this section, including introductions, responses to questions, explicit frame-breaks, procedural instructions, prompts, and interference. Each of these types of footing is related in some way to the structure of the interaction. For example, the footing within introductions was seen to influence the opening of the interview. In addition, several footing types, including responses to questions, explicit frame-breaks, and interference, influenced the sequential structure of the interaction.

## Summary

The two different categories of footing shifts discussed in this section are relayings and interactional management. The categories are determined on the basis of thirty-one interpreter-initiated utterances within the data. Of these utterances, ten functions have been identified: four categorized as relayings (source attribution, requests for clarification, explanations, and repetitions), and six as management of the interaction (introductions, responses to questions, explicit frame bracketing, procedural instructions, prompts, and interference). The existence of these utterances and the variety of footings that they represent suggest that interpreters cannot help but be involved in interactions for which they are present. However, the function of many of the footings appears to be related to the goal of providing access to the interaction without participating in it. In future research, with a larger corpus of data, it would be beneficial to attempt to identify consistent patterns within which various types of footing shifts occur, and within which interactional outcomes appear to be effectively realized.

Through examination of the production format within an interpreted encounter, and the different types of footing established by the interpreter with each interlocutor, it has become evident that the interpreter participated, in some capacity, in the interpreted interaction. The interpreter generated utterances for a variety of purposes including relaying information and managing the interactional structure. Because a given footing represents a participant-based frame of an event, the interpreter's footing types provide some insight into the interpreter's negotiation of the interpreter's paradox.

The interpreter appeared to frame her relationship with the Deaf and hearing interlocutors in two different ways. Evidence for this consists of the single utterance directed only to the hearing interlocutor, as compared with the numerous (twenty-six) utterances directed only to the Deaf interlocutor. Moreover, the interpreter directed very different types of utterances to each interlocutor. That is, the interpreter provided explanations, prompts, and source attributions to the Deaf interlocutor while providing introductions and procedural instructions to the hearing interlocutor. Examination of the functions of footing with each interlocutor suggests that the interpreter frames the interaction in two ways: interpreter-Deaf participant and Deaf participant-hearing participant. The interpreter attempted to avoid interpreter-hearing participant interactions so strongly that she actually avoided responding to an interpreter-directed question from the doctor. Whether or not this type of framing occurs in real interpreted encounters, and what effects such an asymmetrical perspective has on the interaction, is an area for future research.

Analysis of the various functions and types of footing in these data also yield an interesting example in which four different footing are employed in one situation. When the doctor asks the interpreter a question, the interpreter shifts footing four times in an attempt to avoid responding. Whether or not the interpreter employed the most effective strategies is beyond the scope of this study; however, the fact that the interpreter appears to have used footing shifts as a series of strategies in coping with the situation is quite interesting. Another area for future research is to identify the role of footing shifts as strategies in pursuing interpreters' perceived goals, such as nonparticipation, and the effectiveness of such strategies.

**REFERENCES**

Bateson, G. 1972. *Steps to an ecology of mind.* New York: Ballantine.
Chafe, W. 1977. Creativity in verbalization and its implications for the nature of stored knowledge. In *Discourse production and comprehension,* ed. R. Freedle, 41–55. Norwood, N.J.: Ablex.
Clayman, S. 1992. Footing in the achievement of neutrality: The case of news interview discourse. In *Talk at work: Interaction in institutional settings,* ed. P. Drew and J. Heritage, 163–98. Cambridge: Cambridge University Press.
Eckert, P. 1993. Cooperative competition in adolescent "girl talk." In *Gender and conversational interaction,* ed. D. Tannen, 32–61. Oxford: Oxford University Press.
Edmondson, W. 1986. Cognition, conversing, and interpreting. In *Interlingual and intercultural communication,* vol. 7, ed. J. House and S. Blum-Kulka, 129–38. Tübingen: Gunter Narr Verlag.
Fillmore, C. 1976. The need for a frame semantics within linguistics. *Statistical methods in linguistics.* Stockholm: Skriptor, 5–29.
Frishberg, N. 1990. *Interpreting: An introduction.* Silver Spring, Md.: RID Publications.
Goffman, E. 1974. *Frame analysis.* New York: Harper & Row.
———. 1981. *Forms of talk.* Philadelphia: University of Pennsylvania Press.
Gumperz, J. J. 1982. *Discourse strategies.* Cambridge: Cambridge University Press.
Hoyle, S. 1993. Participation frameworks in sportscasting play: Imaginary and literal footings. In *Framing in discourse,* ed. D. Tannen, 114–45. Oxford: Oxford University Press.
Keith, H. 1984. Liaison interpreting—an exercise in linguistic interaction. In *Translating theory and its implementation in the teaching of translating and*

*interpreting,* ed. W. Wilss and G. Thorme, 308–17. Tübingen: Gunter Narr Verlag.

Labov, W. 1972. *Sociolinguistic patterns.* Philadelphia: University of Pennsylvania Press.

Locker McKee, R. 1992. Footing shifts in American Sign Language lectures. Unpublished doctoral diss., University of California, Los Angeles.

Lucas, C., and C. Valli. 1992. *Language contact in the American Deaf community.* San Diego: Academic Press.

Roy, C. 1989. A sociolinguistic analysis of the interpreter's role in the turn exchanges of an interpreted event. Unpublished doctoral diss., Georgetown University, Washington, D.C.

———. 1993. A sociolinguistic analysis of the interpreter's role in simultaneous talk in interpreted interaction. *Multilingua* 12(4):341–63.

Schegloff, E., and H. Sacks. 1973. Opening up closings. *Semiotica.* 7:289–327.

Schiffrin, D. 1993. "Speaking for another" in sociolinguistic interviews: Alignments, identities, and frames. In *Framing in discourse,* ed. D. Tannen, 231–63. Oxford: Oxford University Press.

Smith, F. 1993. The pulpit and woman's place: Gender and the framing of the "exegetical self" in sermon performances. In *Framing in discourse,* ed. D. Tannen, 146–75. Oxford: Oxford University Press.

Tannen, D. 1979. What's in a frame? Surface evidence for underlying expectations. In *New directions in discourse processing,* ed. R. Freedle, 137–38. Norwood, N.J.: Ablex.

———. 1986. *That's not what I meant.* New York: Ballantine Books.

———. 1989. *Talking voices: Repetition, dialogue, and imagery in conversational discourse.* Cambridge: Cambridge University Press.

Tannen, D., and C. Wallat. 1987. Interactive frames and knowledge schemas in interaction: Examples from a medical examination/interview. *Social Psychology Quarterly* 50(2):205–16.

Wadensjö, C. 1992. *Interpreting as interaction: On dialogue-interpreting in immigration hearings and medical encounters.* Linköping University: Linköping Studies in Arts and Science.

Zimmer, J. 1989. ASL/English interpreting in an interactive setting. In *Proceedings of the 30th Annual Conference of the American Translators Association.* Medford, N.J.: Learned Information.

## Transcription Conventions

The use of a musical score transcript allows the interpretation to coincide with the interpreted utterances as they do in the data. The interpreter has two lines for utterances that are both spoken and signed.
Overlapping utterances within a single "line" indicate overlaps. The use
of small caps or noncaps indicates whether interpreters are using ASL or
English, respectively.

| Notation | Explanation |
|---|---|
| SMALL CAPS | used for English glosses of signs |
| U-L-C-E-R | a fingerspelled word |
| HYPHENATED-WORDS | represent a single sign |
| ++ | reduplication of a sign |
| PRO:1 | PRO = pronoun, 1 = first person, 2 = second person, 3 = third person |
| POSS:1 | possessive pronoun (and person) |
| CL | classifier predicate |
| Bob-ASK-TO-Mary | indicating verbs include the subj/obj referents |
| (actions) | indicate paralinguistic content |
| ... | pause of a half-second or more |
| : | the preceding vowel was elongated |
| - | interrupted utterance |
| (?) | unclear from the video recording |
| . | sentence final prosody |
| , | clause final intonation |
| ? | rising intonation (Engl) or nonmanual signals indicating a question form |
| = | utterances continuing to the following, or from the preceding line |
| *italics* | translation of text on preceding line |

# Index

Page numbers followed by *n* indicate footnotes.

Absolute frame of reference in spatial
  discourse, 21–25
Academic bilingualism. *See*
  Bilingualism
Accommodation theory, 159
Affect, emphasis, and comment in text
  telephone conversations, 89–101
  cues to connote, 90–99, 102
American Sign Language (ASL). *See
  also* Bilingualism
  contact signing, 149
  discourse features, 166–67, 178–80
  discourse structure, 164
  interpretation of interview. *See*
    Interpreting an interview
  interpreters' professional code of
    ethics, 190
  pronominal points in, 32
  reference in, 31
  repairing mistakes in, 167
  spatial discourse, 3–26. *See also*
    Spatial discourse
  storytelling, 59–82. *See also*
    Storytelling
Anaphoric references within discourse, 21, 33
Aristotle, 137
Asides
  codeswitching to indicate, 195
  eye gaze to indicate, 197
  narrators in British Sign Lan-
    guage, 53
ASL. *See* American Sign Language

Backgrounding of events, 37–38
Balinese Deaf community, 109–48
  adoption of national language (Bahasa
    Indonesia), effect of, 142–43

case studies, 130–32
changing linguistic ecology,
  142–44
community and identity, 113–15
contact among deaf people, 134
cultural analysis and linguistic
  analysis, 120–21
cultural class of *kolok,* 134–35
deafness
  age range, 123–24
  attitude of Balinese toward,
    116–17, 141–44
  distribution by district, 123
  identity and, 140–42, 146
  viewed as disability, 141–42
  Western views of, 140–41
deaf schools, 134, 141–43
education, 127, 133, 141
ethnographic summary, 132–33
geography and history of Bali,
  110–13
habitus concept and, 120–21,
  142–43
Hindu-Buddhist cosmos, 115–17
history and mythology of Desa
  Kolok, 117–19
interpretation of study data,
  133–34
linguistic ecology concept and,
  120–21
linguistic ecology of Buleleng,
  142–44
linguistic environment of North
  Bali, 135–36
marriage, 127–29
methodology of study, 122–25
occupations, 125–26, 141
reading and writing skills, 135–36

Balinese deaf community (*continued*)
sign language, 132–33
Desa Kolok's sign language *(kata kolok),* 109, 132, 143
distinctions among uses, 132
national sign language, 142–43
transmission across generations, 124, 128, 136, 144–45
as widespread discursive activity, 128–30
theoretical framework for discursive processes, 119–22
trend toward monolingualism, 121–22
Western language tradition distinguished, 136–40
Bateson, G., 191
Bienvenu, M. J., 164, 167, 178–80
Bilingualism, 150–51. *See also* Italian Sign Language (LIS)
American Sign Language and written English, 162–89
ASL discourse features, 166–67, 178–80
conceptual notations used by Deaf students, 174
cross-cultural analysis, 169, 174–75
definition of discourse, 164–65
definition of register, 165
discourse structures, 163–67
evaluation form for ASL discourse, 170, 181
evaluation form for written English discourse, 171, 187
GET-TO-THE-POINT, 164, 166
instruction in ASL, 169–70
instruction in written English, 170–72
introduction and conclusion techniques, 172–74
metacognitive skill development, 169
methodology of study, 168–69
student creation of ASL narrative, 170, 184–86
student creation of written English essay, 171–72, 188–89
teaching contrastive discourse, 174–75
transference abilities, 169
Body position. *See* Shift in body position
Bourdieu, P., 120–21
British Deaf community. *See* Text telephone conversations
British Sign Language (BSL). *See* Event packaging in British Sign Language
BSL. *See* British Sign Language

Cardinal directions (north/south/east/west), 11–13, 24–25
Chafe, W., 39–40, 192–93
Clarification requests when interpreting an interview, 206
Classifiers, 63–71, 67*n*, 68*n*, 79
constructions in spatial discourse, 8–9, 20–24
Clayman, S., 196
Codeswitching and code mixing
interpreter's use of, 206
in Italian, 152, 155–56, 160
quotations and asides using, 195
Coherence in discourse, 28, 33
Cohesion in discourse, 28, 40
Comparisons and spatial reference, 40
Composition skills, variations among language groups, 163
Comprehension checks, 30
Conceptual notations used by Deaf students, 174
Convergence, 159
Conversation. *See* Discourse
Cross-cultural analysis, 136–40, 169, 174–75
Cultural analysis. *See* Balinese Deaf community
Cummins, J., 163, 169

Deaf parents and hearing children
(Italy), 149–61
Deaf schools in Bali, 134, 141, 143
Desa Kolok. *See* Balinese Deaf
community
Diagrammatic space in spatial discourse, 13–14, 18–20, 22–25
Diglossia, 151
Disability, deafness treated as,
141–42
Discourse
bilingual. *See* Bilingualism
definition of discourse, 164–65
simultaneity in British Sign Language, 27–58. *See also* Event
packaging in British Sign
Language
spatial discourse, 3–26. *See also*
Spatial discourse
structures, 163–67
text telephone conversations,
83–106. *See also* Text telephone conversations
Discourse markers, 58

Ecology, linguistic, 120–21, 142–44
Edmondson, W., 199
Education
ASL and written English, 162–89.
*See also* Bilingualism
Balinese Deaf community, 127,
133, 141
deaf schools in Bali, 134, 141, 143
Emmorey, K., 41
English language
bilingual with ASL. *See* Bilingualism
gaze tour, 19
Spanish language vs., 60
spatial description and perspective
choice, 4–12, 23–24
storytelling, 59–82. *See also*
Storytelling
temporal connectives, 38–39
Environmental description, 3–26. *See
also* Spatial discourse

Ethnography of Balinese Deaf community, 132–33
Europe and evolution of language,
136–40
Evaluation forms
ASL discourse, 170, 181
written English discourse, 171, 187
Event packaging in British Sign Language, 27–58
anaphora, 33
backgrounding of events, 37–38
coherence in discourse, 28, 33
cohesion in discourse, 28, 40
comparisons and spatial
reference, 40
comprehension checks, 30
directional verbs, 35
discourse markers, transcription
conventions, 58
eye-closes, use of, 30, 53
eye gaze, use of, 30, 32n, 33, 37,
40, 45–46, 53
transcription convention, 57
face-to-face communication, 30–31
fixed referential framework, use of,
30, 33–35, 47, 53
flashback construction, 51, 53
foregrounding of events, 37–38
index-fingers points, 32, 33n
material used in study, 42–43
measuring extent of event packaging, 42
methodology of study, 41–42
mixed perspective, 37
movement between representational
spaces, 30, 42, 47–48,
50–51, 53
narrative filling information, 30
narrator asides, 53
narrator space, use of, 30
nonmanual markers, use of, 30,
32, 34
notation convention to indicate reference points, 32n
noun phrases, 31–32

Event packaging in BSL (*continued*)
  perceptual verbs, 53
  performatives and spatial
      reference, 40
  perspective choice, 37
  proforms, 30, 33–34, 53
  discourse markers, transcription
      conventions, 58
  pronominal points, 32–33, 40
    transcription convention, 57
  real-world space, 30
  referential forms, 31–41, 53
  representation of discourse, 30
  results of study, 43–50
  role prominence, 37
  scene setting, 30, 42, 46–47, 50, 52
  secondary perspective, 52
  shifted referential framework, use
      of, 29–30, 35–37, 40, 42,
      46–47, 50, 52–54
  sign discourse vs. spoken discourse,
      28–31
  sign space, use for reference, 28–29
  simultaneity in discourse, 37–41
  temporal connectives, 38–39
  temporal devices, 37–39, 42, 48,
      51–53
  thematic perspective, 52
  time mapping and spatial
      reference, 40
  transcription conventions, 57–58
  verb agreement morphology,
      34–37, 57
Existential verbs, use in English de-
    scriptions of space, 8, 24
Explanations by interpreter, 206–8, 214
Explicit frame bracketing by inter-
    preter, 211–12
Eye-closes, use of, 30, 53
Eye gaze. *See also* Gaze-tour description
  asides specified by, 197
  event packaging in British Sign Lan-
      guage, 30, 32*n*, 33, 37, 40,
      45–46, 53
    transcription conventions, 57

shift, 17*n*
storytelling in ASL, 64

Facial expressions
  ASL storytelling, 64, 67, 69–72, 78
  English verbal storytelling, 73, 78
  Italian communication between
      Deaf and hearing, 155,
      157–58
Ferguson, C. A., 151
Fillmore, C., 192
Fingerspelling, 151, 155
Fixed referential framework, use in
      British Sign Language, 30,
      33–35, 47, 53
Flashback construction, 51, 53
Footing shifts, 190–217. *See also* In-
      terpreting an interview
Foregrounding of events, 37–38
Frames in interpreting an interview,
      191–93
Frames of reference, 21–25
  absolute, 22
  intrinsic, 21
  relative, 22

Gaze-tour description, 19–20, 25
Gestures. *See also* Pointing by signer
  Italian communication between
      Deaf and hearing, 152, 155,
      157–58
  verbal speech storytelling and, 66,
      72–78
GET-TO-THE-POINT. *See* Bilingualism
Giles, H., 159
Goffman, E., 191–92, 193–95, 198
Gumperz, J. J., 195

Habitus concept, 120–21, 142–43
Hartmann, A., 140–41
Hearing children of deaf parents
      (Italy), 149–61
High signing plane, use in spatial dis-
      course, 17, 25
Hindu-Buddhist cosmos, 115–17

Horizontal signing space in spatial
    discourse, 14–15
  vs. vertical plane, 20–21, 25
Hoyle, S., 196–97

Identification of parties in text
    telephone conversations,
    84–86, 102
Index-finger points, 32, 33n. *See also*
    Gestures
Indonesia. *See* Balinese Deaf
    community
Interactional management in inter-
    preting an interview, 209–14
Interference in interpreting an inter-
    view, 211, 213
Interpreter's paradox, 202, 214
Interpreters' professional code of
    ethics, 190
Interpreting an interview, 190–217
  analysis of study, 202–15
  clarification requests, 206
  data of study, 200
  explanations by interpreter,
    206–8, 214
  explicit frame bracketing, 211–12
  footing, 193–99
    application to discourse, 195–97
    interpreted encounters and,
      198–99
    shifts, 190–215
  frames, 191–93
  informant and situational character-
    istics, 200–202
  interactional management, 209–14
  interference, 211, 213
  interpreter-generated utterances,
    203–4, 213
  introductions, 210–11, 214
  literature review, 191–99
  methodology of study, 199–202
  prompting, 211–12, 214
  relayings, 204–9, 214
  repetitions, 208–9
  responses to questions, 210–12

role-playing in medical interview,
    200–202
  self-generated utterances of inter-
    preters, 204–5
  simultaneous signing and
    speaking, 199n
  source attribution, 204–6, 214
  taxonomy of interpreter footings,
    204–13
Interruptions in text telephone conver-
    sations, 85–86, 102, 105
Intrinsic frame of reference in spatial
    discourse, 21, 23–25
Introduction and conclusion tech-
    niques, 172–74
Introductions in interview, 210–11, 214
Italian Sign Language (LIS), 149–61
  interactions between Deaf
    bilinguals and hearing
    bilinguals, 154–58
  interactions between Deaf bilinguals
    and hearing monolingual,
    158–60
  LIS grammar used instead of Italian
    grammar, 155–56, 160
  methodology of study, 152–54
  situation of Italian Deaf people,
    150–52
  spoken sign language, 154, 160–61

Joos, M., 153, 165

Keith, H., 198, 199
Kolok. *See* Balinese Deaf community

Labov, W., 59, 190
Language contact, 149–50. *See also*
    Italian Sign Language (LIS)
Lee, D. M., 151
Left directional term. *See* Viewer-
    relational terms (left/right)
Liddell, S., 13–16
Linguistic ecology, 120–21, 142–44
Linguistic habitus. *See* Habitus
    concept

Linguistic mosaic concept, 138, 138n, 139n
LIS. *See* Italian Sign Language
Literature review of interpreting, 191–99
Locker McKee, R., 197
Lucas, C., and C. Valli, 17, 17n, 149–50

Manual English, 151
Maps and spatial discourse, 4–7, 24–25
Marriage in Balinese Deaf communities, 127–29
McNeill, D., 66
Medical interview, interpretation of. *See* Interpreting an interview
Metacognitive skill development, 169
Minicom. *See* Text telephone conversations
Mixed perspective in spatial discourse, 6–8, 18, 25, 37
Model space, 13
Monasteries and use of sign language, 138
Monolingualism, trend toward, 121–22, 140, 143
Motion verbs
spatial discourse, 8–9, 24
storytelling, 60, 65
Movement between representational spaces, 30, 42, 47–48, 50–51, 53
Mühläusler, P., 120–22

Nash, J. E., and A. Nash, 84–85, 87, 90
National language of Bali, 142–43
National Technical Institute for the Deaf (NTID), 168–69
Nicaraguan research with school children's acquisition of signing, 136n
Nonmanual features. *See also* Eye gaze; Facial expressions
event packaging in British Sign Language, 30, 32, 34

North Bali. *See* Balinese Deaf community
Noun phrases in British Sign Language, 31–32

Observer's paradox, 190, 210n
Occupations among Balinese Deaf community, 125–26, 141
Ong, W., 137–38
Oralist views of language, 141
Overlaps in text telephone conversations, 85–86, 102, 105

Performatives and spatial reference, 40
Perspective choice
spatial discourse and, 6–8, 24, 37
storytelling and, 60, 78
Perspective type and spatial formats, 13–18
Pidgin Sign English, 149, 151
Play-acting, 64
Pointing by signer
ASL storytelling, 69
event packaging in British Sign Language, 32, 33n, 40
Pro-drop languages, 34
Proforms in BSL, 30, 33–34, 53, 58
Prompting in interpreting an interview, 211–12, 214
Pronouns
in BSL, 32–33, 40, 57
footing shifts, 196
storytelling, 63

Quotations
character's speech in verbal storytelling, 66, 75
codeswitching and, 195
footing shifts and, 195, 197

Reading and writing skills
in Bali, 135–36
English written language. *See* Bilingualism

Real-world space, 15
   BSL, 30
Referential forms in BSL, 31–41, 53
Register, 165
Relative frame of reference, 22–25
Relayings in interpreting, 204–9, 214
Repairing mistakes
   ASL, 167, 207
   self-repairs, 167, 207
   text telephone conversations, 104
Repetitions in interpreting, 208–9
Representation of discourse in British
   Sign Language, 30
Responses to questions in interpreting,
   210–12
Right directional term. *See* Viewer-
   relational terms (left/right)
Role-playing, 200–202
Role-shifting, 63–72, 78–79
Route perspective in spatial discourse,
   3–12, 18, 23–24
Roy, C. B., 167, 190

Satellite-framed languages, 60
Scene setting
   event packaging in British Sign Lan-
      guage, 30, 42, 46–47, 50, 52
   storytelling, 66
Schick, B., 13
Schiffrin, D., 197
Secondary perspective in BSL, 52
Second language skills. *See*
   Bilingualism
Self-generated utterances of inter-
   preters, 204–5
Shared space, 16
Shift in body position
   in ASL storytelling, 64, 67, 71, 78
   in footings in interviews, 197
Shifting between spatial formats
   in ASL, 18–19, 25
   in BSL, 29–30, 35–37, 40, 42,
      46–47, 50, 52–54
Siertsema, B., 137
Signed English, 136n

Sign language. *See also* American
   Sign Language (ASL); Event
   packaging in British Sign
   Language (BSL); Italian
   Sign Language (LIS)
Bali. *See* Balinese Deaf community
   interpreting. *See* Interpreting an
      interview
   monastic use, 138
   vs. spoken discourse, 28–31
   transmission across generations, 124n
   Western views of, 140–41
Silva, M., 39
Simultaneity in discourse. *See* Event
   packaging in British Sign Lan-
   guage (BSL)
Simultaneous signing and
   speaking, 199n
Slobin, D. I., 59–61, 65
Smith, F., 196
Sound-based view of language,
   137–38
Source attribution in interpreting,
   204–6, 214
Spanish vs. English storytelling, 60
Spatial discourse, 3–26
   absolute frame of reference, 21–25
   cardinal directions (north/south/
      east/west), 11–13, 24–25
   classifier constructions, 8–9, 20–24
   diagrammatic space, 13–14, 18–20,
      22–25
   English description and perspective
      choice, 4–12, 24
   event packaging, 27–58. *See also*
      Event packaging in British Sign
      Language
   existential verbs, use in English de-
      scriptions, 8
   gaze-tour description, 19–20, 25
   high signing plane, use of, 17, 25
   horizontal signing space, use of,
      14–15
   horizontal vs. vertical plane,
      20–21, 25

Spatial discourse (*continued*)
  intrinsic frame of reference, 21,
    23–25
  maps and, 4–7, 24–25
  methodology of study, 6
  mixed perspective, 6–8, 18, 25
  model space, 13
  motion verbs in ASL and English,
    8–9, 24
  perspective choice, 6–8, 24
  real-world space, 15
  relative frame of reference, 22–25
  results and analysis of study, 6–12
  route perspective, 3–12, 18, 23–24
  shared space, 16
  spatial formats
    frames of reference and, 21–25
    perspective type and, 13–18
    shifting between, 18–19, 25
  stative verbs, use in English descrip-
    tions, 8
  surrogate space, 15–16
  survey perspective, 3–12, 18, 24–25
  token space, 13–14
  vertical vs. horizontal plane,
    20–21, 25
  viewer-relational terms (left/right),
    3, 9–10, 18–19, 24–25
  viewer space, 13–16, 18–19,
    22–23, 25
Spatial use in ASL storytelling, 63,
  78–80
Spoken sign language (Italy), 154,
  160–61
Stative verbs, use in English, 8, 24
Stokoe, W., 151
Storytelling, 59–82
  ASL resources used in, 64–72
  classifiers in ASL, 63–71,
    67n–68n, 79
  comparison of ASL and spoken
    English, 78–81
  English resources used in, 65–66,
    72–78
  eye gaze in ASL, 64

facial expressions in ASL, 64, 67,
  69–72, 78
facial expressions used with spoken
  rendition, 73, 78
gestures used with, 66, 72–78
linguistic resources, effect of different languages, 59–60, 62–66,
  78–81
methodology of study, 61–62
motion verbs, 60
motion verbs in English, 65
perspective choice, 60, 78
play-acting, 64
pointing in ASL, 69
pronouns, 63
quoting character's speech, 66, 75
role-shifting in ASL, 63–72, 78–79
scene setting, 66
shift in body position in ASL, 64,
  67, 71, 78
spatial use of ASL, 63, 78–80
time concepts, 63
"The Tortoise and the Hare," 61–81
verb-satellite pairings, 60–61, 74
vocal inflections, 66, 73, 76–77
Surrogate space, 15–16
Survey perspective in spatial discourse, 3–12, 18, 24–25

Tannen, D., 192n, 193, 195n, 196
Taxonomy of interpreter footings,
  204–13
Taylor, H., and B. Tversky, 3–9
Teaching American Sign Language
  and written English. *See*
  Bilingualism
Telephone conversations, 83–106.
  *See also* Text telephone
  conversations
Temporal devices. *See* Time constructs
Tessarolo, M., 151
Text telephone conversations, 83–106
  affect, emphasis, and comment in,
    89–102
  analysis of study data, 89–101

comparison to spoken telephone conversation, 84–87, 101
constraints of text-based technology, 84–86, 101–4
conversation analysis of, 86–87, 104–5
cost and time restraints, 85–87, 104
identification of parties, 84–86, 102
interruptions and overlaps, 85–86, 102, 105
junk in transmission, 89, 104
literacy skills and, 85, 104
methodology of study, 87–89
pauses, 86, 89
repair sequences, 104
transcription of data, 88–89
TTY, TDD, TT, and Minicom, 83*n*–84*n*
turn-taking system, 85–86, 102–3
visual alerts for incoming calls, 84, 99–101
vocatives, use of, 105
Thematic perspective in BSL, 52
Time constructs
in BSL, 37–39, 42, 48, 51–53
mapping and spatial reference, 40
storytelling, 63
Time restraints on text telephone conversations, 85–87, 104
Token space, 13–14
"The Tortoise and the Hare," 61–81
Transcription conventions, 57–58, 182–83, 217
Transference abilities between ASL and written English, 169

TDD/TTY. *See* Text telephone conversations
Turkish language and simultaneity, 38
Turn-taking system in text telephone conversations, 85–86, 102–3

Van Dijk, T. A., 125, 144–145
Verbs
agreement morphology, 34–37, 57
directional verbs, 35
motion verbs
English language storytelling, 60, 65
spatial discourse, 8–9, 24
perceptual verbs, 53
stative verbs, 8, 24
verb-framed languages, 60
verb-satellite pairings, 60–61, 74
Vertical vs. horizontal plane, 20–21, 25
Viewer-relational terms (left/right), 3, 9–10, 18–19, 24–25
Viewer space and spatial discourse, 13–16, 18–19, 22–23, 25
Vocal inflections in English storytelling, 66, 73, 76–77

Wadensjö, C., 198–99
Wallat, C., 196
Western language tradition vs. Balinese tradition, 136–40
Western views of deafness, 140–41
Whorf, B., 59
Winston, E., 40
Written English and ASL. *See* Bilingualism

Zimmer, J., 190

comparison to spoken telephone conversation, 84–87, 101

constraints of text-based technology, 84–86, 101–4

conversation analysis of, 86–87, 104–5

cost and time restraints, 85–87, 104

identification of parties, 84–86, 102

interruptions and overlaps, 85–86, 102, 105

junk in transmission, 89, 104

literacy skills and, 85, 104

methodology of study, 87–89

pauses, 86, 89

repair sequences, 104

transcription of data, 88–89

TTY, TDD, TT, and Minicom, 83*n*–84*n*

turn-taking system, 85–86, 102–3

visual alerts for incoming calls, 84, 99–101

vocatives, use of, 105

Thematic perspective in BSL, 52

Time constructs

in BSL, 37–39, 42, 48, 51–53

mapping and spatial reference, 40

storytelling, 63

Time restraints on text telephone conversations, 85–87, 104

Token space, 13–14

"The Tortoise and the Hare," 61–81

Transcription conventions, 57–58, 182–83, 217

Transference abilities between ASL and written English, 169

TDD/TTY. *See* Text telephone conversations

Turkish language and simultaneity, 38

Turn-taking system in text telephone conversations, 85–86, 102–3

Van Dijk, T. A., 125, 144–145

Verbs

agreement morphology, 34–37, 57

directional verbs, 35

motion verbs

English language storytelling, 60, 65

spatial discourse, 8–9, 24

perceptual verbs, 53

stative verbs, 8, 24

verb-framed languages, 60

verb-satellite pairings, 60–61, 74

Vertical vs. horizontal plane, 20–21, 25

Viewer-relational terms (left/right), 3, 9–10, 18–19, 24–25

Viewer space and spatial discourse, 13–16, 18–19, 22–23, 25

Vocal inflections in English storytelling, 66, 73, 76–77

Wadensjö, C., 198–99

Wallat, C., 196

Western language tradition vs. Balinese tradition, 136–40

Western views of deafness, 140–41

Whorf, B., 59

Winston, E., 40

Written English and ASL. *See* Bilingualism

Zimmer, J., 190